The Economics of Child Labour

The Economics of Child Labour

Education, Fertility, and Infant Mortality in Developing Countries

Alessandro Cigno
and
Furio C. Rosati

OXFORD
UNIVERSITY PRESS

OXFORD
UNIVERSITY PRESS

Great Clarendon Street, Oxford, OX2 6DP,
United Kingdom

Oxford University Press is a department of the University of Oxford.
It furthers the University's objective of excellence in research, scholarship,
and education by publishing worldwide. Oxford is a registered trade mark of
Oxford University Press in the UK and in certain other countries

First Edition published in 2005
Second published in paperback in 2024

Published in the United States of America by Oxford University Press
198 Madison Avenue, New York, NY 10016, United States of America

British Library Cataloguing in Publication Data

Data available

Library of Congress Control Number: 2024941524

ISBN 9780198903000

DOI: 10.1093/oso/9780198903000.001.0001

Printed and bound by
CPI Group (UK) Ltd, Croydon, CR0 4YY

To Enrico, Nicola,

Paola and Tommaso,

who do not know child labour

Preface to the Second Edition

Coming as it does twenty years after the first edition, this second edition could have been subtitled 'Better Late Than Never'. It is subtitled 'Education, Fertility and Infant Mortality in Developing Countries' to alert the reader to the fact that child labour is but one aspect of a complex phenomenon. Compared with the original version, the new edition has been extensively rewritten. The theoretical part includes new chapters on family rules and social norms, and on policy optimization. It also provides demonstrations (that the uninterested reader is at liberty to skip) of all analytical results. Reflecting the volume of applied research that has taken place in the last two decades, the empirical part is larger than in the first edition. It presents further evidence of the factors that determine the demand and supply of child labour, the demand for education, and of the nexus between child labour, education, fertility, and health. A new chapter assesses the effectiveness of the policies that are actually carried out in developing countries for the specific purpose of curbing child labour.

Contents

List of Figures

Introduction

Child labour is a common phenomenon in low- and middle-income countries. The latest global estimates in ILO (2020) show that about 160 million children work. Most of them live in rural areas, and are concentrated in Africa and Asia. The vast majority of them work in agriculture or as contributing family workers (see Table 0.1 for details). Across countries (but the same is true across households), child labour is statistically associated with poverty. Figure 0.1 presents a cross plot of child labour incidence, as measured by the share of school-age children who work, and per-capita GDP, for a sample of developing countries. It is evident that child labour is negatively correlated with per capita income (positively correlated with poverty). Also evident is that the dispersion around the interpolating line is much greater at low, than at high per-capita GDP levels. Equally poor countries have greatly different child labour rates. Medium-income countries have similarly low child labour rates.

Figure 0.2 plots the child labour rate against the total fertility rate (number of children born to a woman over her entire life), and Figure 0.3 against a measure of infant mortality (the probability that a child will not survive to one year of age), again for a sample of developing countries. In both cases, the correlation is clearly positive. A negative correlation exists, by contrast, between child labour and any synthetic measure of education (time spent working is not the complement of time spent in education, because some children are engaged in both). As Figure 0.4 shows, a negative correlation is what we find also if we plot child labour against a measure of participation in international trade (exports minus imports, over exports plus imports). Knowing from trade theory that participation in international trade enhances productivity, and from Figure 0.1 that child labour is negatively correlated with per-capita GDP, that is hardly a surprise, but it runs counter to the popular view, born of media reports of children in poor countries producing goods for rich ones, that international trade encourages child labour.

As these diagrams identify only crude correlations between endogenous variables, we must refrain from inferring any causal relationship from them, let alone speculating about the direction of causation (do children work

The Economics of Child Labour. Second Edition. Alessandro Cigno and Furio C. Rosati, Oxford University Press.
 DOI: 10.1093/oso/9780198903000.003.0001

Table 0.1 Child labour by age, region and sector of employment

		Total							
		5–11 years		12–14 years		15–17 years		5–17 years	
		%	No.	%	No.	%	No.	%	No.
World total		9.7	89,300	9.3	35,600	9.5	35,000	9.6	160,000
Residence	Rural	14.6	72,400	13.7	27,700	12.4	22,600	13.9	122,700
	Urban	4.0	16,900	4.4	7,900	6.6	12,400	4.7	37,300
ILO regions	Africa	22.1	54,900	23.5	21,800	18.2	15,500	21.6	92,200
	Sub-Saharan Africa	24.7	51,900	25.8	20,500	19.5	14,200	23.9	86,600
	Arab States	4.8	1,200	6.4	600	7.8	700	5.8	2,400
	Asia and the Pacific	5.4	25,000	4.8	9,600	7.1	14,100	5.6	48,700
	Americas	3.0	3,100	4.3	1,900	7.2	3,300	4.3	8,300
	Latin America and the Caribbean	4.2	3,100	6.1	1,900	9.8	3,100	6.0	8,200
	Europe and Central Asia	6.4	5,200	5.1	1,700	4.6	1,400	5.7	8,300
Children in child labour who are not attending school	Total	27.7	24,700	35.2	12,500	53.2	18,700	35.0	55,900
	Rural	28.3	20,500	35.8	9,900	54.1	12,200	34.8	42,700
Children in child labour by sector of economic activity	Urban	24.9	4,200	33.1	2,600	51.6	6,400	35.5	13,300
	Agriculture	76.6	68,400	75.8	27,000	47.6	16,700	70.0	112,100
	Industry	6.0	5,400	7.5	2,700	24.0	8,400	10.3	16,500
	Services	17.4	15,500	16.7	5,900	28.4	10,000	19.6	31,400
Children in child labour by employment status	Of which domestic work	4.6	4,100	3.0	1,100	5.6	2,000	4.5	7,100
	Employees	9.2	8,200	12.9	4,600	42.3	14,800	17.3	27,600
	Own-account workers	8.2	7,300	12.6	4,500	15.0	5,300	10.7	17,000
	Contributing family workers	82.6	73,800	74.5	26,500	42.8	15,000	72.1	115,300

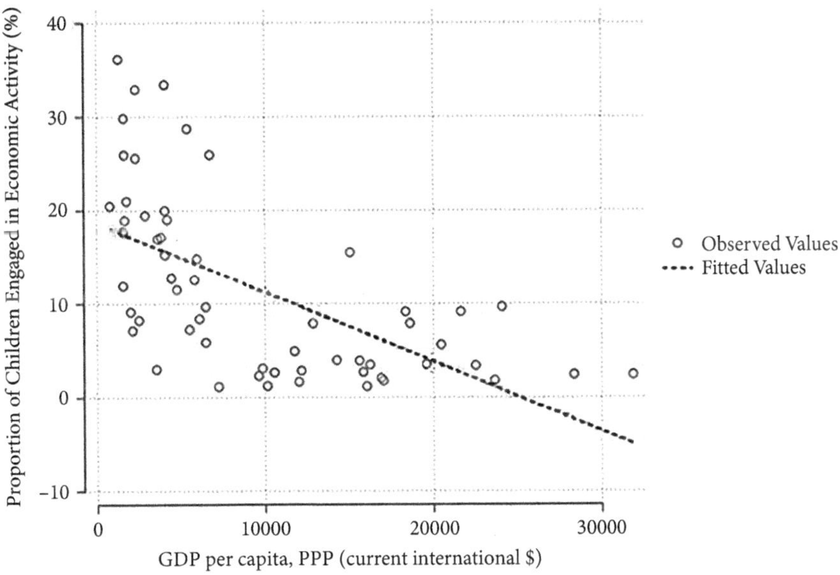

Figure 0.1 Child labour and per capita GDP

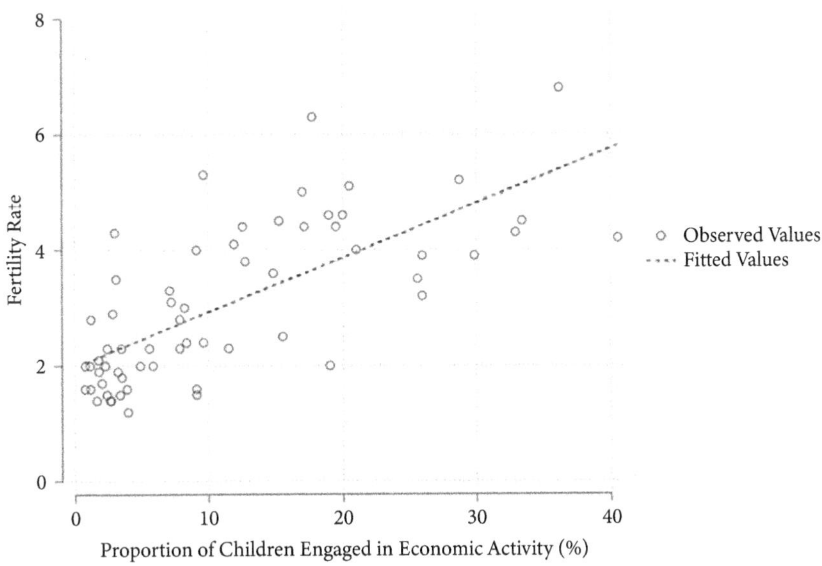

Figure 0.2 Fertility and child labour

because adults are poor, or are adults poor because children work?). All we can say, on the basis of the broad-brush picture these figures provide, is that children tend to work more in poorer countries, and in countries that are less well integrated in the world economy. And also that the countries where

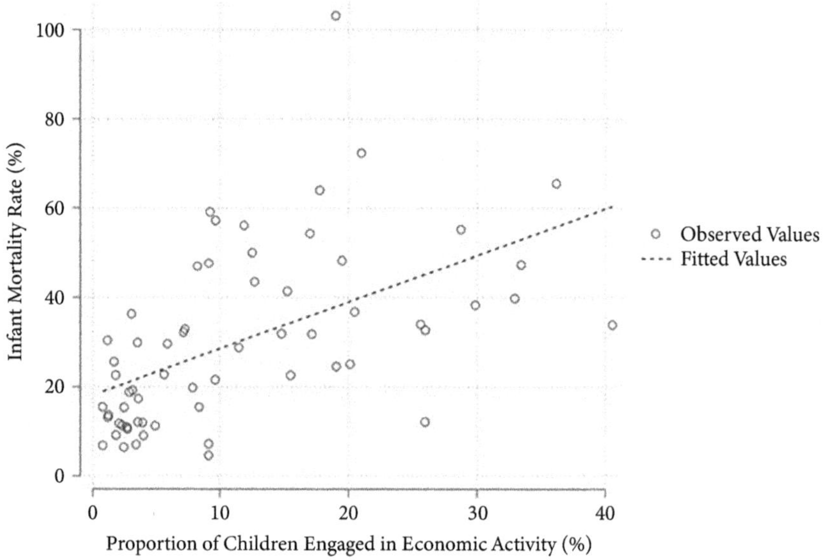

Figure 0.3 Infant mortality and child labour

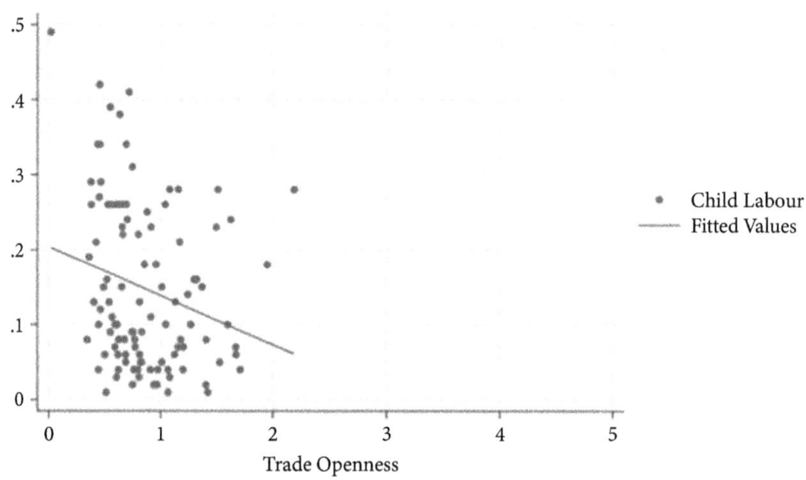

Figure 0.4 Child labour and trade openness

children work more tend to be those where more children are born, fewer survive to school-age and fewer of those who do receive an education. It is the purpose of the present book to explain why, and what can be done about it. The human suffering that child labour and infant mortality cause, puts governments under a special obligation to intervene.

1
Child Labour, Education, and Saving

In this and the next chapter, we construct a comprehensive theory of household behaviour with a focus on child labour, education, fertility, and infant mortality. To do that seriously, one has to take account of the sequential nature of domestic decisions, and of the uncertainty surrounding some of their outcomes. Failing to account for that misses out crucial aspects of the decision process. The simplest decision sequence includes three decision steps, or stages. At Stage 1, the couple choose the level of birth control, and the amount of food, clothing, medical care, etc. to buy for themselves and for each of their children. The latter will condition their children's probability of surviving to the next stage. At Stage 2, the surviving children reach school age. Parents then decide whether and for how long to send these children to school or to work, how much to save, and how much to spend for themselves, and for each of their children's consumption, education, and medical care. Since premature mortality is heavily concentrated in the perinatal period, and in the first year of life, we shall assume that, if a child survives to Stage 2, he or she is certain to be alive also at Stage 3. Stage 2 decisions determine the stock of human capital and other assets with which each child enters adult life at Stage 3. When the latter comes, the children are adults and the parents old. That is the last stage where the original couple are alive.

The decision problem is solved by backward induction. At Stage 3, the parents cannot produce income. All they can do is divide the assets accumulated at earlier stages between themselves and their children. In the absence of uncertainty, however, that is a decision they can take, together with all the others, at Stage 2. Where the original couple is concerned, the last decision stage is thus Stage 2. Subsequent decisions will be taken by their children. In the present chapter, we mentally place ourselves at Stage 2, where the number of school-age children is a constant determined by earlier decisions, and by chance. Throughout, we shall assume that indifference curves are parallel to each other along a ray from the origin (homotheticity). That facilitates the geometry. If all families have the same preferences, it also allows us to derive the aggregate demand for a good, and the aggregate supply of labour, from the optimization of a family with income or wealth equal to the sum of those of the individual families.

The Economics of Child Labour. Second Edition. Alessandro Cigno and Furio C. Rosati, Oxford University Press.
 DOI: 10.1093/oso/9780198903000.003.0002

1.1 Human Capital

The stock of human capital, h, with which a currently school-age person will enter adult life at the next stage of the decision process is partly innate, and partly the result of education. We write:

$$h = h_0 + g(e, k), \tag{1.1}$$

where h_0 is the innate component of h, e the amount of time that the child spends in education, k the amount of educational inputs other than own time (books, tuition, writing material, etc.), and $g(.)$ the production of human capital function. Given that school results depend not only on school attendance, but also on homework and on how rested and alert the child is during lessons, e is defined to include not only time spent at school, but also time allocated to rest and carrying out school assignments outside school hours.

Let w_c be the child wage rate, and p_k the price of the other educational inputs. Assuming for the time being that, if children work, they do so in the labour market (we will see later on what happens if children work for their parents), w_c is the opportunity-cost of e. The full cost of providing the future adult with h units of human capital is given by

$$Q(h, w_c, p_k) = \min_{e,k} (ew_c + kp_k) \text{ s.t. } h_0 + g(e, k) = h. \tag{1.2}$$

The $Q(.)$ function shows the minimum cost of producing the specified amount of output, given the prices of the inputs.

If we assume that the production of human capital function is characterized by constant returns to scale, each unit of h will be produced with the same cost-minimizing combination of e and k up to the point where the child's time endowment, normalized to 1, is fully occupied in education. From that point onwards, any increase in the production of human capital will require an increase in the quantity of the other factors. That is illustrated in Figure 1.1, where the convex-to-the-origin curves are isoquants, and the vertical line through points **E** and **F** represents the constraint that the time spent in education cannot exceed the endowment. For any given (w_c, p_k), the production of human capital will then expand along a given isocline (in the figure, the one through point **F**) to the point where $e = 1$. From that point onwards, h can be increased at a rising marginal cost by moving on to a steeper isocline (in the figure, to the isocline through point **E**). Even with constant returns to scale, the cost function is thus convex in h.

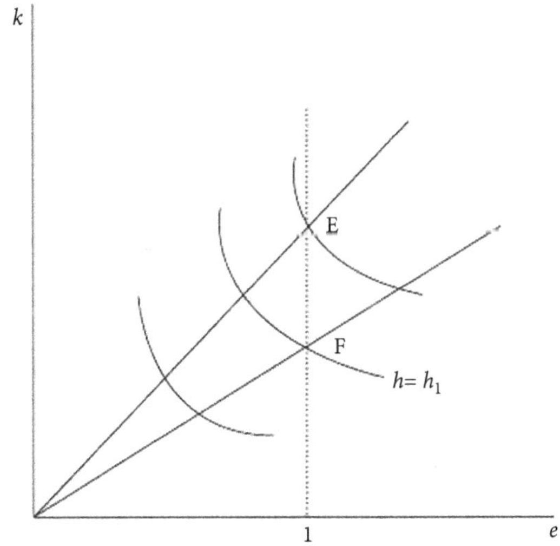

Figure 1.1 Production of human capital

Let h_1 be the level of h where the child's time becomes fully employed in education. Between h_0 and h_1, the Marginal Cost of h is a constant determined by input prices,

$$Q_h(h, w_c, p_k) = q(w_c, p_k) \text{ for } h_0 \leq h \leq h_1.$$

At higher levels, it is an increasing function of h,

$$Q_h(h, w_c, p_k) > q(w_c, p_k) \text{ for } h_1 < h.$$

Figure 1.2 shows the behaviour of the Marginal Cost of h for a given (w_c, p_k) combination. Point **L** is where the child's time becomes fully employed in education. The kinked line through that point may be interpreted as the parents' supply of human capital to each of their children. Had we assumed decreasing returns to scale, this supply curve would have been upward sloping throughout, but there would still have been a discontinuity at point **L**. Therefore, the constant returns to scale assumption does not affect the substance of the argument.

If w_c rises, the horizontal segment of the Marginal Cost of h curve shifts upwards. The point where the child starts to study full time moves to the right, because the parents economize on the child's time. The new Marginal Cost curve then looks like the kinked line through point **M**. Alternatively, suppose that p_k rises. The horizontal segment of the curve will again shift

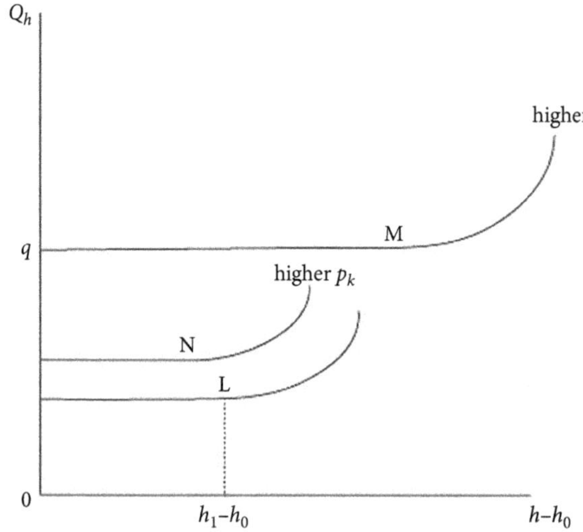

Figure 1.2 The marginal cost of human capital

upwards, but the point where the child starts to study full time will now move to the left, because parents economize on educational inputs other than the child's own time. The new Marginal Cost curve will then look like the kinked line through point **N**.

We have thus established that, like all cost functions, $Q(.)$ is increasing in output, and in input prices. The relationship with the prices is concave, because the amount used of an input is reduced as its price increases. The relationship with the output is non-concave: linear up to the point where the own-provided input is fully employed, convex from there onwards. If we drop the assumption that the production of human capital is characterized by constant returns of scale at all h levels, and assume diminishing returns over the relevant range,[1] Q_h will be an increasing function of h. The curves representing this function in Fig. 1.2 will then be convex everywhere, but there will still be a kink at the point where the child's time becomes fully occupied in education.

1.2 Parental Decisions

At Stage 2, the couple have n school-age children. Assuming, for the time being, that all children are treated the same, and that the outcome of current

[1] At very low levels of h, the production function may well be characterized by increasing returns to scale, but it would obviously be inefficient to stop there. We shall assume that, if children receive an education at all, they will receive enough of it to be in the constant or decreasing returns range.

parental decisions is certain, parental utility at this stage of the decision process may be written as

$$U_2 = u_2(a_2) + u_3(a_3) + \beta n U^*(c_2, y), \tag{1.3}$$

where a_t denotes parental consumption at Stage $t = 2, 3$, and c_2 is the amount that each child consumes (including medical care, as well as food and clothing, but excluding education) at Stage 2, and y is the income that each of the present children will have at Stage 3. Decisions may be taken by either parent, or by the two of them jointly. We may interpret (1.3) as a family welfare function reflecting the relative bargaining power of the two spouses. Notice that leisure does not figure anywhere in (1.3). That is because, in a developing country, leisure is a luxury good that only a few can afford. Therefore, children divide their time between work and education, and adults work full time.

The first and the second term on the right-hand side of (1.3) represent the utility that the parents derive from their own consumption over what is left of their life. They are thus the selfish components of U_2. The $u_t(.)$ functions are increasing and concave, and may differ according to t because of time-preference. The third term is the altruistic component of U_2, proportional to the maximum utility, denoted by $U^*(c_2, y)$, that each of the couple's children will enjoy in life, given c_2 and y. The $U^*(.)$ function is increasing and quasi-concave. The β constant is an altruism parameter that transforms the children's into the parents' utility.[2] Notice that altruism is unidirectional. It descends from parents to children. Becker (1976) justifies this assumption in evolutionary terms by saying that a couple or a species are successful in transmitting their genes to posterity if they take good care of their offspring.[3]

Parents maximize (1.3) subject to a number of restrictions. The first one is the couple's Stage 2 budget constraint,

$$a_2 + [c_2 + Q(h, w_c, p_k)]\, n + s = W_2 + w_c n, \tag{1.4}$$

where s denotes Stage-2 saving, and W_2 is the sum of the couple's earnings and assets. Given that $Q(h, w_c, p_k)$ includes not only the monetary cost, but also the opportunity-cost, of providing each child with h units of human capital, the left-hand side of (1.4) is the family's full cost. The right-hand side is the family's full income, the maximum that they would have to spend or save if

[2] For any given β, the restrictions on the form of $u_t(.)$ and $U^*(.)$ imply that selfish considerations have more weight if a_2 and a_3 are low, less weight if they are high. In the presence of uncertainty, to be introduced later in the chapter, concavity implies risk aversion.

[3] See also Becker (1981) and Cigno (2022b).

all of them, children included, worked full time. The second restriction is the couple's stage-3 budget constraint,

$$a_3 + mn = rs, \tag{1.5}$$

where m is defined as a transfer from the parents to each of the children (we may think of this as an inter vivos transfer in the course of Stage 3, or a bequest at the end of it), and r is the interest factor.

The third restriction expresses each child's Stage 3 income as the sum of the future adult's earnings and transfers received,

$$y = h\omega + m, \tag{1.6}$$

where ω is the coefficient that transforms human capital into money. We may think of this coefficient as the skill premium, the amount by which a person's earnings increase with each additional unit of human capital. In general, h could be positively affected not only by e and k as (1.1) says, but also by c_2, because school-age consumption may enhance the future adult's health and thus ability to work. It could also be negatively affected by the amount of work $(1 - e)$ that the person does while of school age, because this work could be detrimental to her or his future health, and thus reduce h. Given, however, that these additional effects have the same sign as those considered, we shall ignore them for the moment. We will take them into account in the empirical part of the book, where the size as well as the sign of an effect matters.

In addition to (1.4)–(1.6), the parents face a number of inequality constraints. One is that h cannot be less than h_0,

$$(h - h_0)\,n \geq 0, \tag{1.7}$$

because parents cannot sell their children's innate human capital without also selling the child (more about this later in this chapter). Another is that, because of credit and asset market imperfections, s cannot be lower than a certain minimum,

$$s + s_1 \geq 0, \tag{1.8}$$

where s_1 is a nonpositive number, or higher than a certain maximum,

$$s_2 - s \geq 0, \tag{1.9}$$

where s_1 is a nonnegative number. We may interpret $-s_1$ as the amount of assets that the couple has to sell or stake as collateral, or as the maximum that they can borrow without collateral (see Stiglitz and Weiss 1981; Hoff and Lyon 1995), and s_2 as the maximum that the couple can safely lend, or the maximum amount of assets there is to buy (as pointed out by Biswanger et al. 1995, in a developing country, there may be a shortage of assets, in particular land, worth buying).

Yet another restriction is that parents cannot oblige their grown-up children to pass them any of their income at Stage 3,

$$mn \geq 0. \tag{1.10}$$

That is because, when that time comes, the parents will be old, and the children working-age adults. Finally, there are the constraints that a_t and y cannot fall below the minimum, denoted by a_s, that is necessary for an adult to survive, and c_2 cannot fall below the minimum, denoted by c_s, that is necessary for a school-age child to survive. Hence,

$$(a_2 - a_s)\, n \geq 0, \left(y - \frac{a_s}{2}\right) n \geq 0, (c_2 - c_s) \geq n. \tag{1.11}$$

In the present section, we shall assume that these subsistence constraints are not binding. We shall see in a later section what happens if any of them is.

The (1.4)–(1.6) equations can be used to eliminate a_2, a_3 and y from the utility function. For the Kuhn–Tucker theorem, we multiply each inequality constraint by a Lagrange-multiplier, and add it to the utility function, with the proviso that either the constraint is binding (holds as an equation at the optimum) and its multiplier is positive, or it is slack (holds as a strict inequality) and its multiplier is zero. The maximand then becomes

$$\begin{aligned}\Lambda = {} & u_2\,(W_2 - s - zn) + u_3\,(rs - mn) + \beta n U^*\,(c_2, h\omega + m) \\ & + \gamma\,(h - h_0)\, n + \lambda_1\,(s + s_1) + \lambda_2\,(s_2 - s) + \mu mn,\end{aligned}$$

where

$$z = c_2 + Q\,(h, w_c, p_k) - w_c \tag{1.12}$$

is the net cost of a child, and $\gamma, \lambda_1, \lambda_2$ and μ are the multipliers of, respectively, (1.7), (1.8), (1.9), and (1.10).

The first-order conditions on the choice of s, c_2, h, and m are, respectively,

$$-u_2'\,(W_2 - s - zn) + ru_3'\,(rs - mn) + (\lambda_1 - \lambda_2)\, n = 0, \tag{1.13}$$

$$-u_2'\,(W_2 - s - zn)\, n + \beta n U_{c_2}^*\,(c_2, h\omega + m) = 0, \tag{1.14}$$

$$-u_2'\,(W_2 - s - zn)\, Q_h\,(h, w_c, p_k)\, n + \omega\beta U_y^*\,(c_2, h\omega + m)\, n + \gamma n = 0 \tag{1.15}$$

and

$$-u_3'(rs - mn)\,n + \beta n U_y^*(c_2, h\omega + m) + \mu n = 0. \tag{1.16}$$

Condition (1.13) may be re-written as

$$\frac{u_2'(W_2 - s - zn)}{u_3'(rs - mn)} = r + \frac{\lambda_1 - \lambda_2}{u_3'(rs - mn)}.$$

This tells us that the parents' Marginal Rate of Substitution of present for future consumption, $\frac{u_2'(W_2-s-zn)}{u_3'(rs-mn)}$, may be higher or lower than the interest factor depending on whether credit or investment is rationed ($\lambda_1 > 0$ or $\lambda_2 > 0$). Otherwise (i.e., for $\lambda_1 = \lambda_2 = 0$), the Marginal Rate of Substitution will be equated to the interest factor.

Conditions (1.14) and (1.16) together imply

$$\frac{\omega}{Q_h(h, w_c, p_k)} = \frac{\beta U_{c_2}^*(c_2, h\omega + m)}{\beta U_y^*(c_2, h\omega + m) + \gamma}.$$

If the constraint that parents cannot sell their children's innate human capital is binding ($\gamma > 0$), the Marginal Return to Education, $\frac{\omega}{Q_h(h,w_c,p_k)}$, is then smaller than the children's Marginal Rate of Substitution of present consumption for future income, $\frac{U_{c_2}^*(c_2,h\omega+m)}{U_y^*(c_2,h\omega+m)}$. Otherwise ($\gamma = 0$), the Marginal Rate of Substitution will be equated to the Marginal Return to h.

Conditions (1.14) and (1.17) together imply

$$\frac{u_2'(W_2 - s - zn)}{u_3'(rs - mn)} = \frac{\beta U_{c_2}^*(c_2, h\omega + m)}{\beta U_y^*(c_2, h\omega + m) + \mu}.$$

If parents would like to be supported by their children in old age, but cannot oblige them to do so ($\mu > 0$), the parents' Marginal Rate of Substitution of present for future consumption is then lower than the children's. Otherwise ($\mu = 0$), the two marginal rates of substitution will be equalized.

If none of the inequality constraints is binding ($\gamma = \lambda_0 = \lambda_1 = \mu = 0$), the parents and the children's marginal rates of substitution are then equalized, and their common value is equated to the interest factor, which is in turn equal to the Marginal Return to h,

$$\frac{u_2'(W_2 - s - zn)}{u_3'(rs - mn)} = \frac{U_{c_2}^*(c_2, h\omega + m)}{U_y^*(c_2, h\omega + m)} = \frac{\omega}{Q_h(h, w_c, p_k)} = r. \tag{1.17}$$

The allocation is then efficient. It will be efficient also if the constraint that h cannot be lower than h_0 is binding, but none of the other inequality constraints is ($\gamma > 0$, $\lambda_1 = \lambda_2 = \mu = 0$). If that is the case, the first two equations in (1.17) hold, but the third one does not. At $h = h_0$, the Marginal Return to h is lower than the interest factor,

$$\frac{\omega}{q(w_c, p_k)} < r. \tag{1.18}$$

Consider next the constraints that s cannot be lower than s_1, or higher than s_2. If (1.8) is binding ($\lambda_1 > 0$, $\gamma = \lambda_2 = \mu = 0$), meaning that parents cannot borrow as much as they would like, the children's and the parents' marginal rates of substitution are equalized, and their common value equated to the marginal return to education, but the latter is higher than the interest factor,

$$\frac{u_2'(W_2 - s - zn)}{u_3'(rs - mn)} = \frac{U_{c_2}^*(c_2, h\omega + m)}{U_y^*(c_2, h\omega + m)} = \frac{\omega}{Q_h(h, w_c, p_k)} > r. \tag{1.19}$$

If (1.9) is binding ($\lambda_2 > 0$, $\gamma = \lambda_1 = \mu = 0$), meaning that parents cannot lend or invest as much as they would like, the parents and the children's marginal rates of substitution are still equalized, and their common value is still equated to the Marginal Return to Education, but the latter is now lower than the interest factor,

$$\frac{u_2'(W_2 - s - zn)}{u_3'(rs - mn)} = \frac{U_{c_2}^*(c_2, h\omega + m)}{U_y^*(c_2, h\omega + m)} = \frac{\omega}{Q_h(h, w_c, p_k)} < r. \tag{1.20}$$

Consider finally the nonnegativity constraint on m. If (1.10) is binding ($\gamma = \lambda_1 = \lambda_2 = 0, \mu > 0$), meaning that parents would like to lend to their children but cannot, the parents' marginal rate of substitution is still equated to the interest factor, and the children's to the marginal return to education, but the latter is now higher than the former,

$$r = \frac{u_2'(W_2 - s - zn)}{u_3'(rs - mn)} < \frac{U_{c_2}^*(c_2, h\omega + m)}{U_y^*(c_2, h\omega + m)} = \frac{\omega}{Q_h}. \tag{1.21}$$

1.2.1 Saving and Dissaving

Figures 1.3–1.6 illustrate the solution to the parental optimization problem under four different parameter configurations. In all these pictures, the amount currently consumed by each child, denoted by c_2, is measured on the horizontal axis. The vertical axis measures the child's future earnings $h\omega$, and income (earnings plus transfers received) y. If y is higher than $h\omega$, this implies that $m = y - h\omega$ is positive. Otherwise, m will be negative. The kinked curve through point **P** is the domestic production frontier: the locus of $(c_2, h\omega)$ combinations that satisfy the Stage 2 budget constraint (1.4) for any given a_2, if s is constrained to be zero. It thus shows how far the parents can go in providing consumption and education for each of their children, if they can neither save nor dissave. The slope of the curve representing the domestic production frontier, $\frac{\omega}{Q_h}$ (equal to $\frac{\omega}{q}$ up to the point where $h = h_1$, lower than $\frac{\omega}{q}$ for $h > h_1$) is the Marginal Return to Education.[4] The straight line with slope equal to the interest factor r is the intertemporal budget constraint, obtained combining the Stage-2 and Stage-3 budget constraints, to which the parents have access only if they are free to save or dissave. This line has only point **P** in common with the domestic production frontier. The convex-to-the-origin curves are the children's indifference curves, with slope equal to the children's marginal rate of substitution of present consumption for future income, $\frac{U^*_{c_2}}{U^*_y}$.

These diagrams are analogous to those that are used in trade theory to compare a country's equilibrium under conditions of autarchy, with the same if the country is free to trade with the rest of the world. In that context, **P** is called the production point, and **C** the consumption point. In the absence of trade, production and consumption coincide at point **D**. In the present context, the country is replaced by the family, and the rest of the world by the market. Trading now means saving (buying assets, lending) or dissaving (selling assets, borrowing). If parents are free to save or dissave subject only to their intertemporal budget constraint, the solution to the family optimization problem is represented by points **P** and **C**; the allocation is then efficient. If the inequality constraints do not allow parents to save or dissave as much as they like, the solution is at point **D**; the allocation is then inefficient.

[4] We are assuming that human capital is produced under constant returs to scale. The story remains the same, however, if human capital production is produced under diminishing returns to scale, because the slope is then increasing everywhere, but still displays a discontinuously in correspondence with the point where e becomes equal to 1 (see last section).

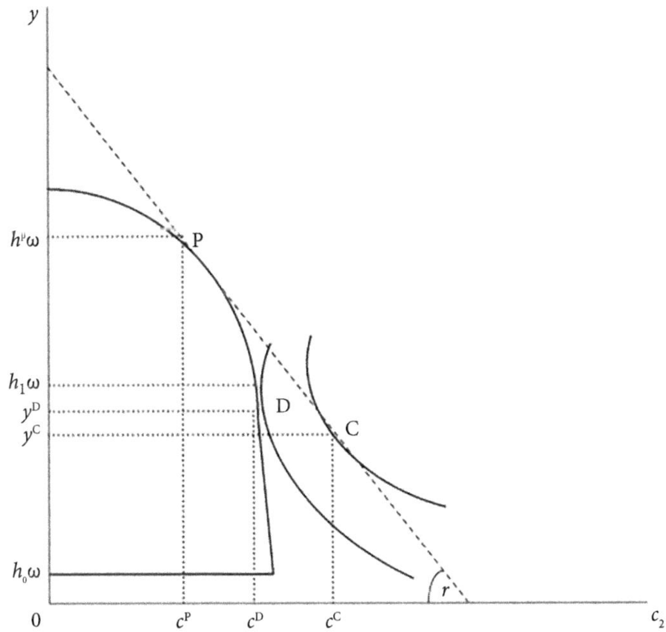

Figure 1.3 Low interest factor, parents would like to dissave

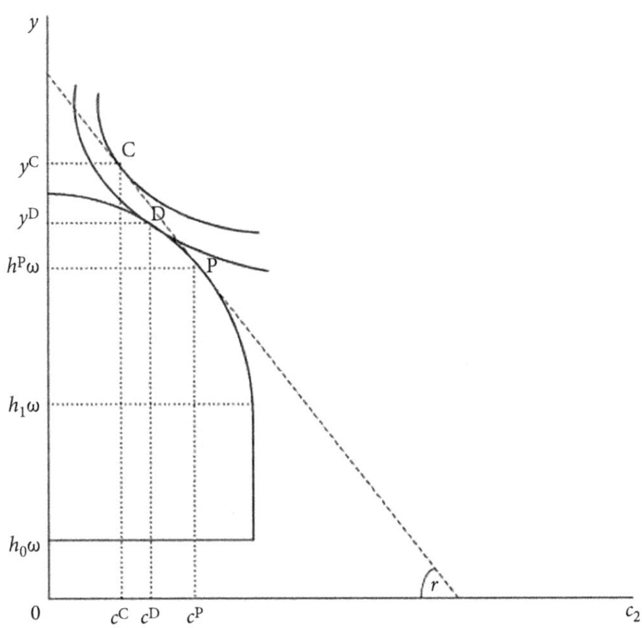

Figure 1.4 Low interest factor, parents would like to save

If the interest factor is low, in the specific sense that

$$r < \frac{\omega}{q(w_c, p_k)}, \tag{1.22}$$

the right-hand side of (1.22) is the highest possible value that the marginal return to education can take. The efficient level of education is then $e = 1$. In Figure 1.3, point **P** lies above the kink in the production frontier ($h^P > h_1$). At that point, children study full time. Point **C** lies south-east of **P**. Parents cannot choose **C**, however, because y would then be smaller than $h\omega$, and m consequently negative. Therefore, **C** violates the constraint (1.10), that children cannot be obliged to give their parents any part of their income when Stage 3 comes. The best parents can do is choose point **D**, where the production and the consumption point coincide,[5] and m is equal to zero. At that point, (1.22) applies. The children's marginal rate of substitution is equated to the marginal return to education, and the parents' to the interest factor, but the former is higher than the latter. As can be seen from the fact that the indifference curve through **D** is lower than the one through **C**, this allocation is inefficient. In particular, child labour is inefficiently high. Children work part-time instead of not at all.

The story that goes with this equilibrium is told in Baland and Robinson (2000, 2002). Children cannot borrow from the credit market because they cannot sign a contract that would legally commit them to paying a loan back with interests. If they could make such a commitment to their own parents, both parties would be better off. Given that $\frac{\omega}{Q_h}$ is greater than r, the children would in fact be willing to pay their parents more than the market does. But, children cannot make such a commitment to their parents any more than they could to anybody else. The reason why the allocation is inefficient is thus that a potentially beneficial contract cannot be implemented (there is a 'hold-up problem'). Now imagine, for a moment, that (1.10) is not binding, but (1.8) is. Given that children cannot commit to paying their parents or anyone else back when they become adults, parents will neither lend to their own children, nor borrow from the credit market on their children's behalf.[6]

In Figure 1.4, point **P** is again above the kink in the production frontier, but **C** lies now north-west of **P**. Given that y^C is larger than $h^P\omega$, m^C is then positive. Parents are so rich and generous that, in addition to letting their children study full time, they would like to save in order to make them gifts

[5] Were we talking of a country rather than a family, **D** would be the autarchic equilibrium, the point where the country does not trade with the rest of the world.

[6] The second part of this statement is not in Baland and Robinson (2000, 2002), but it follows logically from their argument.

when they become adults. If parents cannot do that because (1.9) is binding, however, the solution is at point **D**, where (1.21) applies. Here, education is inefficiently high ($h^D\omega = y^D > h^P\omega$). The reason why education is too high, however, is not that the children spend too much of their time studying. It is too high because parents buy too much k (send their children to unnecessarily expensive private schools, hire personal tutors, etc.). If parents had better investment opportunities (i.e., if (1.9) were not binding), they would spend less for their children's education, and everybody would be happier.

Alternatively, suppose that the interest factor is high, in the sense that

$$r > \frac{\omega}{q(w_c, p_k)}. \tag{1.23}$$

Constraint (1.7) is now binding, meaning that parents would sell off their children's natural talent if they could, but they are not allowed to. The efficient allocation is now at the corner where $e = 0$. Given that the return to lending or conventional forms of investment is higher than the return to education, and having (somewhat restrictively) assumed that the only purpose of education is to produce a future income, if parents want to do their children's good, they should give them money or other conventional assets, not an education.

In Figure 1.5, point **C** lies south-east of point **P**, meaning that, were it possible, parents would do the next best thing to selling off their children's innate

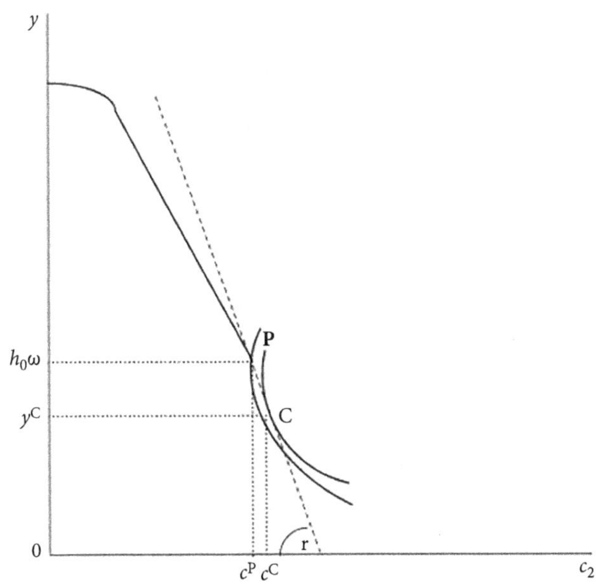

Figure 1.5 High interest factor, parents would like to dissave

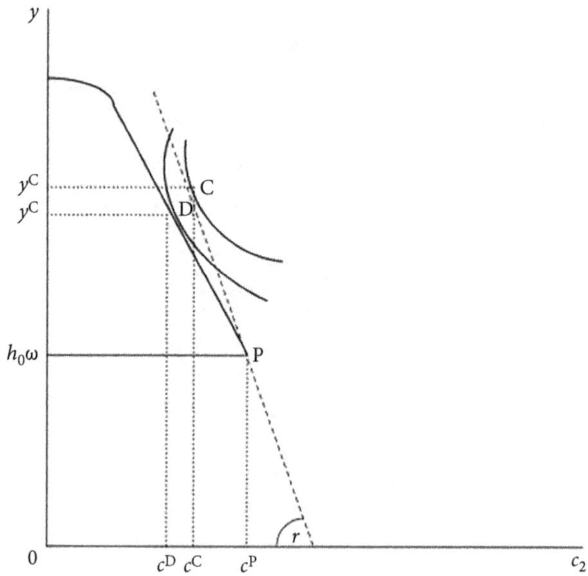

Figure 1.6 High interest factor, parents would like to save

human capital h_0. They would borrow against it. That is not possible, however, because y^C is lower than $h_0\omega$, and m is consequently negative. Therefore, (1.10) is binding. Parents cannot choose **C**. The best they can do is make **P** their consumption as well as their production point. At **P**, the common value of the parents' and the children's marginal rates of substitution is higher than the interest factor. As we can see from the fact that the indifference curve through **P** is lower than the one through **C**, the allocation is inefficient. The inefficiency is not in that the children work too much (given that the marginal return to education is lower than the marginal return to other forms of investment, it is efficient for them to work full time). The inefficiency is in that the children's current consumption is lower that it would be without (1.10).

In Figure 1.6, by contrast, **C** lies north-west of **P**. Parents would now like to save at Stage 2, and use the money to make each of their children a gift equal to $y^C - h_0\omega$ at Stage 3. If they can save as much as they like, they will then do so to the point where their Marginal Rate of Substitution and those of their children are equal to the interest factor. The allocation would then be efficient. If (1.9) is binding, however, parents cannot save as much as they would like (there are not sufficient investment or lending opportunities). The solution is then at point **D**, where children work part-time. As can be seen from the fact that the indifference curve through **D** is lower than the one through **C**, the allocation is inefficient. Child labour is inefficiently low (in contrast with the equilibrium represented by point **P** of Figure 1.5, children study too much).

We have thus established that asset and credit market imperfections may result in either an inefficiently high, or an inefficiently low supply of child labour. The latter may seem paradoxical, but it cannot be ruled out in a developing country where the marginal return to education can be low for a variety of reasons,[7] especially if the world interest rate is high for reasons that nothing have to do with that country.[8] We have also found that asset and credit market imperfections may lead to excessive private expenditure for education. That is unlikely to concern the very poor, but it may well be the case in families that are only just comfortably off.[9]

These conclusions rest on the assumption that child labour is not a bad (it causes disutility only indirectly, by reducing the child's future earning capacity), and that education is not a good (it yields utility only indirectly, by increasing the child's future earning capacity). If child labour is a bad (i.e., it is unpleasant for the children, and thus for their altruistic parents), or education is a good (realistically, if it is a luxury good, yielding direct utility when income is above a certain level), an equilibrium with child labour may be inefficiently high even if none of the constraints from (1.8) to (1.10) is binding.[10] In other words, the equilibrium may be inefficient even if parents are sufficiently rich and altruistic to want to give their children money as well as an education, and no credit or asset market imperfection stops them doing so. The same applies if education is a public good, yielding utility for society as a whole (that is widely recognized, and particularly important in a developing country without a long established sense of the state). If that is the case, however the positive education externality may well counterbalance the inefficiency of the opposite sign arising from the parents' inability to invest in assets other their children's human capital as much as they would find optimal.

1.2.2 Domestic Work

So far we have assumed that, if children work at all, they will work in the labour market. In reality, the vast majority of working children work for their parents. We shall call this activity domestic work, even though it includes not

[7] A sparse population, or the presence of a wide variety of dialects, raises the cost of delivering education to all children (makes Q_h larger). A largely uneducated or low educated adult labour force discourages investment in skill-intensive technology on the part of firms, and thus reduces the remuneration of human capital (more about this in Chapter 9).

[8] This may be the case because of restrictive monetary policies on the part of developed countries' central banks concerned about high inflation in their part of the world.

[9] A *New York Times* article cited in Waldman (2003) documents an outburst of spending for private education by only moderately well-off Indian families.

[10] See Bommier and Dubois (2004).

only household chores like cooking, cleaning, fetching water, and gathering fuel, but also working in the family farm or family business. The children engaging in the latter contribute to the family income directly. Those engaging in the former contribute to family income indirectly, by substituting their parents in the performance of those homely activities. Unlike the child wage rate, which is a given constant as far as the family is concerned, the marginal product of domestic work is a decreasing function of the amount worked. If it is everywhere lower than w_c, children do not do any domestic work. If it is higher than w_c up to a certain amount of domestic work, and lower above that, the children's total work time will be divided between the two forms of work. Given that the marginal opportunity-cost of e is still w_c, however, the total amount worked will be the same as it would if the children worked only in the labour market. If the marginal product of domestic work is everywhere higher than w_c, the children will not do any market work. The marginal opportunity-cost of e will then be the marginal product of domestic work. The children will work to the point where the marginal product of domestic work is equal to the marginal return of education.

The distinction between domestic and market work does not upturn our results, but prompts some additional considerations. If at least part of what we are calling domestic work takes place in the family farm or the family business, its marginal product is an increasing function of the amount of productive assets owned by the family. For example, the marginal product of children working in the family farm will be higher, and children may consequently work more, if the family owns land, than if it does not.[11] Similarly, the marginal product of children working in the family workshop will be higher, and children may consequently work more, if the family owns a certain machine. If government policy, or a microcredit scheme, makes it possible for a family to buy such assets on credit, it is then possible that this will induce children to work more rather than less. The empirical evidence reviewed in the empirical chapters of this book confirms this prediction.

1.2.3 Uncertainty

Up to now, we have taken the outcome of Stage 2 decisions as certain. In reality, all investments are risky to some extent. We shall now follow Pouliot (2006) by introducing uncertainty in the outcome of educational decisions, and comparing the solution in the presence of an insurance market that

[11] May rather than will work more, because there is an income effect pulling in the opposite direction of the substitution effect.

allows parents to fully insure against the risk of an unfavourable outcome, with the solution in the absence of such a market. Neither hypothesis is entirely realistic, but the second is more realistic than the first. Perfect insurance is seldom available even in a developed economy, let alone a developing one, because of moral hazard and adverse selection problems. In a developing country context, there may be the possibility of informal insurance arrangements at the local level, where the asymmetric information problem is less severe. This kind of insurance, however, can only cover idiosyncratic risks, like that of a personal accident. Aggregate risks, like that of adverse weather causing crop failure for an entire community, cannot be insured against through local arrangements.

Educational investment is subject to two kinds of uncertainty, one concerning h, and the other concerning ω. The former is uncertain because it depends not only on e and k, but also on the child's learning ability, which may not be known before the investment is made. We have defined h_0 as a constant representing a person's innate human capital. The more is this human capital, the less extra human capital has to be produced using costly inputs to achieve the desired total, represented by h. To the extent that h_0 measures a person's ability to learn, however, this constant is a cost-reducing parameter of the $Q(.)$ function. If it is not known in advance, h is then uncertain. The latter is uncertain, because it depends on market conditions at Stage 3 when the child enters adult life, not known at Stage 2 when educational decisions are taken.

We have expressed a child's lifetime utility U^* as a function of the child's present consumption c_2, and future income $y = h\omega + m$. This implies that the child, and consequently also the child's altruistic parents, are indifferent between a sum of money m for certain, and an uncertain prospect with expected value equal to $h\omega$. That is a legitimate assumption to make under conditions of certainty, but not otherwise, because in that case a risk-averse person prefers the certain m to the uncertain $h\omega$.

In the absence of a perfect insurance market, risk-averse parents will choose an inefficiently low value of h. If this is lower than h_1, children will then study part time or not at all. Child labour will be inefficiently high. In conclusion, insurance market imperfection has qualitatively the same effect as credit market imperfection. The allocation will be inefficient even in the presence of a perfect insurance market if the outcome of educational investment is uncertain for individual families, but not for society as a whole (because families are many). More on this in Chapter 9.

1.2.4 Access Costs

So far, we have not allowed for the possibility that children do nothing. As we shall see in later chapters, however, household surveys report a large proportion of school-age children, as much as a quarter, who neither work, nor attend school. That is puzzling in areas where a large number of families live close to the subsistence line. Comparing surveys relating to different countries, we also find that combining work with study is common in some places, for example in Latin America, but uncommon in others, for example in rural India. The theory predicts that children will not work and study at the same time if their parents are free to save or dissave, insurance is available, and the non-negativity constraint on parental transfers to grown-up children is not binding. Were it true that the places where it is unusual for children to combine work with study are also the places where parents are rich and generous, and financial markets fully operative, that would explain the empirical finding. But we have no reason to believe that this is the case. Scarcity of part-time work opportunities could be another explanation. Yet another could be that, as we will see in the policy chapter, child labour may be officially prohibited, but the work that children do for their parents is not observable by the competent authorities and thus goes on undetected. Reportedly non-working children could thus be actually working in the family farm or family business, or substituting for their parents in the performance of domestic chores.

Actual (rather than apparent) idleness can be explained also by the presence of fixed costs of access to school and work. Fixed means that the cost must necessarily be incurred if a child is to carry out a certain activity, but does not vary with the number of hours spent carrying it out. Such costs may include travel to school or place of employment, and living expenses away from home while at school or working. Where education is concerned, they may include also school fees, expenditure for essential educational material, and possibly also for clothing (in some surveys, children give lack of decent clothing as a reason for not attending school). The fixed costs of access to work may include also search costs, or paying a labour 'recruiter'. If the fixed cost of education is sufficiently high, a child will not go to school even if the marginal return is high. If the fixed cost of access to the labour market is sufficiently high, a child may work only for her or his parents even though, as assumed, the marginal product of this type of work is lower than w_c. If both types of fixed cost are high enough, the child will neither study nor work in the labour market, and only engage in domestic work.

1.2.5 Extreme Poverty

Extreme poverty cannot be defined with reference to a single family characteristic such as full income. We characterize it as a configuration of initial assets, interest and wage rates, marginal return to education, and number and preferences of children, such that parental choice is effectively constrained by one or more of the subsistence constraints in (1.11). Figures 1.3–1.6 were drawn under the assumption that a_2 and a_3 are fixed at their utility-maximizing levels. To deal with the consequences of extreme poverty, we now assume that $a_2 = a_3 = a_s$. We then consider the point, call it **S**, with coordinates ($c_2 = c_s, y = a_s$). The position of this point determines whether a solution exists, and which of the subsistence constraints is binding. If (1.7)–(1.10) are not binding, for a feasible solution to exist, **S** must lie on or below the intertemporal budget line. If any of those constraints is binding, however, **S** must lie on or inside the domestic production frontier. In this case, if a solution exists, it is inefficient for the reasons we know. If a solution does not exist, the family cannot survive under the assumptions made so far.

Take for example the situation portrayed in Figures 1.3 or 1.4. Parents choose the efficient allocation described by points **P** and **C** if they have access to the intertemporal budget line, or the inefficient one represented by point **D** if they do not. Given the subsistence constraints, however, the choice of **C** is not possible if y^C is lower than a_s, or c_2^C lower than c_s. Therefore, extreme poverty may prevent an efficient solution. The choice of **D** is not possible either if y^D is lower than a_s, or c_2^D lower than c_s. If that is the case, the optimization does not have a solution. The family is so abjectly poor that, if the government does not come to the rescue,[12] slavery, 'tied' or 'bonded' labour are the only means of survival. We talk of tied labour if a person is committed to work for a certain employer over a long period of time in exchange for a stream of predetermined wage payments. We talk of bonded labour if the worker, or the worker's family, gets a lump-sum payment at front. The difference between slavery and tied or bonded labour is the same that there is between outright sale and a long lease, but the difference is immaterial if the length of the lease is very long. In ancient times, slavery was legal.

[12] In the case illustrated, a lump-sum income subsidy would strongly reduce child labour in households close to subsistence, weakly in other strata of society. This seems to carry the policy implication that a government primarily concerned with child labour should give priority to bringing families out of extreme poverty. Using data from Vietnam, Edmonds (2005) finds that improvements in household income (proxied by per capita expenditure) explain 80 per cent of the decline in child labour observed between 1993 and 1997 in households that moved out of poverty over that period. The effect on non-poor households is much weaker. This is consistent with the common belief that child labour is caused by extreme poverty. But, we have seen that child labour may arise even without extreme poverty.

In less distant ones, bonded labour was. At the end of the nineteenth century, a young London-trained barrister, the future Mahatma Gandhi, made his first appearance on the international political scene by campaigning for the rights of bonded labourers originating from the Indian sub-continent in South Africa. Nowadays, slavery and bondage are illegal, but they persist nevertheless. According to the latest estimates (ILO 2022) 24.9 million people are obliged by private individuals, or even by the State authorities, to work under threat or coercion as domestic workers, on construction sites, in clandestine factories, on farms and fishing boats, and in the sex industry. One-fifth of these forced labourers are in debt bondage, mostly in mining, agriculture, or construction, but also in the services sector, especially domestic service.

Consider a family living close to subsistence at the best of times. Suppose that an uninsured, catastrophic event (e.g., repeated crop failures) brings the family below the subsistence threshold. If the government does not intervene, and further credit is not available, parents have no option but to deliver themselves, or some of their children, into bondage or slavery in order to pay back the debt. Genicot (2002) demonstrates that the possibility of delivering oneself, or one's children, into bonded labour makes it less likely that assetless households will get credit from legitimate lenders, and thus more likely that desperate people will resort to borrowing from unscrupulous lenders. If a borrower defaults on his repayments to a bank, he will in fact be denied credit by that and any other bank the next time round. If bonding were effectively outlawed, potential borrowers would know that the penalty for defaulting is death by starvation. If debt bondage is only nominally outlawed, however, it is possible for the defaulter to survive. The existence of this safety net makes the borrower's commitment to pay back a debt a little less credible, and consequently restricts the range of loan applications that financial institutions are willing to accept. Given that children are more docile than adults, and easier to restrain by force if need be, we shall assume (though it is not universally true) that only children are acceptable as bonds. Even though it is unfortunately not always true, we shall suppose that parents resort to giving their children away only if the family cannot survive by any other means.[13]

Let us then suppose that parents cannot borrow, and that full household income is not sufficient to keep all existing family members above the subsistence level ($a_2 \geq a_s$ and $c_2 \geq c_s$) even if education and any other form of investment is set equal to zero ($h = h_0$ and $s = 0$). Imagine that an unscrupulous buyer is willing to pay the parents a sum of money A in exchange for a child. This price must be larger than the net contribution that the child would

[13] Bales (1999) brings evidence of girls delivered into prostitution not to stave off starvation, but in order to buy a consumer durable.

make to the family budget if he or she were kept in the family,

$$A \geq w_c - c_s, \tag{1.24}$$

for otherwise there would be no point in giving her or him away. This condition implies that a child's work is worth more to the buyer than to an ordinary employer, suggesting that the former can get away with using the child for activities that are either illegal, or illegally carried out. At best, a bonded or enslaved child will in fact work excessively long hours. At worst, he or she will be engaged in physically dangerous, or morally objectionable activities (what the international conventions classify as 'unconditional worst' forms of child labour).

Let **B** denote the number of bonded or enslaved children. Obviously,

$$0 \leq B \leq n. \tag{1.25}$$

Given that all variables other than B are fixed, there is no utility maximization. B is determined by solving the Stage 2 budget constraint, which now reads

$$a_s + (c_s - w_c)(n - B) = W_2 + AB, \tag{1.26}$$

subject to the condition that

$$W_2 + An \geq a_s, \tag{1.27}$$

or nobody would survive even if all the children were bonded. If a value of B satisfying (1.25)–(1.27) exists, it is

$$B^* = \frac{a_s + (c_s - w_c)\,n - W_2}{A + c_s - w_c}. \tag{1.28}$$

The numerator on the right-hand side of (1.28) is positive for the starting assumption that nobody would survive if none of the children were bonded. The denominator is positive for otherwise there would be no point in bonding a child. Therefore, B^* is positive. As A figures in the denominator, B^* is a decreasing function of it. Given that

$$\frac{dB^*}{dw_c} = -\frac{W_2 + An - a_s}{(A + c_s - w_c)^2}$$

is non-positive in view of (1.27), B^* is a non-increasing function (a decreasing one if $W_2 + An$ is greater than a_s) of the child wage rate.

Put another way, if parents do not need to dispose of all their children in order to survive, B decreases as w_c increases. Having established in the last subsection that an increase in the child wage rate makes it more likely that a child will work, this raises a difficult moral question. Imagine that a multinational company opens a factory in a very poor area, where children are at risk of being bonded. If the factory can pay child workers more than local employers do, because it uses a more productive technology or sells its product in richer markets, the equilibrium w_c rises. The probability that a child will be bonded or sold then falls, but the probability that a child will work in the ordinary way rises. Is that better or worse than the status quo? Answering this question requires a value judgement. If the answer is that it is better, one is saying that an increase in the number of children working in an ordinary way is a price worth paying to prevent even only one child being abused. If the answer is that it is worse, it means that one is not willing to pay that price.

1.3 The Market for Child Labour

So far we have taken all prices, including wage rates, as given. We now examine the way a price of particular interest for our subject, the child wage rate w_c, is determined. To do that, we revert to the simplifying assumption that ω is certain. The effect of uncertainty will be addressed in Chapter 9. We start by deriving the supply of child labour, and then examine the possible child labour market equilibria.

We saw in Section 1.2 of the present chapter that the parents' choice of h, s and m is efficient if the parents can borrow or lend as much as they like, and are rich enough to make presents or leave bequests to their grown-up children if they so wish. If (1.7) is not binding either (meaning that parents would not sell off their children's innate human capital even if they could), parents then invest in their children's human capital h to the point where the Marginal Return to this asset, $\frac{\omega}{Q_h(h,w_c,p_k)}$, equals the opportunity-cost represented by the interest factor r. Otherwise, h will be set equal to its lowest possible value h_0. The solution is still efficient, but it is at a corner.

Since the Marginal Return to h is a non-increasing function of h and a decreasing function of w_c, any increase in the latter must be accompanied by a reduction in the former for (1.18) to remain true. That is possible, however, only if h is greater than h_1. Below that value of h, the Marginal Return becomes $\frac{\omega}{q(w_c,p_k)}$, independent of h. That is the highest possible value of that marginal return. Let $\widetilde{w}_c$ denote the threshold value of the child wage rate, the one that equates the highest possible value of the Marginal Return to education to the exogenously given interest factor,

$$\frac{\omega}{q(\widetilde{w}_c, p_k)} = r. \tag{1.29}$$

So long as h is larger than h_1, the parents' demand for h will then decrease as w_c rises. The moment h reaches h_1, a small increase in w_c will have no effect on h because, at the point where $h = h_1$, the frontier has a kink (see Figures 1.1–1.6). An increase large enough to make w_c equal to $\widetilde{w}$, however, will cause h to fall discontinuously to h_0. What about e? So long as w_c is low enough for h to be at least as high as h_1, children study full time, $e = 1$. For w_c equal to, or just lower than, $\widetilde{w}$, e is indeterminate, it can take any value between 1 and 0. For w_c higher than, $\widetilde{w}$, $e = 0$, children work full time.

In Figure 1.7, the vertical axis measures the child wage rate w_c. The horizontal axis measures child labour $(1 - e)$ from left to right, and education e from right to left. The (per-child) supply of child labour function is represented by the broken **SS** line. This has two vertical segments, one perpendicular to $e = 1$ in correspondence with the $w_c < \widetilde{w}_c$ wage rate range, and the other perpendicular to $e = 0$ in correspondence with the $w_c > \widetilde{w}_c$ wage rate range, joined together by a horizontal segment in correspondence with the threshold value of $w_c = \widetilde{w}_c$. Given an efficient allocation therefore, child labour responds to a change in w_c only if this change is large enough (or w_c is close enough to $\widetilde{w}_c$) for w_c to jump from below to above $\widetilde{w}_c$, or vice versa.

Let us now introduce the demand for child labour. As the supply is expressed in per-child terms, we do the same with the demand. Figure 1.7 illustrates the different possibilities. If the demand is represented by the **DD** line, the equilibrium wage rate is $\widetilde{w}_c$. Children then divide their time between work and education. They will study full time if the demand line is **DD"**, in which case the equilibrium wage rate is w_c'', lower than $\widetilde{w}_c$. By contrast, if the demand line were **DD'**, the equilibrium wage rate would be w_c', higher than $\widetilde{w}_c$, and children would work full time. Remember that all these equilibria, including the one where children work full time, are derived under the assumption that none of the (1.8)–(1.10) constraints is binding, and thus that the allocation is efficient.

If any of those inequality constraints is binding, the resource allocation chosen by the parents is inefficient. In Figures 1.1–1.6, this type of solution is represented by point **D**. If (1.7) is not binding as in Figures 1.3, 1.4, and 1.6, the inefficient solution is interior. Depending on which of (1.8), (1.9) or (1.10) is binding, it then satisfies (1.20), (1.21) or (1.22). In each

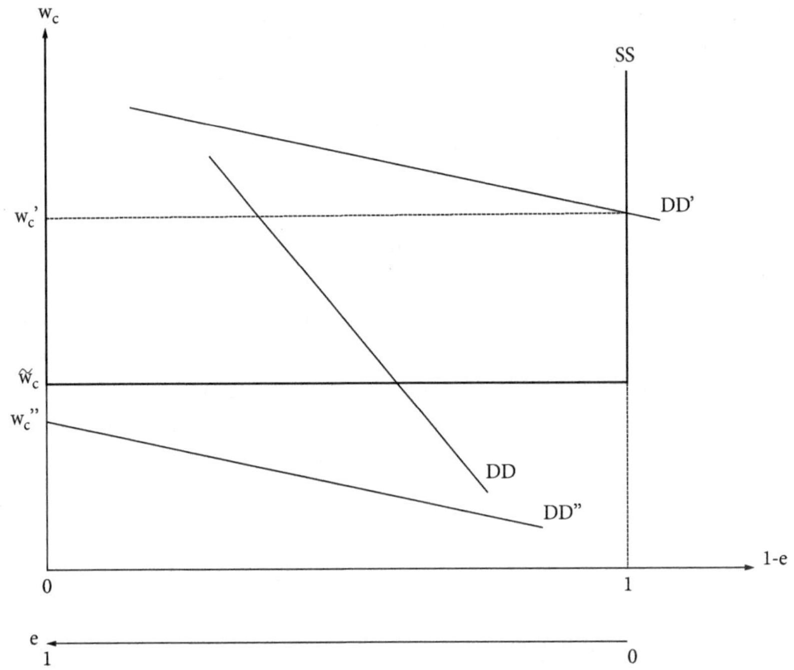

Figure 1.7 Efficient child labour equilibria

case, the Marginal Return to h, $\frac{\omega}{Q_h(h,w_c,p_k)}$, is thus equated to the children's Marginal Rate of Substitution of current consumption c_2 for future income y, $\frac{U^*_{c_2}(c_2,h\omega+m)}{U^*_y(c_2,h\omega+m)}$. In the first and the third case (when parents cannot borrow from the credit market as much as they would like, or would like to lend to their children but cannot), however, the Marginal Return to h is now lower than the interest factor r. In the second case (when parents cannot lend to the credit market, or invest in conventional assets, as much as they would like) the Marginal Return to h is higher than r. If (1.7) is binding as in Figure 1.5 (where point **D** coincides with point **P**), the inefficient solution is at the $h = h_0$ corner, Like the efficient solution, the inefficient one then satisfies (1.19).

If the allocation is inefficient, therefore, the Marginal Return to h, $\frac{\omega}{Q_h(h,w_c,p_k)}$, is not equated to the interest factor r, which is a constant, but to the children's Marginal Rate of Substitution of c_2 for y, $\frac{U^*_{c_2}(c_2,h\omega+m)}{U^*_y(c_2,h\omega+m)}$, which is a decreasing function of h like $\frac{\omega}{Q_h(h,w_c,p_k)}$. We cannot then be as definite about the effect of w_c on h, as we would if the allocation were efficient. As w_c rises, the frontier will in fact become less steep (the Marginal Return to h will decrease), but the area under it will expand (the budget constraint will become less

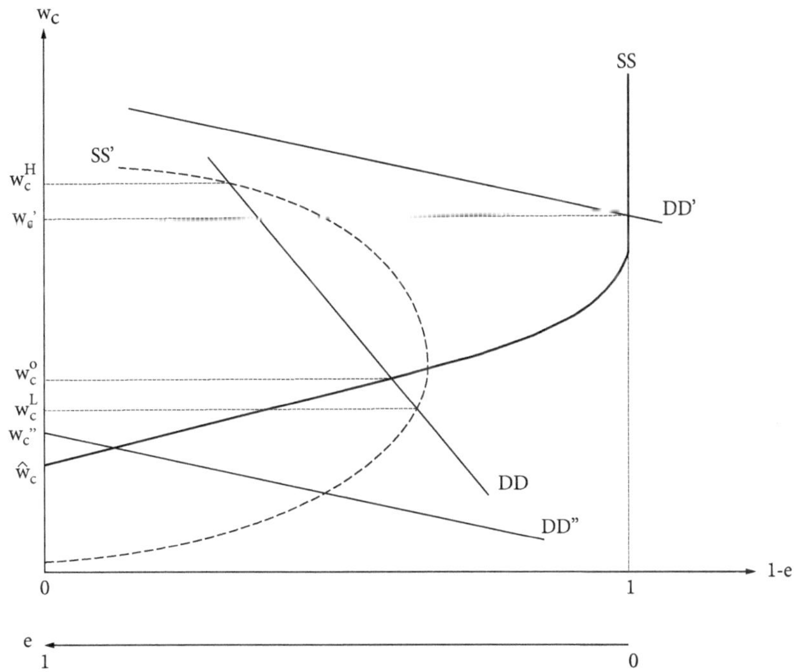

Figure 1.8 Inefficient child labour equilibria

stringent). There will thus be a substitution-effect pulling h downwards, and an income-effect pulling it upwards. Let $\widehat{w}_c$ be the value of w_c such that

$$\frac{\omega}{q\left(\widehat{w}_c, p_k\right)} = \frac{U^*_{c_2}\left(c_2, h\omega + m\right)}{U^*_y\left(c_2, h\omega + m\right)}. \tag{1.30}$$

For $w_c = \widehat{w}_c$, $h = h_1$. Given that $\widehat{w}_c$ depends on preferences rather than r, there is no reason why it should be equal to $\widetilde{w}_c$.

If W_2 is not so small that the family would fall below subsistence if the children did not work, we can make the common assumption that the income-effect is dominated by the substitution-effect. The supply curve then looks like the broken **SS** curve of Fig. 1.8. As w_c rises, point **D** slides down the frontier. For $w_c \leq \widehat{w}_c$, h will then fall, but e will remain equal to 1, because h is at least equal to h_1. Up to $\widehat{w}_c$, the supply of child labour curve is thus vertical. At $w_c = \widehat{w}_c$, however, the frontier has a kink. At that child wage rate level, as w_c rises above $\widehat{w}_c$, and point **D** gets over the kink, h will then fall discontinuously, but not all the way down to h_0. As h falls, $\frac{U^*_{c_2}(c_2,h\omega+m)}{U^*_y(c_2,h\omega+m)}$ will in fact fall too. Eventually, h will become equal to h_0 and stop there. For $h \geq h_1$, e is fixed at 1. Below $h = h_1$, e falls with h. Indeed, e falls faster than h, as w_c rises, because parents 'produce' each unit of h with less and less e, and more and more k (as shown in Figure 1.1, they move on to a steeper isocline). The reduction in e is thus the result of two substitution-effects, of c_2 for h, and k for e. When w_c is so high that h is equal to h_0, e is equal to 0. At that wage rate, the supply of child labour is again vertical.

The story changes a little if W_2 is sufficiently small for the substitution-effect to prevail over the income-effect only at low w_c values. If that is the case, parents are so poor that children will start working at a wage rate that is only just higher than zero. Given this head start, however, there may be a w_c value high enough for the income produced by the children to be so large, that the income-effect is larger than the substitution-effect. At that w_c level, a further increase would raise the demand for h, and thus the demand for e, instead of lowering them. The supply curve would then bend back like the dashed **SS'** curve shown in Figure 1.8.

The possible equilibrium types are illustrated in Figure 1.8. Suppose that the supply curve is **SS**. If the demand line is **DD**, the equilibrium wage rate is w_c^0, higher than $\widehat{w}_c$. Children then work part time. They would work full time if the demand line were **DD'**, in which case the equilibrium wage rate would be w_c', higher than w_c^0. If the demand line were **DD"**, the equilibrium wage rate would be w_c'', lower than $\widehat{w}_c$, and children would study full time. Alternatively, suppose that the supply curve is **SS'**. If the demand line were sufficiently inelastic like for example **DD**, it could then cut the supply curve at two points, one where the equilibrium wage rate is low, $w_c = w_c^L$, and child labour is relatively high, the other where the equilibrium wage rate is high, $w_c = w_c^H$, and child labour is relatively low. Depending on the properties of the demand and supply curves, there is thus a range of possible equilibrium types. All these equilibria, including those where children study full time, are inefficient however, because the supply curve is derived under the assumption that the inequality constraints prevent parents from choosing point **C**. The policy implications of multiple equilibria, some with less and some with more child labour, are examined in Chapter 9.

All of this was on the assumption that human capital production is characterized by constant returns to scale (see Section 1.1), that child labour is not a bad, and that education is not a good. As already noted, if human capital production is characterized by diminishing returns to scale, the Marginal Cost of h is increasing, and the Marginal Return to Education decreasing, for all values of h greater than h_0. Even in the efficiency case, there will then be a range of wage rate values for which e decreases as w_c increases, and a lump-sum subsidy would thus reduce child labour. If that is so, the supply of child labour curve will look like **SS** of Figure 1.8 no matter whether the allocation is efficient or inefficient (the only difference is that, in the inefficiency case, $\widehat{w}_c$ may differ from $\widetilde{w}_c$). Allowing for the possibility that the Marginal Cost of h is increasing even before h reaches h_1, therefore, an income elasticity of child labour different from zero does not imply inefficiency. As pointed out in Section 1.2, if child labour is a bad, or education a good, an equilibrium with $e = 0$ is unlikely to occur, and may be inefficient if it does. If education is a public good, the equilibrium level of e will be inefficiently low even if none of the (1.8)–(1.10) inequality constraints is binding.

2

Fertility, Infant Mortality, and Gender

With this chapter, we enter a sphere of human endeavour where the rationality assumption underlying economic analysis is stretched to the limit. But, a theoretical proposition must be judged by its ability to explain statistical regularities, not by its conformity with our preconceptions. Time, and the vast theoretical and empirical literature sparked off by Gary Becker's 1960 seminal contribution to the economics of fertility, have quelled the initial furore.[1]

In what follows, we deal with a number of questions relating to fertility, infant mortality, and gender. Section 2.1 draws on Cigno (1998), Section 2.2 on Cigno (2012b, 2014). Somewhat restrictively, we assume that babies are born within a stable relationship ('marriage') between a man and a woman. The term 'gender' is used in its current sociological connotation alluding to the social implications of sex differences, but our line of reasoning is strictly economic. In the first section, we retain the simplifying assumption made in the last chapter that parents act as if they were one person. In the second, we distinguish between mother and father, and between daughters and sons. At the end of each section, we point out some of the policy implications as a premise for the fuller discussion in Chapter 9.

2.1 Fertility and Infant Mortality

We have seen how parents choose c_2, h, m, and s at stage 2 of their decision process, given the number of school-age children n they have, and the economic environment they face at that stage. Remember that the stage-2 environment includes the couple's wealth W_2, the child wage rate w_c, the price of educational inputs p_k, the interest factor r, a possible ceiling on the amount the couple can borrow or lend (s_1 or s_2), and the return to human capital

[1] For textbook expositions, see Becker (1981) and Cigno (1991). For a taste of the initial controversy, see Schultz (1974).

The Economics of Child Labour. Second Edition. Alessandro Cigno and Furio C. Rosati, Oxford University Press.
 DOI: 10.1093/oso/9780198903000.003.0003

ω. For any given environment, the chosen values of the decision variables, denoted by c_2^*, h^*, m^*, and s^*, are functions of n. Substituting these values into the stage-2 utility function makes the maximized value of U_2,

$$U_2^* = u_2(W_2 - z^*n - s^*) + u_3(s^*r - m^*n) + \beta nU^*(c_2^*, y^*),$$

where

$$z^* = c_2^* + Q(h^*, w_c, p_k) - w_c$$

denotes the net cost of a child at stage 2, and

$$y^* = h^*\omega + m^*$$

the income with which that child will enter adult life at stage 3, a function of n,

$$U_2^* = v(n).$$

The function $v(.)$ is a maximum-value function, analogous to the indirect utility function, expressing the maximized value of utility as a function of all the parameters that affect the decision maker's (in the present case the parents') decisions. Although not explicitly listed, the arguments of $v(.)$ include, therefore, not only n, but also W_2, w_c, p_k, r, ω, s_0, and s_1.

The curve representing $v(n)$ is shown in Figure 2.1. Choosing the utility scale so that $v(0) = 0$, the curve goes through the origin. The slope is given by the first derivative of $v(n)$,

$$v'(n) = -z^*u_2'(W_2 - z^*n - s^*) - m^*u_3'(s^*r - m^*n) + \beta U^*(c_2^*, y^*). \quad (2.1)$$

The third term on the right-hand side of this equation is a positive constant. Given that the amount of money m^* transferred to grown-up children at stage 3 cannot be negative, the second term is either zero or negative and increasing in size as n increases (because u_3' is a decreasing function of a_3, but a_3 becomes smaller as n gets larger). If z^* is positive, meaning that school-age children cost more than they earn, the first term is negative and increasing in size as n increases (because u_2' is a decreasing function of a_2 but a_2 becomes smaller as n gets larger). If z^* is negative, meaning that school-age children

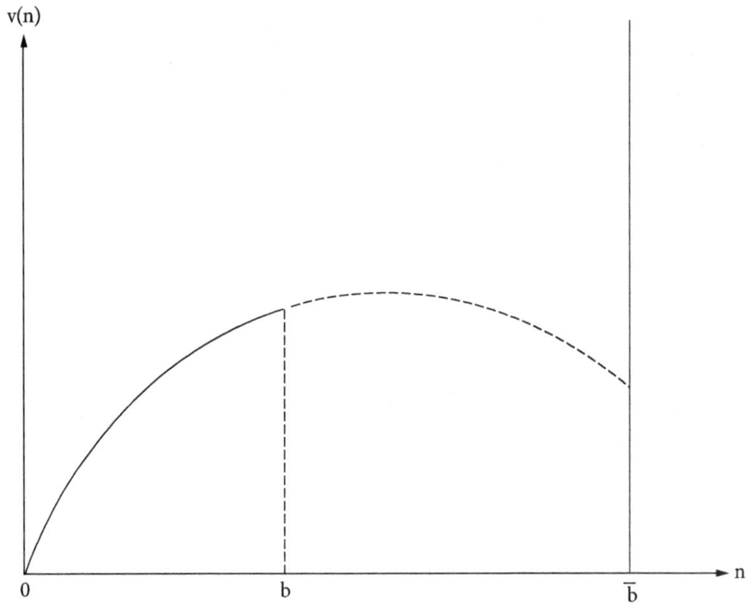

Figure 2.1 The value of school-age children

earn more than they cost, the first term is positive and decreasing in size as n increases (because u_2' is a decreasing function of a_2, but a_2 gets smaller as n becomes larger). In either case, $v'(n)$ is thus a decreasing function of n. The curve representing $v(n)$ is likely to be hump-shaped as shown in Figure 2.1, upward-sloping at low values of n, downward-sloping at high ones. Up to a certain number, an extra school-age child would have made parents happier. Above that number, an extra school-age child would have made parents less happy. The value of n at which $v(n)$ reaches a maximum decreases as z^* increases. At stage 2, however, there is nothing that parents can do about that. The number of school-age children they have at that stage is a given constant. The properties of $v(n)$ matter because they will guide parental decisions at stage 1. We are now ready to climb down the decision tree.

2.1.1 Parental Decisions Once Again

A woman's probability of becoming pregnant after unprotected intercourse decreases with age. It is very high soon after menarche, but it falls precipitously when the woman passes the age of 30, and approaches zero as menopause comes into sight. In developed countries, where women tend to marry after a long spell in education, and more years spent establishing themselves in their profession, the probability that a married woman will become pregnant after unprotected intercourse is thus low. In those countries, birth control may consequently mean seeking medical assistance to procure a first birth, rather than preventing a second or third one. By contrast, in developing countries, where women tend to marry very young, birth control generally means birth limitation.

At stage 1 of their decison process, the couple is just married. Let $\bar{b}$ denote the number of babies that would be born in the absence of birth control. For simplicity, we assume that the couple can deterministically choose how may births (less than $\bar{b}$) they want to avoid. That is a reasonable simplification, because it may not always be possible to procure a birth, but it is generally possible to prevent one. And, if prevention fails, there is always abortion or infanticide. Denoting by c_0 the number of births avoided, the number of babies the couple will have is then

$$b = \bar{b} - c_0, \tag{2.2}$$

with

$$b \leq \bar{b}. \tag{2.3}$$

Let p_0 be the price that has to be paid to avoid a birth. If the method by which this is done is modern contraception, p_0 is a monetary expenditure. If it is abstinence or *coitus interruptus*, p_0 is the money-equivalent of the disutility of carrying out such a practice. If it is abortion or infanticide, p_0 will typically have both a money and a disutility component. Among the birth control methods that are locally available, the couple will choose the one which minimizes p_0.

The probability that a baby will reach school age (and thus, for the assumption made in the last chapter that premature mortality is concentrated in the early part of life, the probability that the baby lives to be an adult) depends on a number of survival-enhancing factors beyond parental control (some totally exogenous like climate, others exogenous only where parents are concerned, but under government control like sanitation, hospital availability, etc.)[2] represented by the vector μ. This probability depends also on the amount of food, clothing, medical care, etc., denoted by c_1, that the couple give the baby. Simplifying in the extreme, we assume that the

[2] In a democracy, government-controlled variables are affected by voting behaviour, but the effect of the single voter is very small.

probability distribution is binomial.[3] There is a probability $\pi(c_1, \mu)$ that every baby will survive, and a probability $1 - \pi(c_1, \mu)$ that every baby will die. The $\pi(.,.)$ function is increasing and concave in all its arguments, with $\pi(0, \mu) = \pi(c_1, 0) = 0$. If b babies are born, the number of children expected to reach school age is then

$$E(n) = \pi(c_1, \mu)\, b \leq b. \tag{2.4}$$

Assuming that children who die before reaching school age do not yield utility, the couple's stage-1 expected utility is

$$E(U_1) = a_1 + \pi(c_1, \mu)\, v(b), \tag{2.5}$$

where a_1 stands for current parental consumption. The couple maximize (2.5) subject to (2.2)–(2.3), to the subsistence constraint

$$a_1 \geq a_s, \tag{2.6}$$

to the nonnegativity constraints

$$b \geq 0, \tag{2.7}$$

$$c_0 \geq 0 \tag{2.8}$$

and

$$c_1 \geq 0, \tag{2.9}$$

and to the budget constraint,

$$a_1 + p_0 c_0 + b p_1 c_1 = W_1, \tag{2.10}$$

where p_1 is the price of c_1, and W_1 represents parental wealth (current earnings, plus any assets). Realistically assuming that W_1 is low, because the couple are still young and have not yet inherited from their own parents, we have set stage-1 savings equal to zero. If W_1 is lower than the couple's subsistence consumption a_s, the maximization does not have a solution. We

[3] Cigno (1998), on which the present section draws, assumes a more general probability distribution, the Gamma function. For different values of its shape-parameter, this function reproduces the most common probability distributions, including Normal and Pareto. Here, we capture the essentials of that analysis in a more student-friendly way.

are then in the extreme poverty situation already encountered at stage 2, with the extra problem that, at the present stage, there are no children to bond or sell.

Using (2.2) to eliminate b, and (2.10) to eliminate a_1, the maximand becomes

$$E(U_1) = W_1 - p_0 c_0 - \left(\overline{b} - c_0\right) p_1 c_1 + \pi(c_1, \mu)\, v\left(\overline{b} - c_0\right). \tag{2.11}$$

An interior solution satisfies the first-order conditions

$$-p_0 + p_1 c_1 - \pi(c_1, \mu)\, v'\left(\overline{b} - c_0\right) = 0 \tag{2.12}$$

and

$$-\left(\overline{b} - c_0\right) p_1 + \pi_{c_1}(c_1, \mu)\, v\left(\overline{b} - c_0\right) = 0. \tag{2.13}$$

Dividing term by term and re-arranging, these conditions give us

$$\frac{\xi}{\psi} = \frac{p_1 c_1 - p_0}{p_1 c_1}, \tag{2.14}$$

where

$$\xi = \frac{\overline{b} - c_0}{v\left(\overline{b} - c_0\right)} v'\left(\overline{b} - c_0\right) \tag{2.15}$$

is the elasticity of $v(n)$ with respect to n, and

$$\psi = \frac{c_1}{\pi(c_1, \mu)} \pi_{c_1}(c_1, \mu) \tag{2.16}$$

the partial elasticity of $\pi(c_1, \mu)$ with respect to c_1. The latter is positive. Being proportional to $v'\left(\overline{b} - c_0\right)$, the former will be positive for n small, negative for n large.

There are thus two types of interior solution. In one, parents spend on each baby more than it would have cost them to prevent that baby being born,

$$p_1 c_1 > p_0. \tag{2.17}$$

As $v'(b)$ is then positive, n is small. Given that the number of children who survive to stage 2 cannot be larger than the number who are born at stage 1,

b will be small too (c_0 will be large). In the other type of interior solution, parents spend on each baby less than it would have cost them to prevent that birth,

$$p_1 c_1 < p_0 \tag{2.18}$$

As $v'(b)$ is then negative, n and b are large (c_0 will be small). The question one might ask at this point is, why should a couple go on having children beyond the point where an extra birth increases the couple's expected utility? The answer is that, given (2.17), it would cost the parents more to prevent that extra birth, than to let it happen.[4]

Given the inequality constraints, there are also possible corner solutions. One occurs if (2.7) is binding, in which case no babies are born ($c_0 = \overline{b}, b = 0$). Another arises if (2.8) is binding, in which case the couple have as many babies as nature permits ($c_0 = 0$, $b = \overline{b}$). Yet another comes about if (2.6) is binding. In this case the couple is too poor to use birth control, but also too poor to feed and care for a baby.[5] They will then have as many babies as nature permits ($b = \overline{b}$) as in the previous case, but with the difference that, in this case, none of the babies will survive. That is the most appalling outcome possible. In what follows, we examine how the choice of c_0 and c_1 is affected by the economic environment, under the assumption that the solution is interior.

2.1.2 Comparative Statics

The choice of c_0 is illustrated in Figure 2.2 for the case where $p_1 c_1 - p_0$ and $v'(b)$ are positive.[6] In view of (2.12), and recalling that $v'\left(\overline{b} - c_0\right)$ is decreasing, the chosen value of c_0, denoted by c_0^*, is determined by the intersection of the upward-sloping line representing $\pi(c_1, \mu)\, v'\left(\overline{b} - c_0\right)$, with the horizontal one representing $p_1 c_1 - p_0$. If we took a lower value of p_0, the $p_1 c_1 - p_0$ schedule would shift upwards, and the chosen value of c_0 would consequently rise,

$$\frac{db}{dp_0} = -\frac{dc_0}{dp_0} > 0. \tag{2.19}$$

[4] There is actually a third possibility, namely that $p_1 c_1$ equals $p_0 c_0$, and $v'(n)$ equals zero, in which case c_0 is indeterminate. As there is only one point out of infinity where this can occur, the probability of it occurring is zero. Therefore, we desregard it.

[5] As already noted, if the couple are so poor that they cannot even support themselves ($W_1 \geq a_s$), there is no solution.

[6] The case where $p_1 c_1 - p_0$ and $v'(b)$ are negative is analogous, but the solution is then in the fourth quadrant.

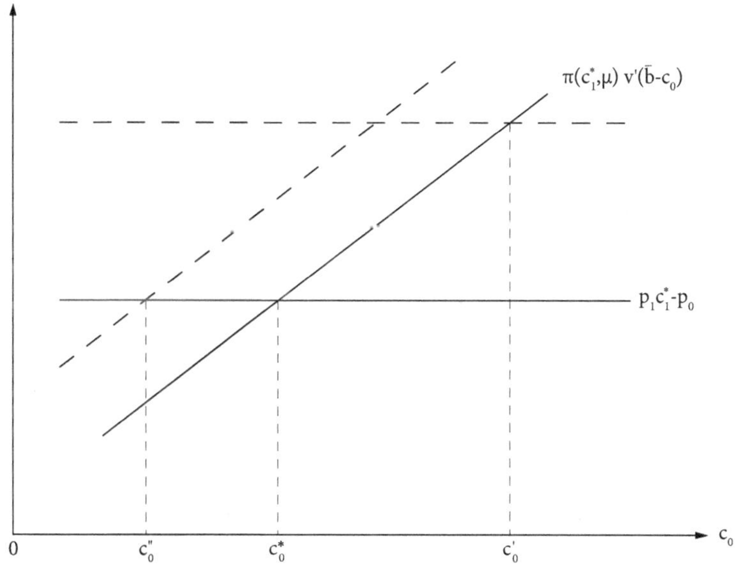

Figure 2.2 Birth control

In other words, if birth control were more expensive, parents would practise it less and have more babies.

The choice of c_1 is illustrated in Figure 2.3. In view of (2.13), the chosen value of this variable, c_1^*, is determined by the intersection of the downward-sloping line representing $\pi_{c_1}(c_1, \mu)\, v\left(\overline{b} - c_0\right)$, with the horizontal one representing $\left(\overline{b} - c_0\right) p_1$. If we took a higher value of p_1, the $\left(\overline{b} - c_0\right) p_1$ schedule would shift upwards, and the chosen value of c_1 would fall from c_1^* to c_1'',

$$\frac{dc_1}{dp_1} < 0, \frac{d\pi}{dp_1} = \pi_{c_1}(c_1, \mu) \frac{dc_1}{dp_1} < 0. \tag{2.20}$$

If survival-enhancing goods were more expensive, parents would give their babies less food, health care, etc., and fewer of these babies would consequently survive to school age.

An exogenous increase in an element of μ directly raises the survival probability by $\pi_\mu(c_1, \mu)$.[7] It also shifts the $\pi(c_1, \mu)\, v'\left(\overline{b} - c_0\right)$ schedule shown in Figure 2.2 upwards, thus reducing the chosen value of c_0, say from c_0^* to the c_0'' (as a higher p_0, or a lower p_1 would). Intuitively, that is because an exogenous fall in infant mortality makes it less costly for parents to achieve any desired

[7] The analysis that follows draws on Cigno and Pinal (2004).

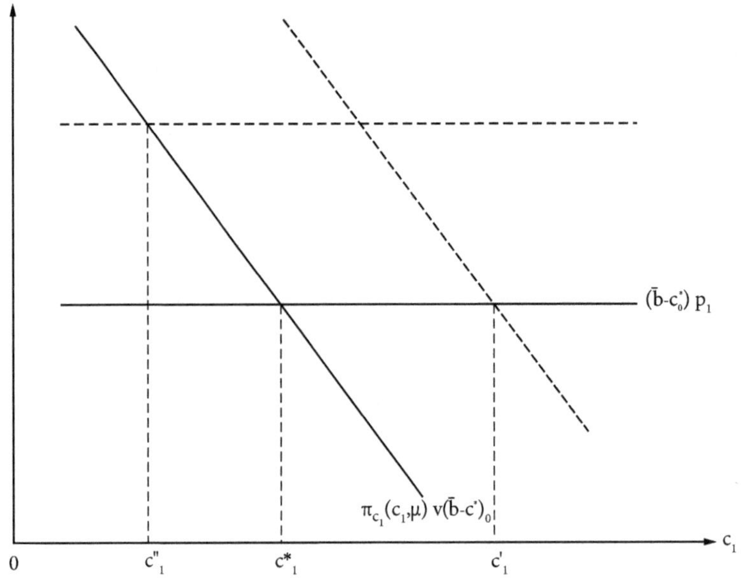

Figure 2.3 Infant survival

$E(n)$ with any given b. Parents then have less incentive to practice birth control. If the element of μ that increased is either a complement or a substitute for c_1 (i.e., if $\pi_{c_1\mu}$ is either positive or negative), there is also an indirect effect. In the complementarity case, the $\pi_{c_1}(c_1,\mu)\,v\left(\overline{b}-c_0\right)$ schedule shown in Figure 2.3 will shift upwards, and the chosen value of c_1 consequently rise from c_1^* to c_1'. Conversely, in the substitutability case, the $\pi_{c_1}(c_1,\mu)\,v\left(\overline{b}-c_0\right)$ schedule will shift downwards, and the chosen value of c_1 will fall from c_1^* to c_1''. Depending on whether the induced change in c_1 is positive or negative, the indirect effect may either reinforce, or weaken the direct effect,

$$\frac{d\pi}{d\mu}=\pi_{\mu}+\pi_{c_1}\frac{dc_1}{d\mu}. \tag{2.21}$$

Let us now look at the effect of the environment facing the parents at stage 2 (W_2, w_c, p_k, r and ω) on their choice of z^* and m^*, and consequently in the value of $v'(n)$ given n. If this value is lower (less positive or more) than in the reference environment, the $\pi(c_1,\mu)\,v'\left(\overline{b}-c_0\right)$ schedule shifts downwards and the chosen value of c_0 consequently rises from c_0^* to c_0'. In other words, the more school-age children cost at stage 2, the more birth control will the couple use, and the fewer babies will they consequently have, at stage 1. This tells us that, at stage 1, the cost of a baby moves in the opposite direction of the number of babies. Similarly, at stage 2, the cost of a child moves in the opposite direction of the number of children. As Gary Becker colourfully puts it, parents then face a trade-off between quantity and quality of children.[8] Keep in mind, however, that quantity and quality are endogenous. If z is high and b low, the reason could be that parental wealth or the rate ω at which human capital is remunerated are high. But, it could also be that the price of educational inputs p_k is low, the price of birth control p_0 high, or the price of survival-enhancing goods p_1 low (the effect of the child wage rate is ambiguous, because w_c raises the cost of education, but contributes also to full income). If m is high and b low, by contrast, the reason could be that the parents are rich (W_2 is large), or that the return to conventional investment is everywhere higher than the return to education ($r > \frac{\omega}{q}$).

2.1.3 Demographic Transition

To the extent that the economic environment can be modified by government intervention, these comparative-statics predictions have important policy implications. If the policy maker wishes to discourage child labour and encourage education, it may raise the marginal return to education (by reducing p_k or procuring an increase in ω). It may also make school attendance compulsory, or prohibit child labour (but we will see that there are implementation difficulties with both). As we have seen, these policies have the side effect of encouraging birth control, because they raise z and thus reduce $v'(n)$ for every n. They thus reduce fertility. That result can be achieved also by subsidizing birth control (reducing p_0). A sufficiently large reduction in the cost of contraception could actually change the characteristics of the solution from (2.18) to (2.17) and thus change the sign of $v'(n)$ from negative to positive. Another way to reduce fertility is to tax b. China's one-child policy, that between 1980 and 2016 imposed penalties on couples who had more than one child, did exactly that.[9]

If the policy-maker wishes to reduce infant mortality, it can achieve that directly by raising an element of μ under its control, or indirectly by subsidizing c_1 (reducing p_1). As in the case of an increase in one of the exogenous

[8] In Becker (1960, 1981), parents choose instantaneously how many children to have, and how much to spend on each child. Here, by contrast, the choice is sequential. At stage 1, parents choose b and c_1 taking into account the effect that this will have on the probability distribution of n. At stage 2, they choose z and m given the realized value of n.

[9] As we will see in the next section, however, such a policy may cause a sex imbalance.

elements of μ, if the policy makes available a good that is either a complement or a substitute for c_1, the direct effect will be either reinforced or weakened by the induced increase or decrease in c_1. There will be complementarity, for example, if the government clears a swamp infested by malaria-carrying mosquitoes, provides sanitation, or builds a public hospital where there previously was none. That is because, without the policy, any amount of food, clothing, medicines and private medical care the parents gave their babies would have done little for the babies' survival chances. There will be substitutability, by contrast, if the government subsidizes private goods, including medicines and private medical care, that parents can buy individually. In the complementarity case, the policy gives parents an incentive to buy c_1, in the substitutability case it gives parents an incentive to buy a_1 (cross-substitution effect), and leaves them more money with which to do so (cross-income effect). Similar effects can be obtained on aggregate, if the government redistributes wealth from rich to poor families, because rich families have fewer children than poor ones, and children born to rich families are more likely to reach school age, and study full time than children born to poor ones.

An appropriate combination of all these policies can induce a switch from the high-fertility, high-mortality, high-child-labour, low-education regime that characterizes developing countries, to the low-fertility, low-mortality, low-child-labour, high-education regime that characterizes the developed part of the world. Such a transition (dubbed 'demographic', but actually economic) could be initiated by domestic policy or triggered by medical advances achieved by research carried out in the developed part of the world (and thus exogenous where the developing country under consideration is concerned).[10] If the latter, domestic policy can reinforce the exogenous stimulus coming from abroad and thus accelerate the transition.[11] In either case, the choice of policy mix will depend on political preferences and cost considerations, but also on the informational requirements of the different policy instruments. We shall discuss this more fully in Chapter 9.

[10] On the role of infant mortality in particular, see the dynamic analysis in Strulik (2004).

[11] In the long run, the transition will generate an increase in per-capita income growth, because education is the mainspring of productivity. In the short run, however, especially if the transition is very sudden, it can have the opposite effect, because the fertility reduction may raise the dependency rate (the ratio of non-working to working age persons). That is a problem especially if the country has a pay-as-you-go public pension system, where current pensions to retired people are paid out of current contributions by working people; see Cigno and Werding (2007).

2.2 Gender

So far, we have talked of the parental couple as if they were one person, and assumed that all children are the same.[12] We shall now distinguish between husband and wife, and allow children to be differentiated by sex and native ability. Where husband and wife are concerned, we shall take into account that, while the benefits of having children accrue to both parents, certain costs accrue only to the mother. Given that only women can have babies, the pain of childbirth, and the health damage caused by repeated pregnancies, is suffered only by the mother.[13] For the same reason, a birth absorbs a certain amount of specifically maternal time in the perinatal period. Put another way, reproduction produces couple-specific public goods, but also mother-specific private bads. That will not upturn the conclusions we have reached so far, but it will enrich the analysis, and bring a new dimension to the policy discussion.[14]

2.2.1 Wage Discrimination

Suppose that women are discriminated against in the adult labour market, meaning that ω (the coefficient which turns human capital into money) takes value ω' in the case of a man, and $\omega'' < \omega'$ in the case of a woman. The marginal return to education, $\frac{\omega}{Q_h(h, w_c, p_k)}$, is then higher for a boy than for a girl. This has implications for the amount of education that girls receive. As we saw in Section 1.2 of the last chapter, at stage 2 of the decision process, if the interest factor r is sufficiently low, parents invest in a child's education to the point where the marginal return equals the interest factor. Otherwise, the child gets no education. Daughters will then get no education for $r > \frac{\omega'}{q}$. They will get some, but less than boys do, for $\frac{\omega''}{q} > r > \frac{\omega'}{q}$. For $r > \frac{\omega''}{q}$, nobody will get any. Therefore, wage discrimination may cause educational discrimination. As we shall see, however, the latter does not imply the former.

[12] Models of that kind, starting with the one in Becker (1981) by which they are all inspired, are referred to as 'unitary'. The moment we recognize that husband and wife may have different preferences and different interests, however, there is a coordination problem. Chiappori (1988, 1992) solves it by assuming that the domestic resource allocation and the distribution of the benefits are Pareto-optimal (he calls his model 'collective'). This assumption is compatible with a range of coordination mechanisms, including the one envisaged by the Nash-bargaining model that we shall use in the present section

[13] This consideration is introduced in the analysis by Eswaran (2002).

[14] This section draws on Cigno (2007, 2012b, 2014).

2.2.2 Marriage

At the start of the last chapter, we defined U^* $(c_2, h\omega + m)$ as the maximum utility that a person can achieve conditional on her or his parents' choice of c_2, h, and m. We did not dwell on the object of the maximization. We now specify that the object includes the decision whether and whom to marry. In the economics literature, marriage is motivated by the production of couple-specific public goods (children, love, companionship) that could not be obtained in any other way.[15] Manser and Brown (1980), and McElroy and Horney (1981), model marriage as a two-person Nash-bargaining game. This type of game has a cooperative moment, where the parties seek an efficient allocation of their joint resources, and a non-cooperative one, where they bargain over the division of the surplus generated by cooperation. For simplicity, we shall assume that the spouses are not altruistic towards each other, but nothing of substance changes if we assume that they are, so long as each spouse cares about the other at least a little less than about her or himself. We said something similar in the last chapter regarding people's attitudes towards their parents.

2.2.2 Efficiency

Take the couple formed by f and m. This is *not* the couple we have referred to up to now. It is the result of the marriage of one of the original couple's children, with one of the children of the original couple's contemporaries. Restricting our attention to sexual reproduction, we shall assume that f and m are of different sex. At this point, however, we do not want to reveal who is the man and who is the woman (f could stand for female and m for male, or f for Frank and m for Mary). At stage 1 of *their* (not their parents') married life, the (f, m) couple have b babies, each of whom has a monetary cost p_1c_1. Given that babies require parental attention,[16] they have also an opportunity-cost. In the last section, there was no need to be concerned with that, because we were treating parents as if they were one person. There is now, however, because the value of the mother's time may be different from the father's, and the opportunity-cost of a baby may consequently depend on how the burden of the care is shared between the parents.

[15] See Becker (1981), Folbre (1994) and Cigno (1991).

[16] School-age children also require supervision. In a developing country context where the children of poor families have to become precociously autonomous, however, we can neglect that further requirement.

Let each spouse be endowed with one unit of time. Let t be the amount of parental time required to care for an infant.[17] Suppose that f and m's time are perfect substitutes where this activity is concerned, so that we can write

$$t = t_f + t_m, \tag{2.22}$$

where t_i is the amount of time contributed by $i = f, m$. If $h^f \omega^f$ is equal to $h^m \omega^m$, the couple's joint opportunity-cost, $h^f \omega^f t_f + h^m \omega^m \left(t - t_f\right) b$, is independent of t_f. If $h^f \omega^f$ is different from $h^m \omega^m$, however, and assuming

$$bt \leq 1, \tag{2.23}$$

so that one parent can attend to all the babies single-handed, the couple's joint opportunity-cost is minimized by setting t_f equal to either t or 0, depending on whether $h^f \omega^f$ is higher or lower than $h^m \omega^m$.[18]

Why should $h^f \omega_f$ be different from $h^m \omega_m$? As we have just seen, a possible reason is wage discrimination. Another is that f's parents were richer (or had fewer school-age children) than m's, in which case h^f would be higher than h^m. The same would be true if f's native ability, measured by f's value for h_0, were higher than m's, for in that case the cost of endowing the new adult with any given amount of human capital would be lower for f's than for m's parents. Yet another reason could be that an adult's human capital increases with work experience ('learning by doing'), in which case there are increasing returns to time worked. For a single, the only difference this would make is that he or she would earn more, because the amount of time worked is a constant equal to 1. Not so for a married person, because the couple's joint opportunity-cost is then minimized if one of the spouses specializes completely in the care of the children, leaving the other free to accumulate as much extra human capital as possible by working full time. If f and m started out with the same amount of human capital, and ω were the same for everybody, it would not matter who specialized in what. The couple would spin a coin. Otherwise, the spouse with the lower initial earning capacity would specialize in the care of the children and the other spouse in making money.[19]

[17] In general, there may be some substitutability between c_1 and t, because the former includes the services of nannies and baby-sitters. That is relevant in a developed country context. In a developing country, however, it applies only to a rich minority. To simplify, we shall then treat t as a constant.

[18] There would be some specialization, but possibly less than total, even if t_f and t_m were not perfect substitutes. Think of child care as a good that is domestically produced using t_f and t_m as factors. Given that $h_f \omega_f$ is different from $h_m \omega_m$, if the Marginal Rate of Technical Substitution decreases as t_m is substituted for t_f, the minimization may have at an interior solution with neither t_f nor t_m equal to zero; see Cigno (2014).

[19] That is indeed the way in which domestic division of labour is explained in Becker (1981).

The picture changes somewhat if we recognize that a baby requires at least a certain amount of specifically maternal time, call it t_0, in addition to the amount t which can be either maternal or paternal. As a parent's sex then matters, we shall specify that f is the woman, and m the man. The maximum amount of time that f can dedicate to paid work is then $1 - bt_0$., rather than 1 as in m's case. In the absence of wage discrimination (i.e., for $\omega^f = \omega^m = \omega$), and assuming that f's human capital endowment is not sufficiently larger than m's to compensate for the handicap of being a woman,

$$(1 - bt_0)\, h^f \leq h^m, \tag{2.24}$$

it is then clear that the couple's joint opportunity-cost is minimized for $t_f = t$ and $t_m = 0$. Assuming (2.23), he will then specialize completely in paid work. She will take care of the children, $t_f = t$, and do some paid work if she has any time left. Otherwise, the opportunity-cost is minimized by setting $t_f = 0$ and $t_m = t$, in which case the woman will put in only the minimum amount of child care time bt_0 that the man cannot do, and he will do the rest.[20]

To capture the idea that human capital accumulates with work experience, we assume that h increases at the rate α, where α is a positive constant, per unit of time worked. Assuming (2.24), the woman's stage-1 human capital will then become

$$\widehat{h^f} = \left\{1 + \alpha\left[1 - \left(t_0 + t_f\right) b\right]\right\} h^f, \tag{2.25}$$

and the man's

$$\widehat{h^m} = (1 + \alpha)\, h^m. \tag{2.26}$$

Given their money and human capital endowments, the maximum income that the couple can jointly achieve at stage 1 is thus a decreasing function of the number of babies b they jointly choose to have,

$$Y(b) = m^f + m^m + \{1 + \alpha\,[1 - (t_0 + t)\, b]\}\, h^f\omega + (1 + \alpha)\, h^m\omega. \tag{2.27}$$

2.2.2 Bargaining

John Nash demonstrates axiomatically that the bargaining equilibrium maximizes the product of the utility gains obtained by the two players by participating in the game. In our context, participating means marrying. Taking

[20] Evidence that this is what actually happens is reported by Siminski and Yetsenga (2020).

into account the fact pointed out at the start of the section, that the pain and health hazard associated with childbirth accrue only to the mother, f's expected utility of marriage is

$$E(U_1^f) = a_1^f - D(b) + \pi(c_1, \mu)\, v\left(\overline{b} - c_0\right),$$

where a_1^f is her current consumption in the married state, and $D(b)$ her disutility for having b babies, increasing and convex in the argument. By contrast, m's expected utility is

$$E(U_1^m) = a_1^m + \pi(c_1, \mu)\, v\left(\overline{b} - c_0\right), \tag{2.28}$$

where a_1^m is his current consumption in the married state. Notice that the $\pi(c_1, \mu)\, v\left(\overline{b} - c_0\right)$ term is the same for both spouses, because the expected value of n is a couple-specific public good.

The alternative to marrying is to stay single, in which case i's utility would be certain and equal to i's income in the unmarried state,

$$\overline{U}_1^i = a_1^i = (1 + \alpha)\, h_i \omega + m_i, \tag{2.29}$$

for $i = f, m$.[21] $\overline{U}_1^i$ is i's fall-back position. By analogy with the reserve price in an auction (the minimum that the seller is willing to accept), we shall refer to it as i's reserve utility.

The Nash-bargaining equilibrium then maximizes the product

$$N = \left[E\left(U_1^f\right) - \overline{U}_1^f\right]\left[E(U_1^m) - \overline{U}_1^m\right], \tag{2.30}$$

subject to the couple's joint stage-1 budget constraint,

$$a_1^f + a_1^m + p_0 c_0 + \left(\overline{b} - c_0\right) p_1 c_1 = Y\left(\overline{b} - c_0\right), \tag{2.31}$$

to the couple's subsistence constraints (one for each spouse)

$$a_1^i \geq a_s, \tag{2.32}$$

and to the same feasibility constraint we had before introducing sex differentiation, (2.3), (2.7), (2.8), and (2.9).

[21] Recall that h_i and m_i were chosen by i's parents, and are thus given constants where i is concerned.

Using (2.31) to eliminate a_1^m, the maximand becomes

$$N = FM, \tag{2.33}$$

where

$$F = a_1^f - D(b) + \pi(c_1, \mu)\, v\left(\overline{b} - c_0\right) - \overline{U}_1^f \tag{2.34}$$

constitutes f's gain, and

$$M = Y\left(\overline{b} - c_0\right) - a_1^f + D(b) - c_0 p_0 - \left(\overline{b} - c_0\right) c_1 p_1 + \pi(c_1, \mu)\, v\left(\overline{b} - c_0\right) - \overline{U}_1^m \tag{2.35}$$

m's gain.

An interior solution satisfies the first-order condition with respect to a_1^f,

$$F - M = 0, \tag{2.36}$$

the one with respect to c_0,

$$\left[D'\left(\overline{b} - c_0\right) - \pi(c_1, \mu)\, v'\left(\overline{b} - c_0\right)\right] M - \left[Y'\left(\overline{b} - c_0\right) + p_0 - c_1 p_1 + \pi(c_1, \mu)\, v'\left(\overline{b} - c_0\right)\right] F = 0, \tag{2.37}$$

and the one with respect to c_1,

$$\pi_{c_1}(c_1, \mu)\, v\left(\overline{b} - c_0\right) M + \left[-\left(\overline{b} - c_0\right) p_1 + \pi_{c_1}(c_1, \mu)\, v\left(\overline{b} - c_0\right)\right] F = 0. \tag{2.38}$$

Using (2.36) and

$$Y'(b) = -\alpha(t_0 + t)\, h_f \omega, \tag{2.39}$$

dividing term by term and re-arranging, (2.37)–(2.38) give us

$$\frac{\xi}{\psi} = \frac{(c_1 p_1 - p_0) + \alpha(t_0 + t)\, h_f \omega + D'\left(\overline{b} - c_0\right)}{p_1 c_1}, \tag{2.40}$$

where ξ and ψ are defined by (2.15) and (2.16) as in the last section. This condition looks very much like (2.14). The left-hand side is the same.

The right-hand side differs in that the numerator is augmented by the sum of the marginal opportunity-cost of a birth, and the mother's marginal disutility of the same. Since ξ is proportional to $v'\left(\overline{b} - c_0\right)$, in equilibrium, the marginal utility of b will then be larger, and $\overline{b} - c_0$ correspondingly smaller, than it would have been if (as in the last section) an extra birth did not have an opportunity-cost for the couple, and did not cause disutility to the mother.

Given that, in the Nash-bargaining equilibrium, the couple split the surplus generated by cooperation equally between them, the gain from marriage is the same for both spouses. Given that the pain and health hazard are suffered only by the mother, she will then get extra consumption as compensation. If the spouses have different reserve utility, however, the one with the higher reserve utility will have also the higher expected utility. A colourful way to put this is to say that the spouse with higher reserve utility has greater bargaining power. The spouses will then have the same bargaining power, and the same expected utility, if they have the same reserve utility. Assortative mating (marriage of equals) is indeed what most theoretical economic models of marriage predict. Of course, it may be argued that passionate young people are not guided by such considerations in the choice of mate, but this objection carries less force in developing countries, where marriages are often arranged by the bride and the groom's parents. That is indeed the justification adduced to justify this otherwise objectionable practice. But there still is a problem.

Suppose that the division of the surplus is bargained before marriage, and that the betrothed have the same reserve utility,

$$m_f + \widehat{h}_f\omega = m_m + \widehat{h}_m\omega. \tag{2.41}$$

If each spouse had control over her or his own earnings and money endowment, $E(U_1^f)$ would then be equal to $E(U_1^m)$ and all would be well. In many developing countries, however, any money a married woman earns is her husband's property.[22] In such circumstances, a husband may be tempted to renege on the division of the surplus agreed before marriage and renegotiate the allocation from a position of strength.[23] Such opportunistic bargaining would not be allowed if the pre-marital agreement were enshrined in a legally enforceable contract, but such a contract is either not available, or

[22] The same was true of some developed countries until not so long ago.

[23] Eswaran (2002), already mentioned, does not allow for the possibility of divorce. The assumption is that, if bargaining fails, the couple will stay together and behave non-cooperatively as in Lundberg and Pollak (1996). Thinking of the United States rather than developing countries, Bergstrom (1996) vividly describes this as a case of 'harsh words and burst toast'.

prohibitively costly.[24] In the absence of alternative forms of protection, a married woman would then have no bargaining power at all. Her husband would take all the decisions.

If f has no say in the matter, m will choose a_1^f, c_0, and c_1 so as to maximize his expected utility (8.42), subject to the couple's joint (but effectively his) budget constraint (2.31), and to the inequality constraints (2.3), (2.32), (2.7), (2.8), (2.9), and (2.22). Using (2.39), the first-order conditions with respect to c_0 and c_1 may then be written as

$$-\alpha\left(t_0+t\right)h_f\omega+p_0-c_1p_1+\pi\left(c_1,\mu\right)v'\left(\overline{b}-c_0\right)=0 \tag{2.42}$$

and

$$-\left(\overline{b}-c_0\right)p_1+\pi_{c_1}\left(c_1,\mu\right)v\left(\overline{b}-c_0\right)=0. \tag{2.43}$$

As there is no bargaining, (2.36) does not apply. Instead, m will fix f's consumption at the lowest level allowed by (2.32),

$$a_1^f=a_s. \tag{2.43}$$

As we can see from (2.42), c_0 is chosen so as to equate the marginal cost to the expected marginal benefit of b. The marginal cost does not include $D'(b)$, because f's disutility is none of m's business. As a consequence, the chosen value of c_0 will be smaller, and b will consequently be larger, than it would if f had a say in the matter. Given also that f's consumption is fixed at the subsistence level, the allocation decided by m is thus inequitable. It is also inefficient, because it does not take into account the full social cost (social from the point of view of the society formed by f and m) of giving birth to another baby. Combining (2.42) with (2.43), we get

$$\frac{\xi}{\psi}=\frac{\left(c_1p_1-p_0\right)+\alpha\left(t_0+t\right)h_f\omega}{p_1c_1}, \tag{2.44}$$

which differs from (2.40) in that the numerator is smaller because of the missing $D'(b)$ term.

[24] In developed countries, a premarital contract may be enforceable, but few couples have one because of the legal and emotional costs. Provided that divorce courts can be relied upon to find in favour of the woman, the remedy for opportunistic bargaining is then divorce rather than a contract; see Cigno (2012b, 2014).

We have thus found that, if a married woman has no control over the money she brings into the family, her husband is a dictator. By the assumption made at the start of the present section, that spouses are not altruistic towards each other (they are only altruistic towards their children), he is a selfish dictator. If we relax this assumption by realistically saying that the spouses may care about each other, the husband may then be a benevolent dictator. He will consequently give his wife more than the subsistence level of consumption and take her disutility into account in deciding how many babies to have. To the extent that he cares about her less than he cares about himself,[25] however, there will still be some inequity, and some inefficiency left.

2.2.2 Dowries

In many of the countries where a married woman cannot own anything, there is a counterweight to the absolute power that the husband would otherwise have over his wife and children. In these countries, any money (or other assets) the bride gets from her parents at the time of marriage, called 'dowry', enjoys special protection.[26] In some of them, a dowry cannot be disposed of by the husband without the wife's assent given before a court of law, and must be returned intact to her family of origin if the marriage breaks down. In others, the dowry is protected by local customs rather than by law (we shall come back to that in Chapter 8). That is good, because it gives a married woman some bargaining power, but it distorts incentives. Caring parents will in fact give a daughter a dowry, rather than an education,[27] because her earnings will be appropriated by her husband, but her dowry cannot.[28] This goes to show that propositions such as 'if parents educate only their sons, it is because they prefer sons to daughters, and are too poor to educate all their children' are wrong. Parents may educate sons rather than daughters for their own good (given the circumstances).

Unless the interest factor is so high that parents give no education to any of their children irrespective of sex, the dowry institution is a source of

[25] Remember that, if m cared about f as much as about himself (and f about m as much as about herself), it would not be possible to model the marital relationship as a Nash-bargaining game. That is not a great loss if there actually is no bargaining, but it is better to keep the same basic assumptions throughout the exposition.

[26] That is now true only of developing countries, but it used to be true also of some developed ones. In Italy, for example, the dowry disappeared from the statute book only in 1975.

[27] If there is a legal minimum, she will get just that. In some countries, however, there is actually a legal maximum, rather than a minimum, to the amount of education a girl can get!

[28] If a married woman's education is valued by her husband for its positive effect on their children's education, however, there is some substitutability between money and human capital. Parents with an educationally talented daughter will then give her education instead of money. Evidence of that is found by Behrman et al. (1999).

inefficiency, because it induces parents to educate sons rather than daughters irrespective of native ability. It is also inequitable (towards women) if human capital means not only ability to make money, but also ability to appreciate the finer things of life, or if paid work brings personal satisfaction and social status as well as income.[29] The consequences of the dowry institution are dramatically worse if parents are so poor that putting together a dowry for each daughter they happen to have is an insurmountable obstacle. In an 'extreme poverty' situation like that examined in Section 1.4 of the last chapter, the dowry institution makes it more likely that girls, rather than boys, will be bonded or sold at stage 2 of their parents' decision process.[30] At stage 1, it also makes it likely that baby girls rather than baby boys will be either aborted or suppressed at birth,[31] and that any baby girl who is allowed to come into the world will have a lower probability of surviving to school age than a baby boy, because she will receive less food and medical care. This explains why, in the developing world as a whole, women are not only less educated but also fewer in number than men (this is known as the 'gender gap') even though there is the same probability that a baby will be male or female and, given the same treatment, a girl's life expectancy at birth is at least as high as a boy's.

2.2.3 Gendered Policy

Accounting for gender and marriage as we have done in this section has implications for the policy conclusions we reached at the end of the last one. Restraining fertility and encouraging education are important for the development process. Educating girls in particular is doubly important, because it raises the age at which women marry and thus reduces the maximum number of children a woman can have (it lowers $\overline{b}$). In the presence of legislation or social norms (to be examined in Chapter 8) that give the husband control over the wife's earnings, however, educational incentives are not sufficient because the return to a girl's education will be appropriated by the husband. They are totally ineffective in the presence of the dowry institution because this institution makes it is more advantageous for girls to receive money from their parents, rather than an education.

[29] On the other hand, if a married woman's education confers status not only on her but also on her husband, or makes conversation more pleasant, it will give her some extra bargaining power.

[30] A third-century bishop by the name of Nicholas (better known as Santa Claus) earned his sainthood by providing a dowry for two young women who were about to be sold into prostitution.

[31] Where medical services are sufficiently developed for the sex of the baby to be detected before birth, as for example in India, selective abortion takes the place of selective infanticide.

Making education compulsory, rather than just cheaper, would correct the distortion caused by the dowry institution to some an extent, but the only radical remedy is 'empowerment', a change of legislation or social norms giving the wife the same bargaining power as the husband. Combined with measures to combat wage discrimination, educating girls is important also because it increases the opportunity-cost of children, thereby encouraging birth control (raising c_0) and reducing fertility (lowering b). The low fertility and high productivity that characterize the developed part of the world are to some an extent a reflection of the relatively low wage discrimination, and relatively high female education, that prevail there. As already noted in the last section, a fertility reduction can be achieved also in a more direct way by subsidizing contraception (lowering p_0), or taxing b.

The gender perspective adopted in the present section prompts additional considerations. The fact that the benefit of having an extra child, $v'(n)$, accrues to both spouses, but the disutility of having another pregnancy, $D'(b)$, is felt only by the mother, gives rise to an externality, as a result of which, if the woman's bargaining power is lower than the man's, fertility will be inefficiently large.[32] It may thus be thought that a subsidy on c_0, or a tax on b (like the already mentioned one-child policy in China), would redress the balance because taxes and subsidies also affect the husband. It would thus reduce inequity as well as inefficiency. That is indeed true where the subsidy on contraception is concerned, but not necessarily where the tax on fertility is. If wage discrimination or the dowry institution make it less beneficial or more costly for a couple to have a daughter rather than a son, a baby girl is in fact more likely to be suppressed at birth (or aborted, if her sex is detectable before birth) than a baby boy is. In this respect, a fertility tax has the same gruesome consequences as the dowry institution and reinforces its effect if that institution is in place. In the quarter of a century that it was in operation, the Chinese one-child policy produced a strong imbalance between the sexes (widened the gender gap), thus magnifying the intended fertility reduction.

[32] The point made by Eswaran (2002).

3

Child Labour Effects of Credit Rationing and Uninsured Shocks

Evidence

Were there perfect capital and insurance markets, human capital accumulation would depend only on the relative costs and benefits, and its path over time would not be influenced by idiosyncratic shocks. But we know that capital markets are far from perfect, especially in developing countries, and that this is even truer of insurance markets. We saw in Chapter 2 that, in the absence of perfect asset and credit markets, investment in human capital may be either inefficiently low or inefficiently high. We also saw that, without insurance, risk-averse parents invest less than the efficient amount in their children's education. An erratic shock can put a family in a state of extreme poverty.

In the present chapter, we assess the extent to which capital market imperfections, and lack of insurance, actually affect the supply of child labour. In particular, we review the relevant empirical literature, and present some of the results in more detail. From a theoretical point of view, changes in child labour supply and human capital investment are two of the possible responses to an adverse event. If education is used as a buffer against uninsured shocks, policies aimed at reducing risk may then have a substantial bearing on child labour.

3.1 Testing for the Effects of Incomplete Markets

The evidence of the effects of market imperfections on child labour is limited. In a seminal paper, Jacoby and Skoufias (1997) look at the role of education as a buffer with respect to expected and unexpected shocks. Assuming that child labour is regarded as the only alternative to attending school, their analysis also defines the supply of child labour. When financial markets are complete, investment decisions, including those in human capital,

The Economics of Child Labour. Second Edition. Alessandro Cigno and Furio C. Rosati, Oxford University Press.
 DOI: 10.1093/oso/9780198903000.003.0004

are determined solely by comparative rates of return. But, when markets are incomplete or imperfect, the separability of consumption and human capital investment decisions no longer holds, and the supply of child labour is affected by the level of resources available to the household. Those authors focus on rural areas, making use of the Village Level Studies (VLS) survey conducted by the International Crops Institute for the Semi-Arid Tropics (ICRISAT), that collected extensive panel data on ten villages to represent four broad agroclimatic zones of semi-arid India.

They develop a theoretical model that includes the presence of complete markets, which in their case implies access to credit and complete insurance (through informal income sharing arrangements) within and between villages. As already said, in the presence of complete markets, decisions concerning child labour supply are separable with respect to (current) household income and only depend on relative prices. If elements of the relevant markets are missing, school attendance (and, in their case, child labour supply) fluctuates with expected and unexpected changes in current income, depending on the specific market failures considered. Below we present some of the main conclusions.

Complete intra-village and inter-village markets define a situation in which households are able to reallocate consumptions across time and states of the world at a fixed price, so that their decisions about school attendance depends only on their lifetime expected wealth constraint. As markets become less perfect, shocks affect household decisions till the extreme case in which household do not have access to any form of insurance or credit market, in which case there are affected both by expected or unexpected shocks both aggregate and idiosyncratic. The authors estimate a structural model to sequentially test the presence of the various market imperfections. The results show that in general child labour is used as an important element of the self-insurance strategy of rural Indian households. Even if the data do not contain all the relevant information, the authors use the estimated parameters to assess the cost in term of human capital accumulation of the observed 'excess' variability of school attendance. The cost turns out not to be high in a single year, but it likely to get higher as the effects cumulate over the years.

From a policy perspective, these results suggest that trying to reduce child labour by increasing educational opportunities for the poor (e.g., building more rural schools) without taking into consideration the economic risks and constraints that they face might have a limited impact. Moreover, compulsory schooling laws, or laws against child labour, to the extent that they can be enforced in rural areas, could substantially lower household welfare. Conversely, interventions in rural financial markets, not to mention financial market development, may have unexpected consequences for human capital accumulation.

3.2 Assessing the Impact of Shocks and of Access to Credit and Insurance

In what follows we present in some detail an analysis that relies on the direct observation of the effects of credit and insurance. This study complements the results of Jakoby and Skoufias, which relies on indirect tests of the effects of markets on child labour. We draw on Guarcello, Mealli, and Rosati (2003) to show how access to credit, and the presence of insurance programmes, affect domestic responses to several kinds of shocks. The ENCOVI 2000 survey, carried out by the Government of Guatemala, covers 7,276 (3,852 rural and 3,424 urban) households following a probabilistic survey design. As most of our attention will be devoted to the effects of shocks, and access to credit and insurance, we start by providing precise definitions, and presenting summary statistics.

Credit rationing. The survey contains questions relating to access to credit. In particular, households are asked whether they have applied for credit and, in case of application, whether they were denied credit. We define as 'credit rationed' households that did not apply for credit for one of the following reasons:

(*a*) institutions offering credit are not available,
(*b*) does not know how to ask for credit,
(*c*) does not have the required characteristics,
(*d*) does not have collateral,
(*e*) interest rates too high,
(*f*) insufficient income,
(*g*) institutions do not give credit to this kind of household.

Households that applied for, but were denied, credit will also be classified as credit rationed.

Table 3.1 shows descriptive statistics of credit-rationed households, broken down by poverty level.[1] About 50% of the households in Guatemala are credit rationed according to our definition. The incidence rises with poverty,

[1] The 'extreme' poverty line is defined as the yearly cost of the *canasta basica*, the food basket that provides the minimum daily caloric requirement, estimated in Q. 1912. The 'non-extreme' poverty line (being just poor) is defined as the extreme poverty line plus an allowance for non-food items, estimated in Q. 4319.

Table 3.1 Distribution of credit-rationed households by poverty level

	Extremely poor	Poor	Not poor	Total
Reasons for not applying for credit	5.13	1.98	1.86	2.39
Institutions offering credit not available				
Does not know how to ask for credit	5.92	4.78	3.05	4.2
Does not have the required characteristics	8.28	11.34	11.02	10.76
Does not have the collateral	12.23	12.5	8.43	10.7
Afraid of losing collateral	5.13	5.53	4.58	5.06
Interest rates too high	5.33	6.56	12.42	8.92
Insufficient income	34.12	36.82	37.85	36.87
Institutions do not give credit to households in that condition	22.09	18.24	13.01	16.54
Other reasons	1.78	2.25	7.77	4.57
Total	100	100	100	100
Credit refused following application	14.43	14.47	10.71	12.28
Credit-rationed households	67.84	58.65	39.78	49.41

Source: *Encuesta de condiciones de vida* (ENCOVI) 2000. Instituto Nacional de Estadísticas (INE) Guatemala.

ranging from about 40% for households above the poverty line to almost 70% for extremely poor households. In absolute terms, lack of income, lack of collateral, and household conditions are the most common reasons for not applying for credit. Credit rationing through the interest rate mainly applies to non-poor households. The rate of rejection of credit applications is similar for poor and non-poor households.

Shocks. ENCOVI 2000 contains a set of questions pertaining to the occurrence of shocks. Shocks are divided into two broad categories: collective and individual (idiosyncratic). Collective shocks include events like earthquakes, floods, fires, etc. Individual shocks include loss of employment, death, etc.[2] Households can report more than one shock from each category. A household is classified as hit by a shock if it reported at least one shock. The analysis used two dummies, one for each of the broad categories of shocks (collective and individual). Other classifications were also tried, but did not change the main results.

About 50% of the households surveyed reported experiencing one or more shocks in the year 2000, as shown in Table 3.2. Of these, 12% reported experiencing natural or economic shocks affecting the community, 20% shocks directly affecting the family, and 20% affecting both. Of the 7,276 households surveyed, 38% were affected by individual (idiosyncratic) shocks and about

[2] For a detailed description and analysis see Tesliue and Lindert (2002).

Table 3.2 Percentage of households affected by collective or individual shocks

		Individual shock		Shock	No. of households	%
Collective shock		Yes (%)	No (%)			
	Yes (%)	18	12	Individual	2,769	38.06
	No (%)	20	50	Collective	2,142	29.44
			Total 100	Total households surveyed	7,276	

Source: *Encuesta de condiciones de vida* (ENCOVI) 2000. Instituto Nacional de Estadísticas (INE) Guatemala.

30% by collective shocks. The most frequently reported collective shock is a general increase in prices, as shown in Table 3.3. This could reflect a misperception of the economic environment, or just a generic complaint about the cost of living. In any case, excluding this form of shock does not change the results obtained.

Risk reduction and risk-coping mechanisms. The questionnaire permits to identify whether an individual has medical insurance (public or private). A dummy variable (*Insurance*) was created, taking the value of 1 if at least one member of the household has medical insurance. Information was insufficient to identify whether households belonged to an informal social support network.

'Expected' expenditure. Expected expenditure is computed by regressing household expenditure on a set of variables (age and sex of the household head, parents' education, parents' occupation and sector of employment, urban/rural area, regional dummies, household structure).

Child and household characteristics. A set of control variables is used to take into consideration individual and household characteristics. These include: the age of the child (*age*, age^2); a gender dummy (*Female*); a dummy taking value 1 if the child belongs to an indigenous household (*Indigenous*); the number of household members (*Hhsize*); the number of children aged 0–5 in the household (*numkidsy*) and the number of school-age children (*numkidso*); a dummy taking value 1 if the child is a girl and there are children aged 0–5 in the household (*femkidsy*); a series of dummies for the mother's (*M_*) and for the father's (*F_*) education.

Child work is very common in Guatemala. Some 506,000 children aged 7–14 years, one-fifth of total children in this age group, are engaged in work. Most are employed on the family farm or in petty business and live in rural areas.

Table 3.3 Percentage of households affected by different types of shock

Individual shock	%	Collective shock	%
Loss of employment of any member	13.67	Earthquake	0.87
Lowered income of any member	17.42	Drought	6.32
Bankruptcy of a family business	2.55	Flood	2.33
Illness or serious accident of a working member of the household	15.64	Storms	3.28
Death of a working member of the household	2.19	Hurricane	1.66
Death of another member of the household	3.03	Plagues	16.69
Abandonment by the household head	1.67	Landslides	1.41
Fire in the house/business/property	0.27	Forest fires	1.1
Criminal act	4.79	Business closing	0.81
Land dispute	1.56	Massive lay-offs	0.85
Family dispute	1.82	General increase in price	63.01
Loss of cash or in-kind assistance	1.82	Public protests	0.87
Fall in prices of products in the household business	7.54	Other covariate shocks	0.82
Loss of harvest	24.95		
Other idiosyncratic shocks	1.08		
Total	100	Total	100

Source: *Encuesta de condiciones de vida* (ENCOVI) 2000. Instituto Nacional de Estadísticas (INE) Guatemala.

The decision to consider the 7–14 age range in order to define child work is based on several considerations. School in Guatemala starts at seven and no significant amount of child labour is found below the age of seven. The basic education cycle (*ciclo basico*) requires, in most cases, nine years of study. It should also be noted that current legislation allows children to work legally from the age of 14.

Table 3.4 gives more detailed information on children's activities in Guatemala. It shows that a significant proportion of children, 17%, are reportedly neither working nor attending school. This group includes children, mainly girls, performing full-time household chores, undeclared workers, and children who cannot attend school (either because there is no school near home, or because getting to the nearest school is too expensive), but do not have the opportunity to perform any productive activity. These 'idle' children are nearly as numerous as working children and constitute as great a policy concern. This group is the most sensitive to changes in policy and in exogenous variables. The table shows important gender differences in child activity status. Boys are more likely to work, but girls are more likely to be neither working nor attending school. It also shows that indigenous

Table 3.4 Children aged 7–14, by sex, type of activity, and residence

Sex	Activity	Urban		Rural		Total	
		%	No.	%	No.	%	No.
Male	Work only	4.3	19,285	12.3	104,161	9.5	123,446
	Study only	73.9	334,299	53.9	455,964	60.9	790,263
	Work and study	10.1	45,587	19.7	166,924	16.4	212,511
	Total work[a]	14.4	64,872	32.0	271,085	25.9	335,957
	Total study[b]	78.2	379,886	73.6	622,888	67.3	1,002,774
	Neither	11.8	53,308	14.1	119,329	13.3	172,637
Female	Work only	4.1	17,820	6.8	54,249	5.9	72,509
	Study only	74.6	323,451	58.4	464,030	64.1	787,764
	Work and study	7.6	32,764	8.3	66,386	8.1	99,546
	Total work[a]	11.7	50,584	15.1	120,635	14.0	172,055
	Total study[b]	82.2	356,215	66.7	530,416	72.2	887,310
	Neither	13.8	59,770	26.5	210,491	22	270,371
Total	Work only	4.2	37,105	9.7	158,410	7.7	195,515
	Study only	74.2	657,750	56.1	919,994	62.4	1,577,744
	Work and study	8.8	78,351	14.2	233,310	12.3	311,661
	Total work[a]	13.0	115,456	23.9	391,720	20.0	507,176
	Total study[b]	83.0	736,101	70.3	1,153,304	74.7	1,889,405
	Neither	12.8	113,078	20.1	329,820	17.5	442,898

[a] 'Total work' refers to children that work only *and* children that work and study.
[b] 'Total study' refers to children that study only *and* children that work and study.
Source: *Encuesta de condiciones de vida* (ENCOVI) 2000. Instituto Nacional de Estadísticas (INE) Guatemala.

children have a lower school attendance rate, and a higher work participation rate than the rest.

The theoretical analysis in Chapter 1 leads us to expect that parental decisions regarding whether a child will study only, work only, work and study, or do neither are guided by an unobservable utility index,

$$I = f(Z, X, C, S),$$

where Z is a vector of household characteristics (including household expected or 'permanent' income net of children's contribution), X a vector of proxies for the marginal rates of return to child work and education, *C* a vector of variables relating to credit rationing, and access to public or private insurance mechanisms, and *S* a vector of realized shocks.

The main econometric problem is endogeneity. Being credit rationed, belonging to an insurance scheme, or being part of a social security system, may all be endogenous to a certain extent. Not even the occurrence of certain idiosyncratic shocks is entirely exogenous. Whether strong winds will take the roof off a house may partly depend on how well the house is built. The decision to spend more or less money on making the house safe is not independent of decisions regarding the labour supply and school attendance of the children who will live in it.

The approach followed by Guarcello, Mealli, and Rosati (2003) is based on propensity score matching methods, and regression analysis. Given that adjusting for unobservables tends to be quite subjective, very sensitive to distributional and functional assumptions, and usually relying on the existence of a valid instrument, the analysis rests on the so-called unconfoundedness assumption. The latter is similar to the so-called selection-on-observables assumption: exposure to treatment is random within cells defined by the observed variables X. We now discuss how the propensity score is to be specified and used for analysing the child labour and school attendance effects of shocks, insurance, and credit rationing.

Shocks, insurance, and credit rationing are defined at the household level. A child is said to be 'treated' if his or her household is affected by the shock. This implies that, even though we want to analyse the effects of the treatment variables on children, these variables are assigned at the household level. The clustered structure of the units of analysis (children) has some methodological implications. First of all, since the assignment is at the household level, assignment can be assumed ignorable (or even unconfounded) only if we condition on the household and its characteristics. The propensity score is thus defined at the household level and represents the probability that a single household with vector of characteristics x is credit rationed (or subject to a shock, or insured). In order to be consistent with the hypothesized assignment mechanism, x should include also summary characteristics (e.g., number and age) of the children in each household. Once the propensity scores are estimated using households as units of analysis, the estimated propensity score for treated and untreated households can then be used to check the degree of overlap between the two groups in terms of the distribution of their characteristics.

The propensity score can also be used to estimate the ATT using a matching strategy. Even if the outcome involves the children within the household, the outcome Y must be defined in this case at the household level. Summary measures of child labour or school attendance, such as the proportion of school-age children going to school, to work, etc. are appropriate.

Matching is done by a nearest neighbour matching procedure that, for each of the N^T treated (e.g., rationed) households, looks for the nearest neighbour matching sets in the group of control households, defined as

$$C(i) = \min_j p_i - p_j,$$

which usually contains a single control unit (household). Denoting the number of controls matched with treated observation i by N_i^C, the matching estimator of ATT is an estimate of the variance of this estimator that can be derived either analytically, or using bootstrap methods (for details, see Becker and Ichino 2001).

$$\hat{ATT} = \frac{1}{N^T} \sum_{i \in T} \left[Y_i^1 - \sum_{j \in C(i)} \frac{1}{N_i^T} Y_j^0 \right]$$

A further complication is that we are interested in at least three potentially endogenous variables, namely credit rationing, insurance, and the occurrence of shocks. The order of these treatments cannot be determined from the questionnaire. In principle, one could define a treatment variable as the combination of the three, but that would render the propensity score based analysis, as well as the interpretation of the results, more complicated. Propensity scores and ATT estimates are thus obtained separately for each variable.[3]

The consequences that a violation of the unconfoundedness hypothesis could have on any causal conclusion are tested by performing the sensitivity analysis proposed by Rosenbaum and Rubin (1983a), extended here to a multinomial outcome. This method allows one to assess the sensitivity of the causal effects to assumptions about an unobserved binary covariate that is associated with both the treatments and the outcome. The results are reported in Appendix 3.1 indicate that our estimates are robust also to relatively high level of correlation between the outcome and the treatment.

Household decisions concerning the four possible activities in which a child can engage (work only, work and study, study only, or do neither) are modelled as a multinomial logit. The detailed results are reported in Table A3.2. As reported in Appendix 3.1, the results are robust with respect to the sensitivity analysis carried out to assess the consequences of a violation of the unconfoundedness assumption. This gives us confidence in the causal interpretation of the results.

Table 3.5 reports the marginal effects calculated (at the mean) from the estimated coefficients of the multinomial logit model. All the coefficients for individual and household-level characteristics are significant and have the

[3] Preliminary tests showing conditional independence of the occurrence of the three variables considered confirm the validity of this procedure.

expected sign. Holding expenditure and other characteristics constant, girls are less likely than boys to become part of the labour force. They are more likely to attend school, and even more likely to be 'idle'. This indicates that girls are more likely than boys to be involved full time in household chores. Indigenous children are more likely to be working than other children (the probability of work increases by 8 percentage points). Parents' education (above primary education, the omitted category) has a negative effect on child labour, and a positive one on school attendance. A child with an uneducated father is about 5 percentage points more likely to work full time, and 13 percentage points more likely to be idle, than a child with an educated father. It appears that, in Guatemala, there are no large differences between the impact of the mother's and the father's education. Household expenditure reduces child labour and increases full-time school attendance. At the mean, a 10% increase in income reduces the probability that a child works only, or works and studies, by about 7 percentage points.

The proxies for access to credit and insurance, and shocks, are significant, and have strong effects on household decisions regarding the children's activities. These results are consistent with those found in the propensity score-based analysis. Credit rationing strongly reduces school attendance. The probability that a child belonging to a credit-rationed household attends school is about 7 percentage points lower compared with an unrationed household. Children from credit-rationed households are more likely to be not only out of school, but also out of the labour force. This finding seems to indicate that credit rationing influences especially investment in the human capital of children. Since credit-rationed parents would send their children to school if they could borrow, this finding seems to indicate that, at the margin, returns to education are higher than returns to work. In the presence of fixed costs of access to work, low returns to child labour would in fact induce credit-rationed parents to keep their children idle.

Households affected by shocks reduce their children's full-time school attendance and increase child labour. Following a collective shock, child participation increases by 5.5 percentage points. Most of the additional participation comes from formerly full-time students, who start to work without dropping out of school. The overall effect of individual shocks is similar to that of collective shocks. Child labour participation in households hit by an individual shock is about 5 percentage points higher than average. Individual shocks, however, affect mainly children attending school, and increase the probability of work full time (by 1.5 percentage points). Idle children are barely affected. About two-thirds of the children that enter the labour force continue to attend school.

Table 3.5 Multinomial logit model marginal effects

Variable	Work only		Study only		Work and study		No activities	
	dy/dx	z	*dy/dx*	z	*dy/dx*	z	*dy/dx*	z
Female	−0.022	−4.02	0.036	2.13	−0.078	−7.26	0.064	4.94
Age	−0.023	−2.48	0.178	7.09	0.094	5.51	−0.249	−13.5
Age2	0.002	4.4	−0.010	−8.6	−0.003	−3.77	0.011	12.76
Indigenous[a]	0.013	3.02	−0.096	−7.19	0.065	7.07	0.018	1.8
Hh expenditure	−0.032	−5.01	0.152	7.95	−0.035	−2.95	−0.084	−5.41
Hhsize	−0.013	−5.89	0.052	7.99	−0.016	−3.74	−0.023	−4.61
Numkidsy	0.009	3.59	−0.013	−1.63	0.012	2.49	−0.007	−1.12
Numkidso	0.003	1.46	−0.018	−2.75	0.008	1.87	0.007	1.42
Femkidsy	−0.004	−1.8	0.003	0.36	−0.009	−1.64	0.010	1.64
M_none[a]	0.050	3.22	−0.155	−5.61	−0.014	−0.84	0.118	4.99
M_primary[a]	0.047	2.36	−0.092	−3.14	−0.006	−0.38	0.051	2
F_none[a]	0.048	3.72	−0.177	−7.13	−0.004	−0.27	0.132	5.7
F_primary[a]	0.023	2.47	−0.099	−4.53	0.002	0.19	0.073	3.8
Collective[a]	0.006	0.96	−0.055	−3.08	0.055	4.62	−0.005	−0.37
Individual[a]	0.015	2.51	−0.051	−3.00	0.039	3.65	−0.002	−0.17
Credit[a]	0.006	1.3	−0.066	−4.49	−0.002	−0.22	0.062	5.55
Insurance[a]	−0.014	−3.38	0.037	2.66	0.039	−4.94	0.016	1.37
Credit Individual[a]	−0.006	−0.97	0.023	1.06	0.017	−1.34	0.000	0.01
Credit_Collectivet[a]	−0.010	−1.54	0.081	3.91	0.037	−3.18	−0.034	−2.11
Regional dummies:								
Norte[a]	−0.008	−0.94	0.067	2.43	0.005	−0.22	−0.054	−3.06
Nororiente[a]	−0.009	−1.08	0.051	1.84	0.003	0.16	−0.045	−2.54
Suroriente[a]	−0.017	−2.44	0.088	3.32	0.021	0.94	−0.092	−6.73
Central[a]	0.008	0.72	0.035	1.25	0.050	2.1	−0.092	−6.66
Surroccidente[a]	−0.021	−3.21	0.113	4.62	0.017	0.81	−0.108	−8.1
Noroccidente[a]	−0.016	−2.08	0.106	4.15	−0.015	−0.78	−0.075	−4.47
Peten[a]	−0.003	−0.32	0.080	3.06	0.003	0.12	−0.080	−5.64

[a] For dummy variables, *dy/dx* is the effect of a discrete change from 0 to 1.

These findings seem to show that inability to obtain credit affects household investment in human capital, rather than child labour participation. Shocks, by contrast, affect child labour participation, most likely because of the need to compensate for an unexpected loss of resources. This confirms the importance of credit rationing for investment in human capital but seems to indicate that improving access to credit is not very useful for removing children from the labour force. Children who do not attend school nor work are at risk of becoming workers (or worse, see Chapter 2), and may be actually worse off than working children, as they might receive a smaller allocation of resources, and do not even benefit from any increase in human capital from on-the-job training that working children might receive.

Information on the availability of formal or informal insurance mechanisms and 'safety nets' is limited to the indicator of whether any household member is covered by health insurance. But the effect of this variable is far from negligible. Children belonging to households where at least one member (usually the household head) is covered by health insurance are about 5 percentage points less likely to work only, or work and study. Such a large effect should not come as a surprise, if one considers that about 15% of the idiosyncratic shocks are linked to health conditions, and that other kinds of shocks can be at least in part influenced by health conditions. Since the estimates are obtained controlling for the income and education of the parents, we **can** be reasonably confident that insurance cover does not act as a proxy for either of those variables.

3.3 Not All Shocks Are Bad for Child Labour

In the previous discussion we focused on shocks that affect resources available to the household without changing relative prices. We have, in other words, looked at the consequences of uninsured, but not necessarily unexpected, pure income shocks. Different conclusion can be reached if the shocks are not pure income shocks but take the form of productivity shocks that might alter the rate of return to different activities.

Consider, for example, the effect of rainfall in rural areas. A higher than average rainfall can increase household income and hence, if market are not perfect, increase investment in education and reduce child labour supply. However, such a positive shock to production can also have a substitution effect. If labour and rain are complements in the agriculture production, then a positive shock might increase labour productivity and, for what we are concerned with, an increase in the incentive for the households to involve children in farm work. If labour, and other, markets were perfect then the usual separability conditions would apply. Households would determine the optimal investment in human capital as a function of relative returns and adjust to productivity shocks by hiring or laying off workers. On the other hand, if labour markets do not exist or are imperfect, then a productivity shock will change the relative returns to human capital and affect child labour.

Utilizing data for rural Tanzania, Dumas (2018) shows that income and substitution effects of rainfall shocks on child labour are linked to the characteristic of the labour market. While positive rainfall shocks tend to increase child labour for farmer households, such an increase is smaller if agricultural households have access to labour markets and can hire additional workers. On the other hand, access to the credit market does not seem to ease the impact on child labour.

Nordman et al. (2021) examine the effects of rainfall shock in India. They combine data from the India Human Development Survey (IHDS), which measures detailed child-specific education expenditures on different categories and engagement in a variety of work activities with rainfall data. They first show that positive rainfall shocks actually increase farm productivity and yield. Then they look at the impact of rainfall shocks on enrolment, educational expenditures and child labour. Children do not appear to be withdrawn from school as a consequence of a positive shock, but expenditures on education are reduced. As the reduction is relative to school fees and transport this seems to indicate that children are reducing their regularity of attendance. This appears to be due to the fact that children work more. The estimates show that child work increases over the board, both in farm and non-farm activities. The latter result could be justified if the non-farm activities are linked to farm production, like stalls for selling agricultural produce etc. Not surprisingly the effects just described are amplified if the household owns land. It would be interesting to see whether such effects were present for landless household, but the authors do not perform such a test.

These results are suggestive of the fact that household are quick to respond to changes in the incentives system they face and adapt their behaviour accordingly. Of course, this does not imply that adverse shocks should be advocated to address child labour, but that policies should take in consideration the change in relative prices they generate in order to avoid undesired effects.

3.4 The Long-Term Effects of War and Violence

The studies discussed till now have focused on the short- or medium-term impact of shocks, looking at how they affect the behaviour of current generations. The consequences of adverse events can, however, extend beyond the current generation, and exert their impact over a long time-span. Not only large-scale natural disasters but also violence and war can project their negative effects on generations to come. As an example of such long-term effects we focus on the study of Chin, Cunningham, and Van (2023) that looks at the long-term impact of the Rwanda genocide.

To estimate the child labour impact of that genocide, the authors use the 2010 Rwanda Demographic Health Survey (RDHS). Utilizing geocodes from the RDHS, they link the current clusters to pre-genocide communes. In this way they can link the number of killings based on a retrospective survey of genocide victims to the clusters of the 2010 surveys.

To address potential endogeneity issues stemming from other factors at the commune level, that may be associated with both the intensity of the genocide and the prevalence of child labour, Chin et al. use the distance from the commune to the Ugandan border as an instrument for measuring the intensity of the genocide. The rationale for this instrument is rooted in the historical context of the genocide. The conflict between the Hutu majority government and the minority Tutsi-led Rwandan Patriotic Front (RPF) saw the RPF launching an offensive from their exile base in northern Uganda in April 1994, advancing southward into Rwanda, eventually toppling the Hutu government in July. This three-month timeframe created a pattern where the genocide endured longer the further one was from the Ugandan border. Consequently, distance provides an exogenous source of variation in the number of killings, which we can use to estimate the causal impact of killing intensity on child labour. Moreover, other potential confounding factors are controlled introducing in the estimate household demographics and pre-genocide commune characteristics.

The genocide appears to have a statistically significant and positive impact of on child labour of the subsequent generations. Specifically, doubling the number of killings in a commune increases the probability of a child working outside the home 15 years later by 3.35 percentage points, representing approximately a 40% increase. Concurrently, school attendance decreases as genocide intensity rises. Doubling the number of killings per capita leads to a 3.68 percentage point reduction in children's school attendance, equivalent to about a 5% decline.

Several mechanisms could explain these results. Firstly, the brutal and targeted nature of the genocide resulted in the destruction of social institutions, potentially leading to subsequent state dysfunction, corruption, and instability. This could depress productive investment and economic exchange, ultimately affecting local economies negatively. The resulting lower incomes may have forced families to send children into the workforce. Second, in low-performing economies, the returns to education are likely to be low, reducing the incentives for investing in schooling and increasing the motivation for children to work. Third, the genocide significantly altered the gender ratio in Rwanda, with a disproportionate loss of more educated men. This, in turn, decreased the incentive for education for both men and women in the marriage matching market.

3.5 Does Insurance Actually Reduce Child Labour?

We have presented ample evidence that incomplete markets have a bearing on child labour. The question naturally arises whether policies aimed at increasing access to credit and insurance markets have an impact on child labour. The analyses in this area are extremely scarce, not least because some of the policies in this domain tend to be implemented in a way that does not lend itself to a rigorous causal evaluation. For example, an expansion of the credit system in a country is unlikely to be orthogonal to the determinants of child labour. Therefore, assessing its impact on it is likely to be difficult.

One of the few studies that bring some solid evidence, albeit with limitations, is relative to a health insurance scheme in Pakistan. Landmann and Frölich (2015) use a randomized control trial relative to the promotion of health insurance. The design is complex and presents some limitations. NRSP is a large non-profit organization that supports the poor countrywide. Among other services, it provides microcredit to vulnerable households. In 2005, in order both to protect their loans and to shelter poor households from health shocks, it bundled a health insurance scheme to the microcredit extension making it mandatory for loan clients, for their spouses, and all children of the client below 18 years.

In 2009 NRSP identified areas with high prevalence of hazardous child labour and introduced a new product in the hope of benefiting the most vulnerable households and thus reducing the incidence of child labour. In particular, in nine randomly selected treatment branch offices only it offered additional household members (adult children of the client and other minor or adult household members—e.g., aunts, cousins, parents) a voluntary insurance. Moreover, the clients were visited monthly and asked whether they had incurred in any medical costs or needed assistance with claims. The clients in the control branches were not aware of the treatment being offered in the other branches.

The take up of the voluntary insurance was relatively high and a substantially higher of claims were filed by the households in the treatment group with respect to the control group. Unfortunately, there is no information on the amounts reimbursed by the insurance.

The results indicate a reduction in the number of children working, especially in hazardous work, and to a lesser extent of their working hours. The impact was larger for boys than for girls. The paper does not identify the mechanism, but one could speculate that the reduction in (expected) out of pocket health expenditures in households where also adult children and other members could insure did reduce the need to utilize child labour to support household income should a health shock occur.

3.6 Summing Up

The empirical findings reported in the present chapter indicate that credit rationing is an important determinant of the household decision to invest in the human capital of children, but less relevant where child work is concerned. The children kept away from school tend to remain idle, rather than work. As idle children may find themselves in circumstances that are much worse than those associated with work in the usual sense (see Chapter 2), credit rationing thus puts children at considerable risk. Shocks substantially alter household decisions. In particular, a negative shock substantially increases the probability that a child will work. Coupled with evidence from other research that child labour shows a high degree of persistence, as in the case of the Rwanda genocide, this finding highlights the importance of protection from shocks for reducing children's labour supply and increasing human capital investment. Risk-reduction schemes, proxied by the availability of medical insurance, also have a beneficial and substantial effect on child work. This is confirmed also by experimental evidence relative to the increase of access to health insurance.

In order to get a rough impression of the size of the effects of the possible policies, consider that in order to achieve an increase in school attendance equal to that due to the elimination of credit rationing, household income would have to increase by as much as 30%. To match the effects of eliminating the consequences of a negative individual shock on child work, household income would have to increase by about 40%. The effects on the other variables have a similar order of magnitude. Policies aimed at improving access to credit and providing safety nets, especially for poorer households, thus appear to be among the most powerful instruments for promoting school attendance and reducing child work. As the amount of income needed to match the effects of a reduction in either shocks or credit rationing is very large, this suggests that policies aimed at reducing risk may be not only effective, but also cost efficient. Finally, a word of caution: as we have seen, shocks might also alter the returns to child labour and lead to unexpected reactions from the households. Such changes in the incentives facing the household must be kept in mind when designing actual policies. Neglecting such changes in the relative returns, as we shall see, has hampered the effectiveness of many programmes and policies implemented.

Appendix 3.1 Sensitivity Analysis

The estimates of the ATT for credit rationing, and different combinations of values for π, α, and δ_{ti}, are reported in Table A3.1. The elements of X are the same as those used in the estimation of the multinomial logit model, and by the propensity score method. The results are clearly not very sensitive to a range of plausible assumptions about U. Notice that an α or δ_{ti} of 0.5 almost doubles the odds of receiving the treatment, or the odds of a certain value of the outcome. These values are larger than most of the coefficients of the estimated multinomial logit. Setting the values of the association parameter to bigger numbers may change the results. Given the large number of observed covariates already included in the model, however, the existence of a residual unobserved covariate so highly correlated with T and Y appears implausible. The sensitivity analysis of the ATT estimates of the effects of individual and collective shocks, and of the availability of insurance, gave similar results.

Table A3.1 Average effects of treatment with 'credit rationing', for different values of the sensitivity parameters

ATT	$\alpha = 0$ $\delta_{0W} = \delta_{1W} = 0$ $\delta_{0S} = \delta_{1S} = 0$ $\delta_{0WS} = \delta_{1WS} = 0$	$\pi = 0.1, \alpha = 0.1$ $\delta_{0W} = \delta_{1W} = -0.1$ $\delta_{0S} = \delta_{1S} = 0.1$ $\delta_{0WS} = \delta_{1WS} = 0.1$	$\pi = 0.5, \alpha = 0.5$ $\delta_{0W} = \delta_{1W} = -0.1$ $\delta_{0S} = \delta_{1S} = 0.1$ $\delta_{0WS} = \delta_{1WS} = 0.1$	$\pi = 0.1, \alpha = 0.1$ $\delta_{0W} = \delta_{1W} = -0.5$ $\delta_{0S} = \delta_{1S} = 0.5$ $\delta_{0WS} = \delta_{1WS} = 0.5$	$\pi = 0.5, \alpha = 0.5$ $\delta_{0W} = \delta_{1W} = -0.5$ $\delta_{0S} = \delta_{1S} = 0.5$ $\delta_{0WS} = \delta_{1WS} = 0.5$
Working only	0.011	0.011	0.012	0.011	0.018
Studying only	−0.049	−0.050	−0.052	−0.053	−0.060
Working and studying	−0.028	−0.023	−0.028	−0.028	−0.031
Idle children	0.066	0.062	0.067	0.070	0.073

Table A3.2 Results of multinomial logit estimates (Reference Group: children neither working nor studying)

Variable	Work only		Study only		Work and study	
	Coeff.	Z	Coeff.	Z	Coeff.	Z
Female	−1.03	−6.11	−0.39	−3.65	−1.20	−8.27
Age	1.06	3.85	1.94	13.04	2.60	11.62
Age squared	−0.02	−1.96	−0.09	−12.77	−0.11	−10.22
Indigenous[a]	0.22	1.68	−0.26	−3.17	0.47	4.18
Hh expenditure	−0.31	−1.5	0.78	6.29	0.23	1.34
Hh size	−0.19	−2.82	0.23	5.61	0.01	0.13
Numkidsy	0.29	3.6	0.03	0.59	0.17	2.44
Numkidso	0.03	0.5	−0.07	−1.8	0.03	0.5
Femkidsy	−0.19	−2.4	−0.07	−1.28	−0.16	−2.19
M_none[a]	0.51	1.13	−1.03	−5.36	−0.94	−3.76
M_primary[a]	0.74	1.65	−0.46	−2.45	−0.39	−1.59
F_none[a]	0.30	1.01	−1.07	−6.78	−0.84	−4.09
F_primary[a]	0.13	0.45	−0.63	−4.14	−0.47	−2.37
Collective[a]	0.18	1.01	−0.04	−0.37	0.52	3.55
Individual	0.40	2.25	−0.06	−0.5	0.38	2.65
Credit[a]	−0.26	−1.74	−0.52	−5.63	−0.45	−3.42
Insurance[a]	−0.52	−3.36	−0.05	−0.6	−0.52	−4.12
Credit_Individual[a]	−0.18	−0.78	0.03	0.21	−0.18	−0.93
Credit_Collectivet[a]	−0.03	−0.13	0.36	2.39	−0.16	−0.78
Regional Dummies Included						
_cons	−7.19	−2.94	−13.35	−9.53	−16.10	−8.12

4
Child Labour Effects of Access to Basic Utilities
Evidence

In the theoretical analysis of Chapters 1 and 2 the availability or otherwise of a number of facilities was subsumed in the parameters of the cost functions (of human capital and of the good consumed by pre-school children) and of the probability distribution of survival. Access to such utilities may well have important effects on the allocation of household resources.

According to UNICEF in 2022 about 700 million people had no or very limited access to water[1] and roughly the same number did not have access to electricity.[2] While it has been often speculated that lack of access to basic services has an impact on the time allocation of children, there is in fact an almost complete lack of evidence on the matter. This is partly due to the complexities of establishing a causal relationship for programs for which a counterfactual is obviously difficult to identify. Moreover, from a policy point of view the discussion on child labour interventions is focused mainly in the area of social policies. Be that as it may, there is hardly any evidence on the impact of access to basic services on child labour, and very few studies on their impact on children time allocation. For example, Khandker, Barnes, and Samad (2013) show that rural electrification in Vietnam led to an increase in school attendance and in school completion, especially for girls.

In the present chapter, we present the results of a study by Guarcello, Lyon, and Rosati (Guarcello et al., 2003), on the effects of electricity and piped water. The only study, to our knowledge, addressing the link between access to basic services and child labour.

Lack of piped water may raise the opportunity cost of time spent studying, as children are needed to fetch water, or to help pay for the cost of purchasing

[1] https://data.unicef.org/topic/water-and-sanitation/drinking-water/.
[2] https://trackingsdg7.esmap.org/data/files/download-documents/sdg7-report2022-ch1-access_to_electricity.pdf.

The Economics of Child Labour. Second Edition. Alessandro Cigno and Furio C. Rosati, Oxford University Press.
 DOI: 10.1093/oso/9780198903000.003.0005

Table 4.1 Water and electricity access, by country and residence(1)

Country	Households with water access(1)			Households with electricity access		
	Rural	Urban	Total	Rural	Urban	Total
El Salvador	40.4	81.0	64.3	70.8	97.3	86.4
Ghana	22.1	84.2	44.8	19.6	78.1	41.1
Guatemala	53.7	88.1	68.7	57.3	93.7	73.1
Morocco	36.9	–	36.9	17.3	–	17.3
Yemen	22.8	81.6	38.1	23.4	89.1	40.5

Notes:
[1] See Appendix A4.1 for questions upon which the access indicators are based.

Sources: UCW calculations based on Ghana: Ghana Living Standard Measurement Survey, 1998–1999; Yemen: National Poverty Survey, 1999; Guatemala: Guatemala, Encuesta de Condiciones de Vida (ENCOVI), 2000; El Salvador: Enquesta de Hogares de Propositos Multiples (EHPM) 2001; Morocco: Living Standard Measurement Survey, 1998–1999.

water. The same may be said about lack of electricity, as children are needed to collect wood and other fuels.

The chapter investigates the link between child labour and access to water and electricity in five countries: El Salvador, Ghana, Guatemala, Morocco, and Yemen. As Table 4.1 shows, a significant proportion of the population of these countries lacks, particular in rural areas, adequate access to water and electricity. The investigation uses datasets from national household surveys containing detailed information both on children's activities and on basic services access. The data sets used are listed in Appendix 4.1.

4.1 Child Activity Status

Two alternative definitions of working children are used. The first classifies as workers all children aged between 7 and 14 who carry out an economic activity for at least one hour a day. The second includes in the number of working children also those performing household chores for at least 28 hours a week. As data on hours spent on household chores are available only for El Salvador and Guatemala, the extended definition is utilized only for these two countries.

Table 4.2 shows the proportion of children who, according to these definitions, work only, work and study, study only, or are involved neither in work nor in education, in the five countries. The proportion of children involved full-time in economic activities ranges from 10% in Morocco to 2% in El Salvador, and rates of children's attending school only from 76% in Morocco to

51% in Yemen. The proportion of children combining school and economic activity varies from 12% in Guatemala to just 1% in Morocco.

All these countries feature a significant proportion of children absent from both school and work. More than one in three children in Ghana and Yemen, and almost one in five in El Salvador and Guatemala, fall into this category. In Morocco, 15% of the 7–14 age group is reported doing nothing. Some of these reportedly 'idle' children may be engaged in unreported work.[3] Others may perform household chores—including water or fuel collection—that allow other household members to engage in productive activities.[4]

As international labour standards make exceptions for household chores performed in a child's own household, these activities are normally excluded from estimates of child labour. Since they can interfere with school and leisure, however, they also merit consideration. As shown in Table 4.3, the inclusion of household chores raises the participation rate and reduces the incidence of children reportedly neither working nor attending school. The effect is particularly strong in El Salvador, where including household chores raises the participation rate from 7% to 43% and reduces the proportion of children reported idle from 18% to 8%.

4.2 The Effect of Access to Water and Electricity

As Figures 4.1 and 4.2 and Tables 4.4 and 4.5 show, the children's activity status in the five countries varies dramatically according to whether the household does or does not have access to water and electricity. With the exception of Guatemala, where the survey does not specify it, access to water is intended to mean that the household has piped drinking water. With the exception of Guatemala and Morocco, where the surveys ask about connection to the electricity network, electricity access refers to the source of lighting for the dwelling. Details of the questions used in the survey and precise definitions of the variables used in the estimates and tabulations are given in Appendix 4.1.

[3] Parents may falsely report their children as not working because (at best) children are forbidden work, or (at worst) because their children are engaged in illegal or dangerous activities. Alternatively, parents may misinterpret the survey question, and report a child as idle because he or she was not working at the time of the interview, although he or she may work in other periods.

[4] A study of the phenomenon of 'idle' children (UCW Project, 'The Puzzle of Apparently Idle Children: Evidence for Six Countries', October 2003) provides evidence suggesting that children can be absent from both school and external work because they are needed to perform household chores, because of their health, or because they are unable to find work after leaving school. But the study indicates that a large proportion of children not in school or economic activity does not fall into any of these categories. In Guatemala, one of the countries considered in the present chapter, the 'unexplained' portion of idle children is 70%.

Table 4.2. Child activity status (excluding household chores), by sex and country

Country	Activity Status	Male		Female		Total[2]	
		%	No.[1]	%	No.[1]	%	No.[1]
El Salvador	Working[3] and not attending school	3.3	25.1	1.3	10.0	2.3	35.1
	Attending school and not working	73.3	564.2	77.4	585.7	75.3	1,150.0
	Working and attending school	6.7	51.9	2.9	22.0	4.8	73.9
	Not working and not attending school	16.7	128.7	18.3	138.7	17.5	267.4
Ghana	Working and not attending school	9.3	282	9.7	287	9.5	569
	Attending school and not working	46.8	1427	46.9	1384	46.8	2811
	Working and attending school	6.5	199	5.5	163	6.03	362
	Not working and not attending school	37.4	1140	37.94	1121	37.67	2261
Guatemala	Working and not attending school	9.5	123	5.9	72	7.7	195
	Attending school and not working	60.9	790	64.1	787	62.4	1,577
	Working and attending school	16.4	212	8.1	99	12.3	311
	Not working and not attending school	13.3	172	22	270	17.5	442
Morocco	Working and not attending school	11.0	297.5	8.6	231	9.8	528.5
	Attending school and not working	80.9	2,198.2	70.3	1,877.8	75.6	4,075.9
	Working and attending school	1.8	49.9	0.8	20.87	1.3	70.7
	Not working and not attending school	8.1	220.5	21.1	563.1	14.5	783.6
Yemen	Working and not attending school	5.0	140.8	10.8	284.8	7.9	425.6
	Attending school and not working	62.6	1,749.3	38.4	1,011.3	50.9	2,760.5
	Working and attending school	6.3	175.2	2.0	51.5	4.2	226.6
	Not working and not attending school	26.1	728.1	48.8	1,283.1	37.1	2,011.2

Notes: (1) Numbers expressed in thousands; (2) totals may not add up due to rounding; (3) Economically active children.

Sources: UCW calculations based on Ghana: Ghana Living Standard Measurement Survey, 1998–1999; Yemen: National Poverty Survey, 1999; Guatemala: Guatemala, Encuesta de Condiciones de Vida (ENCOVI), 2000; El Salvador: Enquesta de Hogares de Propositos Multiples (EHPM) 2001; Morocco: Labour Force Survey, 1998.

Table 4.3 Child activity status (including household chores), by sex and country

Country	Activity Status	Male		Female		Total[2]	
		%	No.[1]	%	No.[1]	%	No.[1]
El Salvador	Working[3] and not attending school	13.4	103	11.0	83	12.2	186
	Attending school and not working	44.0	340	54.0	407	49.0	747
	Working and attending school	36.0	276	26.0	200	31.2	476
	Not working, not attending school	7.0	51	9.0	65	8.0	116
Guatemala	Working[3] and not attending school	10.8	140	11.6	142	11.18	282
	Attending school and not working	57.8	751	53.9	662	55.9	1413
	Working and attending school	19.4	252	18.3	224	18.6	476
	Not working, not attending school	12.0	156	16.3	200	14.2	356

Notes: (1) Numbers expressed in thousands; (2) totals may not add up due to rounding; (3) economically active children and children performing household chores for at 28 hours per week, eliminating the overlapping category doing both.

Sources: UCW calculations based on Guatemala: Guatemala, Encuesta de Condiciones de Vida (ENCOVI), 2000; El Salvador: Enquesta de Hogares de Propositos Multiples (EHPM) 2001.

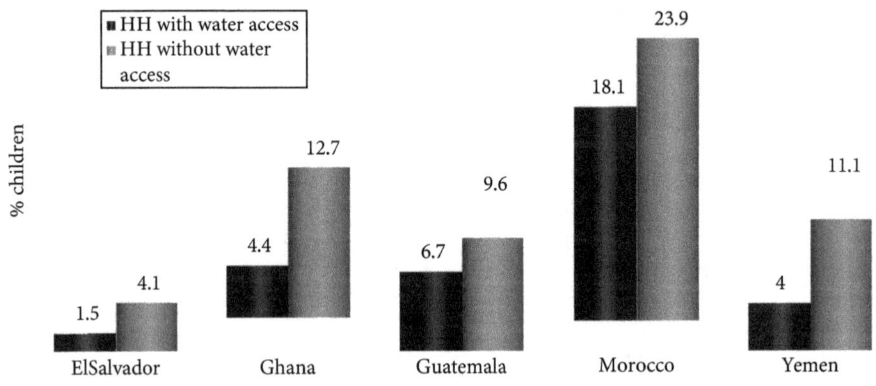

Figure 4.1 Rate of involvement in economic activity only, by household water access

Sources: UCW calculations based on Ghana: Ghana Living Standard Measurement Survey, 1998–1999; Yemen: National Poverty Survey, 1999; Guatemala: Guatemala, Encuesta de Condiciones de Vida (ENCOVI), 2000; El Salvador: Enquesta de Hogares de Propositos Multiples (EHPM) 2001; Morocco: Living Standard Measurement Survey, 1998–1999.

In all five countries, the percentage of children working only is much higher, and the rate of full-time school attendance much lower, among children from households without access to water or electricity. With the

Table 4.4 Child activity status (excluding household chores) by water access, sex, and country[1]

Country	Activity status	Households with water access[2]			Households without water access[2]		
		Male	Female	Total	Male	Female	Total
El Salvador	Working[2] and not attending school	1.9	1.1	1.5	6.1	2.1	4.1
	Attending school and not working	83.1	86.3	84.7	67.4	73.4	70.4
	Working and attending school	6.3	3.4	4.9	9.2	3.0	6.1
	Not working and not attending school	8.6	9.2	8.9	17.3	21.5	19.3
Ghana	Working[2] and not attending school	2.8	5.9	4.4	13.0	12.4	12.7
	Attending school and not working	66.8	63.8	65.2	34.9	35.0	35.0
	Working and attending school	3.1	3.4	3.3	8.5	6.9	7.7
	Not working and not attending school	27.3	26.9	27.1	43.6	45.8	44.6
Guatemala	Working[2] and not attending school	7.8	5.5	6.7	12.8	6.4	9.6
	Attending school and not working	65.9	68.2	67.0	51.1	57.1	54.1
	Working and attending school	15.1	9.3	12.3	18.9	6.0	12.3
	Not working and not attending school	11.3	17.0	14.0	17.2	30.5	24.0
Morocco[3]	Working[2] and not attending school	15.9	20.3	18.1	23.2	24.6	23.9
	Attending school and not working	63.2	38.6	51.1	66.4	41.1	54.3
	Working and attending school	2.3	0.7	1.5	2.4	0.8	1.6
	Not working and not attending school	18.6	40.4	29.4	8.1	33.5	20.2
Yemen	Working[2] and not attending school	3.0	5.1	4.0	6.7	15.8	11.1
	Attending school and not working	79.7	65.0	72.5	61.7	28.3	45.6
	Working and attending school	4.9	1.7	3.3	8.3	2.5	5.5
	Not working and not attending school	12.4	28.3	20.2	23.3	53.4	37.8

Sources: UCW calculations based on Ghana: Ghana Living Standard Measurement Survey, 1998–1999; Yemen: National Poverty Survey, 1999; Guatemala: Guatemala, Encuesta de Condiciones de Vida (ENCOVI), 2000; El Salvador: Enquesta de Hogares de Propositos Multiples (EHPM) 2001; Morocco: Living Standard Measurement Survey, 1998–1999.

Table 4.5 Child activity status (excluding household chores) by electricity access, sex, and country[1]

Country	Activity status	Households with electricity access[2]			Households without electricity access[2]		
		Male	Female	Total	Male	Female	Total
El Salvador	Working[2] and not attending school	2.3	1.3	1.8	9.5	2.5	6.1
	Attending school and not working	81.4	84.7	83.0	56.0	63.1	59.4
	Working and attending school	6.8	3.3	5.0	10.8	2.9	7.0
	Not working and not attending school	9.5	10.7	10.1	23.7	31.5	27.4
Ghana	Working[2] and not attending school	3.8	5.4	4.6	12.2	12.5	12.4
	Attending school and not working	66.4	65.0	65.7	35.7	35.0	35.4
	Working and attending school	5.0	4.7	4.8	7.4	6.0	6.7
	Not working and not attending school	24.8	24.8	24.8	44.7	46.6	45.6
Guatemala	Working[2] and not attending school	6.9	4.8	5.9	15.7	8.1	11.9
	Attending school and not working	67.3	71.0	69.1	45.4	49.2	47.4
	Working and attending school	15.3	8.7	12.2	18.9	6.6	12.7
	Not working and not attending school	10.5	15.5	12.9	20.0	36.0	28.1
Morocco	Working[2] and not attending school	9.9	6.9	8.5	21.3	25.1	23.2
	Attending school and not working	77.5	66.2	72	63.8	36.4	50.6
	Working and attending school	2.9	3.2	3	2.2	0.5	1.4
	Not working and not attending school	9.7	23.7	16.5	12.6	37.9	24.9
Yemen	Working[2] and not attending school	2.4	5.5	3.8	9.0	9.0	9.0
	Attending school and not working	65.4	50.4	59.0	40.8	20.2	32.5
	Working and attending school	1.5	2.3	1.9	5.3	1.3	3.7
	Not working and not attending school	30.6	41.7	35.3	44.9	69.5	54.8

Notes: (1) See detailed table in Appendix A4.2 for disaggregation by both residence and sex; (2) economically active children.

Sources: UCW calculations based on the following surveys. Ghana: Ghana Living Standard Measurement Survey, 1998–1999; Yemen: National Poverty Survey, 1999; Guatemala: Guatemala, Encuesta de Condiciones de Vida (ENCOVI), 2000; El Salvador: Enquesta de Hogares de Propositos Multiples (EHPM) 2001; Morocco: Living Standard Measurement Survey, 1998–1999.

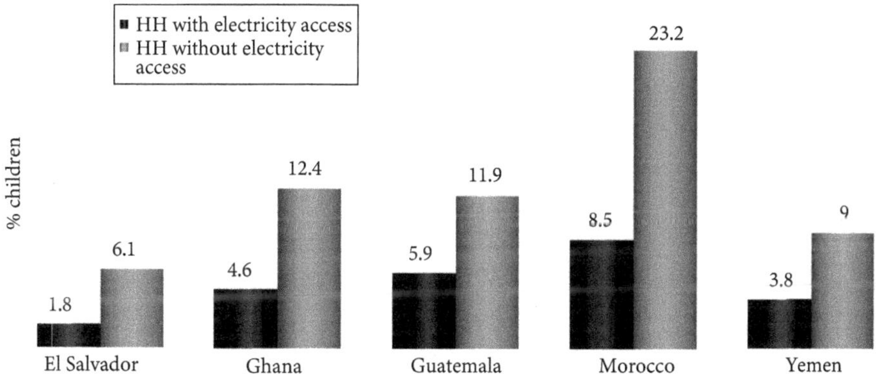

Figure 4.2 Rate of involvement in economic activity only, by household electricity access

Sources: UCW calculations based on data provided by the following surveys. Ghana: Ghana Living Standard Measurement Survey, 1998–1999. Yemen: National Poverty Survey, 1999. Guatemala: Guatemala, Encuesta de Condiciones de Vida (ENCOVI), 2000. El Salvador: Enquesta de Hogares de Propositos Multiples (EHPM) 2001. Morocco: Living Standard Measurement Survey, 1998–1999.

exception of Guatemala, the rate of full-time child involvement in work, for example, is more than three times higher in households without, than in households with water access. In all five countries, a much higher proportion of children from households not served by water and electricity is also reportedly 'idle'. In general, the variation in children's activity status by water/electricity access is higher among girls than boys, and higher in rural compared to urban areas.

Similar patterns prevail in El Salvador and Guatemala also when household chores are counted as work (Tables A4.2.3–A4.2.4, Appendix 4.2). For example, school attendance rates in El Salvador and Guatemala decrease from 85% and 79%, respectively, for household with access to water, to 72% and 66%, respectively, for households without water access.

There is, therefore, a strong correlation between water/electricity access and the activities of children. But is there also a causal link? Disentangling the causal relationship is not straightforward. The observation, for example, that households without water access are less likely to send their children to school is not sufficient to establish a causal relationship, because a household without water access may have a set of characteristics (observable and unobservable) that makes them more likely to send their children to work. The next three sections deal with the issue.

4.3 Econometric Methodology

The main econometric problem in estimating the effects of access to basic services is the potential endogeneity of such variables. Guarcello et al. (2003) estimate the probability ('propensity score') that a household with characteristics X has access to water or electricity. In each case, specification of the propensity score is achieved by checking if the balancing property of the estimated probability is satisfied. Since access to water and electricity is likely to be different for urban and rural households, the propensity scores are computed separately for the two areas of residence.

The distributions of the propensity scores for 'treated' and 'non-treated' groups of households overlap to a large extent for El Salvador (rural areas) and Guatemala (rural and urban areas) in the case of water access, and for Morocco (rural areas) in the case of electricity access. This indicates that the characteristics of the two groups of households that have and do not have access to water (electricity) do not differ in a significant way. In the other cases, however, the 'treated' and 'non-treated' groups of households overlap much less, and the estimates are consequently more sensitive to model specification.

Average Treatment Effects (ATT) are computed using a nearest-neighbour-matching estimator. The results are shown in Tables 4.6 and 4.7. Access to water in rural areas appears to raise school attendance and lower both child participation in work, and the number of children reported doing nothing. The effects are somewhat differentiated by country but have a similar pattern. As to be expected, in urban areas, the pattern is less well defined than in rural areas, and the effects are not always significant.

Access to electricity has broadly similar effects. It significantly increases the proportion of children in school (El Salvador, Ghana, Morocco), and significantly reduces the proportion of economically active children (Morocco) and idle children (El Salvador, Ghana, and Morocco). With the exception of Guatemala, the pattern is again less well defined in urban than in rural areas.

These results should be taken with caution because of the potential endogeneity arising from the existence of unobserved variables, not taken into account in the estimation. We shall deal with the issue in the next section.

Table 4.6 Average treatment effects for water access (results from matching procedure using water access as the treatment variable)

Country	Outcome variable[2]	Urban				Rural			
		treat.	contr.	ATT	t	treat.	contr.	ATT	t
El Salvador	Children attending school	1122	627	0.055	2.87	2887	570	0.028	1.028
	Children working[1]	1122	627	−0.016	−1.131	2887	570	−0.027	−1.397
	Working[2] and not attending school	1122	627	−0.007	−0.885	2887	570	−0.015	−1.12
	Attending school and not working	1122	627	0.004	0.316	2887	570	−0.026	−1.55
	Working and attending school	1122	627	0.05	2.347	2887	570	0.053	1.795
	Not working and not attending school	1122	627	−0.047	−3.244	2887	570	−0.026	−1.55
Ghana	Children attending school	876	174	0.043	0.658	400	319	0.068	1.772
	Children working[1]	876	174	−0.096	−1.937	400	319	−0.088	−3.002
	Working[2] and not attending school	876	174	−0.023	−0.693	400	319	−0.04	−1.754
	Attending school and not working	876	174	−0.073	−1.938	400	319	−0.048	−2.543
	Working and attending school	876	174	0.109	1.63	400	319	0.144	3.875
	Not working and not attending school	876	174	−0.029	−0.47	400	319	−0.028	−0.748
Guatemala	Children attending school	1516	171	−0.059	−1.411	1263	611	0.065	2.784
	Children working[1]	1516	171	0.078	1.295	1263	611	0.015	0.74
	Working[2] and not attending school	1516	171	−0.027	−1	1263	611	0.001	0.06
	Attending school and not working	1516	171	0.112	1.776	1263	611	0.014	0.874
	Working and attending school	1516	171	−0.032	−0.91	1263	611	0.051	2.084
	Not working and not attending school	1516	171	−0.052	−0.961	1263	611	−0.066	−3.272
Morocco	Children attending school	–	–	–	–	726	404	−0.021	0.032
	Children working[1]	–	–	–	–	726	404	−0.053	0.027
	Working[2] and not attending school	–	–	–	–	726	404	−0.046	0.025
	Attending school and not working	–	–	–	–	726	404	−0.007	0.006
	Working and attending school	–	–	–	–	726	404	−0.015	0.032
	Not working and not attending school	–	–	–	–	726	404	0.067	0.026

Notes: (1) Economically active; (2) the outcome variable is the proportion of children in each household involved in the reported activities.
Sources: UCW calculations based on the following surveys. Ghana: Ghana Living Standard Measurement Survey, 1998–1999; Yemen: National Poverty Survey, 1999; Guatemala: Guatemala, Encuesta de Condiciones de Vida (ENCOVI), 2000; El Salvador: Enquesta de Hogares de Propositos Multiples (EHPM) 2001; Morocco: Living Standard Measurement Survey, 1998–1999.

Table 4.7 Average treatment effects for electricity access (results from matching procedure using electricity access as the treatment variable)

Country	Outcome variable[(2)]	Urban				Rural			
		treat.	contr.	ATT	t	treat.	contr.	ATT	t
El Salvador	Children attending school	3598	125	0.011	0.09	1928	478	0.082	2.662
	Children working[(1)]	3598	125	0.006	0.076	1928	478	−0.029	−1.347
	Working[(2)] and not attending school	3598	125	−0.013	−0.186	1928	478	−0.01	−0.748
	Attending school and not working	3598	125	0.08	0.639	1928	478	0.108	3.249
	Working and attending school	3598	125	−0.073	−0.971	1928	478	−0.028	−1.345
	Not working and not attending school	3598	125	−0.016	−0.168	1928	478	−0.075	−2.943
Ghana	Children attending school	847	763	0.079	1.229	395	287	0.107	2.926
	Children working[(1)]	847	163	−0.041	−0.868	395	287	−0.05	−1.708
	Working[(2)] and not attending school	847	163	−0.031	−0.951	395	287	−0.031	−1.386
	Attending school and not working	847	163	0.067	1.035	395	287	0.119	3.282
	Working and attending school	847	163	−0.01	−0.298	395	287	−0.019	−0.946
	Not working and not attending school	847	163	−0.066	−1.062	395	287	−0.077	−2.197
Guatemala	Children attending school	1283	541	0.165	5.775	1557	140	0.168	1.887
	Children working[(1)]	1283	541	0.022	0.912	1557	140	−0.059	−0.958
	Working[(2)] and not attending school	1283	541	−0.028	−1.541	1557	140	−0.027	−0.554
	Attending school and not working	1283	541	0.116	3.929	1557	140	0.2	2.255
	Working and attending school	1283	541	0.05	2.727	1557	140	−0.032	−0.729
	Not working and not attending school	1283	541	−0.131	−5.151	1557	140	−0.141	−1.727
Morocco	Children attending school					393	361	0.189	4.859
	Children working[(1)]					393	361	−0.115	−3.797
	Working[(2)] and not attending school	–	–	–	–	393	361	−0.12	−3.926
	Attending school and not working	–	–	–	–	393	361	0.183	4.631
	Working and attending school	–	–	–	–	393	361	0.005	0.688
	Not working and not attending school	–	–	–	–	393	361	−0.069	−2.145

Notes: (1) Economically active; (2) the outcome variable is the proportion of children in each household involved in the reported activities.
Sources: UCW calculations based on the following surveys. Ghana: Ghana Living Standard Measurement Survey, 1998–1999; Yemen: National Poverty Survey, 1999; Guatemala: Guatemala, Encuesta de Condiciones de Vida (ENCOVI), 2000; El Salvador: Enquesta de Hogares de Propositos Multiples (EHPM) 2001; Morocco: Living Standard Measurement Survey, 1998–1999.

4.4 The Effects of Access to Water and Electricity on Children's School Attendance and Labour Supply: A Bivariate Analysis

The distribution of the propensity scores for 'treated' and 'non-treated' groups of households (not shown here) makes us confident that, under the unconfoundedness assumption, the use of a regression model does not imply that the estimation of treatment effects relies on extrapolation. Because of similar covariates' distributions for the treatment and control groups, also model-based sensitivity should be very limited. This allows us to draw causal inferences from a regression model.

The effects of the explanatory variables are estimated by fitting a bivariate probit model of the probability of work and the probability of school attendance that takes into account the simultaneity of the decisions through the correlation of the error terms. The marginal effects are then calculated from the estimated coefficients of the probit model. Given that the results obtained with the propensity scores indicated clearly that rural and urban areas are not homogeneous, the estimates are carried out separately for the two areas.

Besides access to water and electricity, the list of explanatory variables includes the household's and the child's characteristics. These characteristics include the sex and age of the child, the income or expenditure of the household, the household's size and age composition, the education of the parents. Where available, other relevant variables such as the occurrence of shocks, availability of schools, presence of living parents, etc. are also included. The effects are very similar to those estimated in the last section).

Table 4.8 presents the marginal effects. Those of access to water and electricity are well defined, and relatively large, for almost all countries. Access to water in urban areas tends to increase the number of children that attend school only. This is normally associated with a reduction in the number of children working or who were reported as doing nothing. The size of the effect varies from country to country. Access to water in urban areas is associated with an increase in the probability of attending school of between two (Ghana) and 10 (Yemen) percentage points. In El Salvador and Yemen increased water access reduces the number of 'idle' children more than the number of children who work. In the other countries it is the other way round.

Access to water in rural areas shows a similar pattern. It induces an increase in the number of children attending school and a reduction in the number of children either working or not working nor attending school. Notice that

Table 4.8 a. Bivariate probit model marginal effects of access to water (1)

Country	Residence	Working[5] not attending school		Attending school not Working		Working and attending school		Not attending school not working	
		dy/dx	*z*	*dy/dx*	*z*	*dy/dx*	*z*	*dy/dx*	*z*
El Salvador	Rural	−0.003	−1.36	0.054	4.71	0.003	1.34	−0.055	−5.06
	Urban	−0.004	−3.21	0.041	4.24	−0.007	−1.99	−0.03	–
Ghana	Rural	−0.077	−7.47	0.074	3.02	−0.035	−5.98	0.039	1.59
	Urban	−0.016	−2.13	0.019	0.68	−0.019	−2.25	0.016	0.61
Guatemala	Rural	−0.012	−1.99	0.035	2.43	0.003	0.32	−0.0262	−2.29
	Urban	−0.004	−0.67	0.016	0.73	−0.001	−0.1	−0.011	−0.73
Morocco	Rural	−0.184	−5.28	0.094	1.06	−0.013	−4.98	0.103	1.16
	Urban	–	–	–	–	–	–	–	–
Yemen[4]	Rural	0.002	–	0.014	–	0.006	–	−0.021	–
	Urban	−0.004	–	0.04	–	−0.001	–	−0.034	–

Notes: (1) See Appendix A1 for all control variables; (2) dy/dx is for discrete change in dummy variable from 0 to 1; (3) dy/dx is for discrete change in dummy variable from 0 to 1; (4) simulated effects after bivariate probit; (5) economically active children.
Sources: UCW calculations based on the following surveys. Ghana: Ghana Living Standard Measurement Survey, 1998–1999; Yemen: National Poverty Survey, 1999; Guatemala: Guatemala, Encuesta de Condiciones de Vida (ENCOVI), 2000; El Salvador: Enquesta de Hogares de Propositos Multiples (EHPM) 2001; Morocco: Living Standard Measurement Survey, 1998–1999.

Table 4.8 b. Bivariate probit model marginal effects of access to electricity[1]

Country	Residence	Working[4] not attending school		Attending school not Working		Working and attending school		Not attending school not Working	
		$dy/dx^{(2)}$	z	$dy/dx^{(2)}$	Z	$dy/dx^{(2)}$	z	$dy/dx^{(2)}$	z
El Salvador	Rural	−0.01	−3.83	0.084	6.27	−0.004	−1.26	−0.07	−5.55
	Urban	−0.006	−2.08	0.081	3.87	−0.004	−0.61	−0.072	-
Ghana	Rural	0.025	1.66	0.017	0.74	0.029	2.94	−0.071	−3.04
	Urban	−0.041	−3.96	0.145	4.93	−0.021	−2.44	−0.033	−2.98
Guatemala	Rural	−0.019	−3.06	0.075	4.82	0.031	3.42	−0.037	−7.02
	Urban	−0.024	−2.59	0.144	4.75	0.028	2.5	−0.149	−5.63
Morocco	Rural	−0.097	−4.36	0.188	5.43	0.002	0.46	−0.093	−3.24
	Urban	–	–	–	–	–	–	–	–
Yemen[3]	Rural	−0.02	–	0.07	–	0.001	–	−0.05	–
	Urban	−0.015	–	0.11	–	−0.01	–	−0.09	–

Notes: (1) See Appendix A1 for all control variables; (2) dy/dx is for discrete change in dummy variable from 0 to 1; (3) simulated effects after bivariate probit; (4) economically active children.

Sources: UCW calculations based on the following surveys. Ghana: Ghana Living Standard Measurement Survey, 1998–1999; Yemen: National Poverty Survey, 1999; Guatemala: Guatemala, Encuesta de Condiciones de Vida (ENCOVI), 2000; El Salvador: Enquesta de Hogares de Propositos Multiples (EHPM) 2001; Morocco: Living Standard Measurement Survey, 1998–1999.

the size of the effects is in general larger in rural than in urban areas. Access to electricity increases school attendance in both urban and rural areas, with the exception of rural Ghana. The increase in school attendance is associated with a reduction of the number of both children working and of children neither attending school nor involved in economic activity. The size of the effect ranges between 11% in urban Yemen and 18% in rural Morocco. As the distribution of the propensity scores for the treated group is somewhat different from that of the control group, the effect of access to electricity and children's activities must be treated with more caution than that of access to water.

These estimates make it clear that access to water and electricity is an important determinant of household decisions concerning child labour and education. How important depends on the country. Given that the available controls are not the same for each country, however, it is difficult to draw any conclusion about differences in the size of the effects.

It is also interesting to distinguish the effects of access to water and electricity by the age of the child. Where school attendance is concerned, the effects of access to basic utilities are higher for relatively young and relatively old children. This seems to indicate that availability of water and electricity helps both to increase school enrolment at younger ages and to reduce the drop-out rate at later ages. The effect on labour participation tends to be more negative for relatively older children. 'Idle' children seem to particularly benefit from access to basic services at a young age. At the lower end of the age range, the increase in enrolment seems therefore to be due to children being released from full-time household chores (or to formerly 'idle' children being brought into the education system). At the upper end, access to water and electricity appears to help retain in the school system children who would have otherwise dropped out to join the labour market.

4.5 Causality

As already mentioned, the presence of unobservables influencing both the decision relative to children's activities and the presence of a certain facility could invalidate the casual interpretation of the estimated relationship. Were we talking of schools, for example, parents with stronger interest in education could decide to live in an area served by basic services, or lobby for the improvement of the one that exists in the area where they live. The problem seems less serious where basic facilities like electricity and piped water are concerned. To address this issue, following the methodology proposed by Rosenbaum and Rubin (1982a) a sensitivity analysis was performed considering the possible effects of unobservables correlated with outcomes and the explanatory variables on the estimated coefficients. The results for El Salvador and Guatemala[5] reported in Appendix A4.2 of the present chapter confirm the robustness of the results with respect to the possible presence of unobservables correlated both with children's activities and with access to the utilities. We can thus be reasonably confident that the estimated relations are causal.

The finding of a strong causal link between access to water and electricity has the obvious policy implication that governments concerned about child labour and school attendance should attach a high priority to these basic facilities, as well as to the provision of schools and health.

[5] For the other countries, see Guarcello et al. (2003).

Appendix 4.1 Surveys and questions used to define variables for access to water and electricity

Question used to define access to water

Ghana		Yemen		Guatemala		El Salvador		Morocco (1)	
What is the source of drinking water for your household?		What is the source of drinking water for your household?		What is the main source of water used by the household?		What is the source of drinking water for your household?		What is the main source of drinking water in the 'DOUAR'?	
Indoor plumbing	1	Public net	1	Pipe (network) inside the dwelling	1	Pipe inside the dwelling	1	Public network	1
Inside standpipe	2	Cooperative net	2	the property Pipe, outside the dwelling but within	2	Pipe outside the dwelling but	2	Well	2
Water vendor	3	Private net	3	Pipe from a public well...	3	inside the property	3	Lake, river, spring...	3
Water truck/tanker service	4	Well inside the dwelling	4	Public or private well...	4	Neighbour's pipe...	4	Hill dam...	4
Neighbouring household	5	Well outside the dwelling...	5	River, lake, stream...	5	Fountain or public stream... Cooperative stream.	5	Water truck...	5
Private outside standpipe/tap....	6	Spring...	6	Water truck...	6	Water truck...	6	Other	6
Public standpipe	7	Covered pond...	7	Rain water	7	Private or cooperative well	7	(1) Question applied to the	
Well with pump	8	An open pond...	8	Other (specify)	8	Lake, river, spring.	8	rural questionnaire	
Well without pump	9	Dam...	9			Other (specify)	9		
River, lake spring, pond	10	Other	10						
Rainwater	11								
Other	12								

Note: In bold positive response used to define the variable 'Access to Water'.
Source: Ghana: Ghana Living Standard Measurement Survey, 1998–1999; Yemen: National Poverty Survey, 1999; Guatemala: Guatemala, Encuesta de Condiciones de Vida (ENCOVI), 2000; El Salvador: Enquesta de Hogares de Propositos Multiples (EHPM) 2001; Morocco: Living Standard Measurement Survey, 1998–1999

Question used to define access to electricity

Ghana		Yemen		Guatemala	El Salvador		Morocco (1)
What is the main source of lighting for your dwelling?		What is the main source of lighting in the house?		This dwelling is connected to:	What is the main source of lighting in this house?		**Is there any electricity in this 'DOUAR'?**
Electricity (mains)	1	**Public net**	1	**An electrical energy distribution system?**	**Electricity**	1	Yes.... .1, No......2
Generator...	2	**Cooperation net**	2		Neighbour's electricity connection	2	
Kerosene, gas, lamp...	3	**Private net**	3	Yes.... .1, No.... .2			
Candles/torches (flashlights)...	4	Household private generator	4		Kerosene (gas)	3	
		Kerosene (gas)...	5		Candle	4	
		Gasoline torch...	6		Other	5	
		Other (specify)	7				
							(1) Question applied to the rural questionnaire

Note: In bold positive response used to define the variable 'Access to Electricity'.
Source: Ghana: Ghana Living Standard Measurement Survey, 1998–1999; Yemen: National Poverty Survey, 1999; Guatemala: Guatemala, Encuesta de Condiciones de Vida (ENCOVI), 2000; El Salvador: Enquesta de Hogares de Propositos Multiples (EHPM) 2001; Morocco: Living Standard Measurement Survey, 1998–1999

Definition of variables	
Child activities:	
Employment:	1 if individual currently works
School Attendance:	1 if individual currently attends school
Work only:	1 if individual currently works and does not attend school
Study only:	1 if individual currently attends school and school not work
Work and Study:	1 if individual currently works and attends
school Neither:	1 if individual currently neither works nor attends school
Access to basic services:	
Water	1 if household have access to public network
Electricity	1 if household have access to public network
Other variables:	
Female:	1 if female
Household expenditures:	logarithm of per capita household expenditure
Insurance:	if at least one member of the household has a medical insurance, 0 otherwise
Credit:	1 if a household is credit rationed, 0 otherwise
Father's education:	
Fed_None:	1 if he has no completed education
Fed_Primary:	1 if he has completed primary education
Mother's Education:	
Mother_None:	1 if she has no completed education
Mother_ Primary:	1 if she has completed primary education
(Secondary or higher education is the comparison group)	
Shocks:	
Collective	1 if a household reported experiencing at least a collective shock
Individual	1 if a household reported experiencing at least an idiosyncratic shock

Appendix 4.2 Average treatment effects for 'access to water and access to electricity' for different values of the sensitivity parameters

Table A4.2.1 Sensitivity analysis on the effect of access to water in Urban area

ATT	$\alpha = 0$ $\delta_{0W} = \delta_{1W} = 0$ $\delta_{0S} = \delta_{1S} = 0$ $\delta_{0WS} = \delta_{1WS} = 0$	$\pi = 0.1, \alpha = 0.1$ $\delta_{0W} = \delta_{1W} = -0.1$ $\delta_{0S} = \delta_{1S} = 0.1$ $\delta_{0WS} = \delta_{1WS} = 0.1$	$\pi = 0.5, \alpha = 0.5$ $\delta_{0W} = \delta_{1W} = -0.1$ $\delta_{0S} = \delta_{1S} = 0.1$ $\delta_{0WS} = \delta_{1WS} = 0.1$	$\pi = 0.5, \alpha = 0.5$ $\delta_{0W} = \delta_{1W} = -0.5$ $\delta_{0S} = \delta_{1S} = 0.5$ $\delta_{0WS} = \delta_{1WS} = 0.5$	$\pi = 0.5, \alpha = 0.5$ $\delta_{0W} = \delta_{1W} = -0.5$ $\delta_{0S} = \delta_{1S} = 0.5$ $\delta_{0WS} = \delta_{1WS} = 0.5$
Working only	−0.018	−0.018	−0.018	−0.018	−0.016
Studying only	0.107	0.107	0.106	0.103	0.097
Working and Studying	−0.012	−0.012	−0.012	−0.012	−0.012
Idle Children	−0.077	−0.077	−0.076	−0.073	−0.069

Sources: UCW calculations based on El Salvador: Enquesta de Hogares de Propositos Multiples (EHPM) 2001.

Table A4.2.2 Sensitivity analysis on the effect of access to water in rural area

ATT	$\alpha = 0$ $\delta_{0W} = \delta_{1W} = 0$ $\delta_{0S} = \delta_{1S} = 0$ $\delta_{0WS} = \delta_{1WS} = 0$	$\pi = 0.1, \alpha = 0.1$ $\delta_{0W} = \delta_{1W} = -0.1$ $\delta_{0S} = \delta_{1S} = 0.1$ $\delta_{0WS} = \delta_{1WS} = 0.1$	$\pi = 0.5, \alpha = 0.5$ $\delta_{0W} = \delta_{1W} = -0.1$ $\delta_{0S} = \delta_{1S} = 0.1$ $\delta_{0WS} = \delta_{1WS} = 0.1$	$\pi = 0.1, \alpha = 0.1$ $\delta_{0W} = \delta_{1W} = -0.5$ $\delta_{0S} = \delta_{1S} = 0.5$ $\delta_{0WS} = \delta_{1WS} = 0.5$	$\pi = 0.5, \alpha = 0.5$ $\delta_{0W} = \delta_{1W} = -0.5$ $\delta_{0S} = \delta_{1S} = 0.5$ $\delta_{0WS} = \delta_{1WS} = 0.5$
Working only	−0.018	−0.018	−0.018	−0.018	−0.016
Studying only	0.107	0.107	0.106	0.103	0.097
Working and Studying	−0.012	−0.012	−0.012	−0.012	−0.012
Idle Children	−0.077	−0.077	−0.076	−0.073	−0.069

Sources: UCW calculations based on El Salvador: Enquesta de Hogares de Propositos Multiples (EHPM) 2001

Table A4.2.3 Sensitivity analysis on the effect of access to electricity in urban area

ATT	$\alpha = 0$ $\delta_{0W} = \delta_{1W} = 0$ $\delta_{0S} = \delta_{1S} = 0$ $\delta_{0WS} = \delta_{1WS} = 0$	$\pi = 0.1, \alpha = 0.1$ $\delta_{0W} = \delta_{1W} = -0.1$ $\delta_{0S} = \delta_{1S} = 0.1$ $\delta_{0WS} = \delta_{1WS} = 0.1$	$\pi = 0.5, \alpha = 0.5$ $\delta_{0W} = \delta_{1W} = -0.1$ $\delta_{0S} = \delta_{1S} = 0.1$ $\delta_{0WS} = \delta_{1WS} = 0.1$	$\pi = 0.1, \alpha = 0.1$ $\delta_{0W} = \delta_{1W} = -0.5$ $\delta_{0S} = \delta_{1S} = 0.5$ $\delta_{0WS} = \delta_{1WS} = 0.5$	$\pi = 0.5, \alpha = 0.5$ $\delta_{0W} = \delta_{1W} = -0.5$ $\delta_{0S} = \delta_{1S} = 0.5$ $\delta_{0WS} = \delta_{1WS} = 0.5$
Working only	−0.027	−0.027	−0.027	−0.026	−0.024
Studying only	0.220	0.220	0.218	0.205	0.206
Working and Studying	−0.013	−0.013	−0.013	−0.013	−0.019
Idle Children	−0.180	−0.180	−0.178	−0.166	−0.164

Sources: UCW calculations based on El Salvador: Enquesta de Hogares de Propositos Multiples (EHPM) 2001

Table A4.2.4 Sensitivity analysis on the effect of access to electricity in rural area

ATT	$\alpha = 0$ $\delta_{0W} = \delta_{1W} = 0$ $\delta_{0S} = \delta_{1S} = 0$ $\delta_{0WS} = \delta_{1WS} = 0$	$\pi = 0.1, \alpha = 0.1$ $\delta_{0W} = \delta_{1W} = -0.1$ $\delta_{0S} = \delta_{1S} = 0.1$ $\delta_{0WS} = \delta_{1WS} = 0.1$	$\pi = 0.5, \alpha = 0.5$ $\delta_{0W} = \delta_{1W} = -0.1$ $\delta_{0S} = \delta_{1S} = 0.1$ $\delta_{0WS} = \delta_{1WS} = 0.1$	$\pi = 0.1, \alpha = 0.1$ $\delta_{0W} = \delta_{1W} = -0.5$ $\delta_{0S} = \delta_{1S} = 0.5$ $\delta_{0WS} = \delta_{1WS} = 0.5$	$\pi = 0.5, \alpha = 0.5$ $\delta_{0W} = \delta_{1W} = -0.5$ $\delta_{0S} = \delta_{1S} = 0.5$ $\delta_{0WS} = \delta_{1WS} = 0.5$
Working only	−0.029	−0.029	−0.028	−0.029	−0.025
Studying only	0.141	0.140	0.138	0.140	0.129
Working and Studying	−0.003	−0.003	−0.003	−0.003	−0.004
Idle Children	−0.109	−0.108	−0.107	−0.108	−0.100

Sources: UCW calculations based on El Salvador: Enquesta de Hogares de Propositos Multiples (EHPM) 2001.

Table A4.2.5 Sensitivity analysis on the effect of access to water in urban area

ATT	$\alpha = 0$ $\delta_{0W} = \delta_{1W} = 0$ $\delta_{0S} = \delta_{1S} = 0$ $\delta_{0WS} = \delta_{1WS} = 0$	$\pi = 0.1, \alpha = 0.1$ $\delta_{0W} = \delta_{1W} = -0.1$ $\delta_{0S} = \delta_{1S} = 0.1$ $\delta_{0WS} = \delta_{1WS} = 0.1$	$\pi = 0.5, \alpha = 0.5$ $\delta_{0W} = \delta_{1W} = -0.1$ $\delta_{0S} = \delta_{1S} = 0.1$ $\delta_{0WS} = \delta_{1WS} = 0.1$	$\pi = 0.1, \alpha = 0.1$ $\delta_{0W} = \delta_{1W} = -0.5$ $\delta_{0S} = \delta_{1S} = 0.5$ $\delta_{0WS} = \delta_{1WS} = 0.5$	$\pi = 0.5, \alpha = 0.5$ $\delta_{0W} = \delta_{1W} = -0.5$ $\delta_{0S} = \delta_{1S} = 0.5$ $\delta_{0WS} = \delta_{1WS} = 0.5$
Working only	−0.166	−0.157	−0.157	−0.122	−0.133
Studying only	0.271	0.271	0.266	0.247	0.251
Working and Studying	0.000	0.000	0.000	0.000	0.000
Idle Children	−0.105	−0.113	−0.108	−0.125	−0. 118

Sources: UCW calculations based on Guatemala, Encuesta National Sobre Condiciones De Vida (ENCOVI), 2000.

Table A4.2.6 Sensitivity analysis on the effect of access to water in rural area

ATT	$\alpha = 0$ $\delta_{0W} = \delta_{1W} = 0$ $\delta_{0S} = \delta_{1S} = 0$ $\delta_{0WS} = \delta_{1WS} = 0$	$\pi = 0.1, \alpha = 0.1$ $\delta_{0W} = \delta_{1W} = -0.1$ $\delta_{0S} = \delta_{1S} = 0.1$ $\delta_{0WS} = \delta_{1WS} = 0.1$	$\pi = 0.5, \alpha = 0.5$ $\delta_{0W} = \delta_{1W} = -0.1$ $\delta_{0S} = \delta_{1S} = 0.1$ $\delta_{0WS} = \delta_{1WS} = 0.1$	$\pi = 0.1, \alpha = 0.1$ $\delta_{0W} = \delta_{1W} = -0.5$ $\delta_{0S} = \delta_{1S} = 0.5$ $\delta_{0WS} = \delta_{1WS} = 0.5$	$\pi = 0.5, \alpha = 0.5$ $\delta_{0W} = \delta_{1W} = -0.5$ $\delta_{0S} = \delta_{1S} = 0.5$ $\delta_{0WS} = \delta_{1WS} = 0.5$
Working only	−0.080	−0.074	−0.072	−0.057	−0.067
Studying only	0.140	0.135	0.131	0.124	0.118
Working and Studying	−0.013	−0.013	−0.013	−0.013	0.000
Idle Children	−0.060	−0.061	−0.059	−0.067	−0.051

Sources: UCW calculations based on Guatemala, Encuesta National Sobre Condiciones De Vida (ENCOVI), 2000.

Table A4.2.7 Sensitivity analysis on the effect of access to electricity in urban area

ATT	$\alpha = 0$ $\delta_{0W} = \delta_{1W} = 0$ $\delta_{0S} = \delta_{1S} = 0$ $\delta_{0WS} = \delta_{1WS} = 0$	$\pi = 0.1, \alpha = 0.1$ $\delta_{0W} = \delta_{1W} = -0.1$ $\delta_{0S} = \delta_{1S} = 0.1$ $\delta_{0WS} = \delta_{1WS} = 0.1$	$\pi = 0.5, \alpha = 0.5$ $\delta_{0W} = \delta_{1W} = -0.1$ $\delta_{0S} = \delta_{1S} = 0.1$ $\delta_{0WS} = \delta_{1WS} = 0.1$	$\pi = 0.1, \alpha = 0.1$ $\delta_{0W} = \delta_{1W} = -0.5$ $\delta_{0S} = \delta_{1S} = 0.5$ $\delta_{0WS} = \delta_{1WS} = 0.5$	$\pi = 0.5, \alpha = 0.5$ $\delta_{0W} = \delta_{1W} = -0.5$ $\delta_{0S} = \delta_{1S} = 0.5$ $\delta_{0WS} = \delta_{1WS} = 0.5$
Working only	−0.188	−0.176	−0.185	−0.140	−0.168
Studying only	0.391	0.388	0.389	0.371	0.371
Working and Studying	0.000	0.000	0.000	0.000	0.000
Idle Children	−0.204	−0.212	−0.204	−0.231	−0.203

Sources: UCW calculations based on Guatemala, Encuesta National Sobre Condiciones De Vida (ENCOVI), 2000.

Table A4.2.8 Sensitivity analysis on the effect of access to electricity in rural area

ATT	$\alpha = 0$ $\delta_{0W} = \delta_{1W} = 0$ $\delta_{0S} = \delta_{1S} = 0$ $\delta_{0WS} = \delta_{1WS} = 0$	$\pi = 0.1, \alpha = 0.1$ $\delta_{0W} = \delta_{1W} = -0.1$ $\delta_{0S} = \delta_{1S} = 0.1$ $\delta_{0WS} = \delta_{1WS} = 0.1$	$\pi = 0.5, \alpha = 0.5$ $\delta_{0W} = \delta_{1W} = -0.1$ $\delta_{0S} = \delta_{1S} = 0.1$ $\delta_{0WS} = \delta_{1WS} = 0.1$	$\pi = 0.1, \alpha = 0.1$ $\delta_{0W} = \delta_{1W} = -0.5$ $\delta_{0S} = \delta_{1S} = 0.5$ $\delta_{0WS} = \delta_{1WS} = 0.5$	$\pi = 0.5, \alpha = 0.5$ $\delta_{0W} = \delta_{1W} = -0.5$ $\delta_{0S} = \delta_{1S} = 0.5$ $\delta_{0WS} = \delta_{1WS} = 0.5$
Working only	−0.162	−0.145	−0.157	−0.118	−0.136
Studying only	0.245	0.231	0.239	0.210	0.215
Working and Studying	0.000	0.000	0.000	0.000	0.000
Idle Children	−0.083	−0.086	−0.082	−0.092	−0.051

Sources: UCW calculations based on Guatemala, Encuesta National Sobre Condiciones De Vida (ENCOVI), 2000.

5
The Demand for Child Labour
Evidence

While large attention has been given in the literature to the supply of child labour, there has not been much discussion of the specificity of the demand for child labour. In the majority of the analyses, child work is considered as a form of unskilled work, at times with a lower productivity with respect to unskilled adults. In part, this is due to the fact that the majority of children work with their families in agricultural subsistence production, or in non-agricultural small enterprises. In such a situation, and given imperfect labour and land markets, demand and supply side cannot be separated, and the decision about children's time allocation has to be modelled accordingly. There is, however, a non-negligible number of children who work for a third party for a wage (monetary or in kind). As already mentioned, the demand for these children's labour has been often modelled (at times implicitly) in the same way as that for unskilled adult labour. The hypotheses advanced in the non-economic literature as to why child labour is demanded as such range from 'nimble finger' to docility in the workplace, but the evidence is mixed. Koutstaal and Schacter (1997) and Sloutsky and Fisher (2004) seem to imply that children have an advantage at work that requires pattern memorization, but direct evidence in support of the 'nimble fingers' hypothesis is weak (Levison et al. 1998; Edmonds 2008).

If we consider child labour as a form of labour that does not have a specificity in its use, the question arises of how the demand for child labour is related to aggregate labour demand and industrial structure. If labour markets are tight and wage rates high, economic theory makes ambiguous predictions about child labour. On the one hand, wage rates increase potential household income, but on the other, as we saw in Chapter 1, they increase the opportunity-cost of education. Furthermore, child labour may be present with different intensity in different industries, because of the characteristics of the industry, historical legacy, etc. The question then arises whether changes in industrial structure affect child labour overall, or children just move from one sector to another. We address these issues on the basis of the results presented in Manacorda and Rosati (2010, 2011).

The Economics of Child Labour. Second Edition. Alessandro Cigno and Furio C. Rosati, Oxford University Press.
 DOI: 10.1093/oso/9780198903000.003.0006

5.1 Aggregate Labour Demand and Child Labour

Manacorda and Rosati (2010) examine children's employment responses to changes in local labour demand in Brazil using data from the Brazilian Pesquisa Nacional por Amostra de Domicílios (PNAD) for the period 1981 to 2002.[1] The survey collects detailed individual and household socio economic characteristics as well as information on work activity and school enrolment consistently throughout the period. Information about working activities and hours worked are available for individuals aged 10 or older and include information on hours of work in the week preceding the survey. Work refers to both paid and unpaid (family or non-family) work but excludes household chores. Data on labour earnings are only available for paid workers, a minority of working children especially in rural areas.

The analysis focuses on individuals aged 10–15, with an overall sample of around one million children-observations over 19 waves: about three-fourths in urban areas and one fourth in rural areas. This large sample size allows to investigate in detail heterogeneous responses across gender, residence, and other characteristics of children. Over the period considered, 48% of rural boys were engaged in work, while 70% were enrolled in school. Around 25% of them combined both work and school. Despite the possibility of combining work with education, approximately 7% are classified as inactive, neither working nor attending school; 23% of rural boys work exclusively, and 45% attend school only. For those in the labour force, the average weekly working hours are approximately 35. Trends over age indicate an increase in work participation as children grow older, with a modest rise in the proportion combining work and school. Results for rural girls exhibit similar trends but with lower work involvement (21% versus 48%) and less frequent combination of work and school (10% versus 25%).

Urban boys are less likely to work (15% versus 48%) and more likely to attend school (88% versus 70%) compared to rural counterparts. The option of combining work and school is pursued less frequently in urban areas (10% versus 25%). Differences between urban and rural boys in inactivity and working hours are negligible. Trends over age are generally similar, except for a notable increase in inactivity among urban boys.

Urban girls also display differences relative to boys, working less (9% versus 15%), combining work and school less frequently (5% versus 10%), and being slightly more inactive (8% versus 6%). Trends over age remain comparable

[1] PNAD is a household survey run annually (with the exception of 1991, 1994, and 2000) that is representative of the entire Brazil except the rural North-West.

across gender groups. Note that these figures provide an average overview of Brazilian children's labour market outcomes between 1981 and 2002, masking significant variations in time use over time and across regions.

To assess empirically the effect of improvements in local labour market conditions on child labour and schooling, Manacorda and Rosati (2007), take adult (ages 25–50) employment as an indicator of labour demand that is exogenous to young individuals' labour supply. In particular, they use male prime age employment as an indicator of local labour demand for both boys and girls, since adult female employment might respond to variations in male employment due to added worker or discouraged worker effects. Local markets are defined as either the urban or rural areas of each state.

To analyse the relationship between children's time use and adult employment they use the following regression:

$$T_{\text{ist}} = d_S + d_t + \beta_1 E_{\text{st}} + x_{\text{ist}}{}'\beta 2 + u_{\text{ist}}, \quad (5.1)$$

where T_{ist} is an outcome (work, school, etc.) for child i living in State s at time t, E_{st} is male adult employment to population in State s at time t, the x's are additional controls and the d_s and d_t are state and time dummies respectively. Identification of the coefficient of interest β_1 is based on a simple difference in differences estimator. The model attributes any differential variation in children's time use across states (conditional on the x's) to the differential variation in adults' employment.

Consistency of the OLS coefficient requires unobserved determinants of child labour to be uncorrelated with adult employment. Although this hypothesis is ultimately untestable and we have no credible instrument for local adult employment, we discuss below potential sources of bias in the OLS estimates and we present empirical strategies that attempt to control for such sources of bias.

Table 5.1 presents OLS estimates of model (1).[2] We initiate by showcasing regression outcomes for a model that solely incorporates state and year effects. Once more, we introduce interactions between state indicators and two-decade indicators, aiming to leverage the distinct trends in adult employment within each decade for identification. Furthermore, our model incorporates additive age effects. Despite conducting regressions on micro-level data, our approach primarily capitalizes on the variations in local labour demand

[2] The sample is limited to children living with at least one parent and who are offspring of either the head, the spouse of both. This reduces the original sample by around 8%.

across states and over time for identification purposes. Consequently, standard errors in this and all subsequent regressions are clustered by state and time.

The first row of Table 5.1 highlights a clear impact of adult employment on the time allocation of rural boys. With the exception of school attendance in column 2 and of the household income in column 8, all other coefficients are significant. In column 1, a 1 percentage point increase in adult employment corresponds to a roughly equivalent increase in child employment. Approximately two-thirds of this increase manifests as a combination of work and school (column 3), while the remaining third translates into an increase in work only (column 5). Columns 4 and 6 provide additional insights into the adjustment mechanism adopted by rural children in response to heightened local labour demand. About one-third of the employment increase arises from a decline in inactivity, and roughly two-thirds from a decrease in the number of children attending school only. Column 7 reveals that children's hours of work, inclusive of zeros for non-workers, rise by approximately 2.7 for a 10 percentage point increase in adult employment. Interestingly, column 8 indicates no significant effect on rural household income, likely due to the prevalence of family farm employment reporting no labour income. Lastly, column 9 displays an interesting correlation between children's log wages and adult employment, showcasing a significant increase in wages for rural boys when labour demand strengthens.

Results for girls (presented in the lower section of the table) mirror those for boys, albeit generally smaller in magnitude and not consistently statistically significant. Girls, too, demonstrate an inclination to work more in response to heightened local labour demand, mainly transitioning from attending school only to working in combination with school. Surprisingly, there is no discernible effect of increased labour demand on girls' inactivity rates. Overall, girls exhibit a less pronounced responsiveness compared to boys, suggesting potential advantages in home production or potential labour market discrimination.

Findings for urban children align qualitatively with those for rural children, albeit with generally smaller effects. Urban boys respond to improved labour market conditions by increasing their work and reducing inactivity. Additionally, work combined with school sees an uptick. A notable distinction is observed in the response of household income, which significantly increases by around 20% with a 10 percentage point rise in adult employment. This disparity is attributed to the distinct employment structures in rural and urban areas.

Similar to boys, urban girls display a relatively diminished response to variations in local labour demand. If anything, a marginally significant decrease in hours worked by girls during better times is observed. However, like boys, wages for urban girls rise in favourable conditions.

In summary, an upswing in local labour demand prompts some children to shift from inactivity or exclusive school attendance to combining school with work. Overall work participation, with or without school, increases. However, school attendance seems unaffected by shifts in local labour demand, although a stronger demand for labour results in more children combining work and school while fewer dedicate all their time to schooling. These outcomes align with the idea that children respond to improved labour market prospects by increasing their labour supply to the market, similar to adults. Despite notable increases in household income (particularly in urban areas), the rise in children's labour market opportunities, measured by the wage rate, induces a substitution effect that appears to outweigh the income effect, leading to an increase in hours of work. However, increased labour market participation among children does not seem to come at the expense of school attendance, even though there is growing evidence that combining work and study tends to have negative effects on school survival and achievement.

The authors carried out several robustness checks to validate the results. One potential concern with the results presented in Table 5.1 is the possibility of omitted determinants, correlated with statewide trends in adult employment, influencing children's time use patterns t. This correlation could introduce bias in the Ordinary Least Squares (OLS) estimates in Equation (5.1). For instance, systematic differences in statewide trends in parents' education might lead to an underestimation of the effect of local labour demand on children's employment. If, for example, states with better-educated parents tend to have children less likely to work, the omission of these variables might result in a biased estimate. On the contrary, trends in income or wealth that differ across states for reasons other than variations in aggregate labour demand could spuriously correlate children's and adult employment. In poorer states, both adults and children might tend to work more.

To address these concerns model (5.1) was augmented with an extensive set of household and state characteristics included as controls. The included variables include mother's age and age squared, father's age and age squared, mother's and father's years of education, dummies for missing father or missing mother, number of children in the household by age group, and various indicators for household size and wealth. State controls incorporate the ratio of children (10–15) to adults (25–50) in the population, considered a measure of aggregate child labour supply. The estimates obtained through this extended model are close to those presented in Table 5.1, providing some assurance that differences in adult employment across states are largely orthogonal to unobserved determinants of children's time use.

An additional concern for the consistency of the estimates in Table 5.1 is the possibility of households migrating from rural to urban areas or across states in search of job opportunities. This could lead to an overestimation of the effect of local labour market conditions on children's work if households with children more likely to work disproportionately reside in areas of high labour demand.

As a mitigation strategy, Manacorda and Rosati pursue two paths. Firstly, they recompute the male adult employment-to-population rate in each state and year by pooling urban and rural individuals, allowing the effect to differ between these areas. This pooling eliminates within-state variation in adult employment that might be correlated with unobserved determinants of children's time use due to household sorting across urban and rural areas. The results indicate that endogenous sorting within states does not seriously threaten the consistency of the estimates with the exception of household income.

An additional issue arises if households endogenously migrate across states. To address this, we utilize information on individuals' state of birth from the PNAD. Children are treated as if they were residing in their state of birth, or, if the child resides in his state of birth but parents were born elsewhere, we use the parents' state of birth. The employment-to-population ratio by state is then computed based on adult individuals residing in each state, irrespective of their state of birth. In both cases, the point estimates remain largely unchanged relative to the overall period in Table 5.1.

Table 5.2 examines the differential impact of changes in local labour market conditions on children's time use across households with different levels of income. The sample is divided into three groups: low, medium, and high per capita household income (computed excluding children's earnings). Low (high) income households are those below (above) the bottom (top) tercile of the income distribution. Given that we condition on the household's position in the income distribution, the consistency of these estimates requires the assumption that the household ranking in the income distribution (but not their level of income) is unaffected by changes in local labour demand. This assumption appears relatively mild. The regressions include the full set of controls, and the male employment-to-population rate by state (pooling urban and rural households) serves as a measure of local labour demand.

The results unveil substantial heterogeneity in responses between children from poor and rich households. Generally, in better economic times, children from poorer households seem to increase their labour supply more than their wealthier counterparts. In rural areas, children's participation increases with stronger labour demand across the income distribution, although the rate of increase declines with household income. Conversely, among urban children—especially among urban girls—stronger labour demand is associated with a decrease in children's employment in wealthier families.

While school attendance is, on average, unaffected by increases in labour demand (as shown in column 2), there are significant differences between richer and poorer children. Wealthier children tend to increase their school attendance in better times, while the opposite holds for poorer children. Poorer children experience an uptick in their probability of working only (column 5) and a decline in attending school only (column 6), with the reverse pattern observed for richer children. At the intensive margin, hours of work increase for poorer children in rural areas, while they remain constant or decrease for wealthier children (column 7).

These findings are noteworthy, particularly considering that poorer households seem to disproportionately benefit from temporary increases in local labour demand. As illustrated in column 8, a 10 percentage point increase in adult employment leads to a roughly 25% increase in household income among poorer households, compared to about a third of that amount among wealthier households. Changes in market wages in column 9, on average, appear largely uncorrelated with household socio-economic status.

In line with Krueger (2007), these results indicate that, despite the marginal increase in income being higher for poorer households (with the change in market wages being consistent across household types), the overall impact of a positive labour demand shock for these households is an increase in child labour and some reduction in schooling. Poorer households show a greater willingness to trade their children's leisure or schooling for an additional consumption when the opportunity arises. In contrast, wealthier households find that the increase in consumption from sending their children to work is insufficient to compensate for the associated disutility of work. Consequently, poorer households are more inclined to trade some increase in consumption for their children's leisure or schooling.

Manacorda and Rosati (2007) further explore the differences across age groups. Table 5.3 reports the results of regression (5.1) with the coefficient β1 allowed to vary by age. Significant heterogeneity across different age groups is evident in the response to changes in local labour market conditions. In general, younger children tend to withdraw from the labour market during

Table 5.1 Local labour demand and children's time use—controls separately by household income

	(1) Work	(2) School	(3) Work & School	(4) Idle	(5) Work & no school	(6) School & no work	(7) Weekly work hours	(8) Log household income	(9) Log wages
					RURAL				
					Males				
Low	1.205***	−0.163	0.798***	−0.237*	0.405**	−0.966***	28.352***	2.228***	5.774***
	(0.274)	(0.214)	(0.236)	(0.137)	(0.185)	(0.251)	(10.518)	(0.702)	(1.322)
Middle	1.195***	−0.169	0.806***	−0.213	0.385**	−0.979***	29.577***	1.575**	5.344***
	(0.272)	(0.213)	(0.231)	(0.132)	(0.190)	(0.245)	(10.545)	(0.650)	(1.182)
High	0.644**	0.183	0.626***	−0.196	0.016	−0.446*	8.222	1.672***	4.657***
	(0.267)	(0.225)	(0.237)	(0.139)	(0.191)	(0.256)	(10.309)	(0.638)	(1.191)
					Females				
Low	0.636***	0.280	0.550***	−0.364*	0.085	−0.272	16.971***	2.799***	4.048***
	(0.203)	(0.210)	(0.166)	(0.186)	(0.124)	(0.246)	(6.421)	(0.685)	(1.358)
Middle	0.574***	0.366*	0.471***	−0.467**	0.103	−0.107	14.682**	1.878***	3.490***
	(0.208)	(0.206)	(0.166)	(0.195)	(0.118)	(0.255)	(6.433)	(0.604)	(1.275)
High	0.311	0.545***	0.453***	−0.401**	−0.142	0.090	5.157	2.141***	5.008***
	(0.213)	(0.203)	(0.163)	(0.184)	(0.127)	(0.257)	(6.761)	(0.603)	(1.396)

URBAN

					Males				
Low	0.557***	−0.118	0.270***	−0.169***	0.286***	−0.387***	20.990***	2.805***	2.015***
	(0.101)	(0.088)	(0.082)	(0.064)	(0.063)	(0.113)	(3.561)	(0.318)	(0.599)
Middle	0.273***	0.023	0.222***	−0.074	0.050	−0.198*	6.734*	2.020***	2.510***
	(0.098)	(0.073)	(0.081)	(0.053)	(0.056)	(0.104)	(3.432)	(0.301)	(0.614)
High	−0.050	0.332***	0.184**	−0.099*	−0.233***	0.149	−10.718***	1.226***	2.281***
	(0.098)	(0.079)	(0.078)	(0.054)	(0.058)	(0.106)	(3.460)	(0.317)	(0.675)
					Females				
Low	0.292***	−0.263***	0.151***	0.121*	0.142***	−0.414***	9.087***	2.722***	3.107***
	(0.077)	(0.084)	(0.058)	(0.062)	(0.043)	(0.104)	(3.211)	(0.323)	(0.764)
Middle	0.013	0.018	0.056	0.024	−0.041	−0.039	−3.409	2.014***	4.302***
	(0.068)	(0.072)	(0.057)	(0.057)	(0.034)	(0.089)	(2.676)	(0.313)	(0.784)
High	−0.287***	0.315***	−0.072	−0.100*	−0.213***	0.386***	−16.926***	1.259***	3.977***
	(0.070)	(0.078)	(0.057)	(0.059)	(0.038)	(0.093)	(2.844)	(0.329)	(0.904)

favourable economic conditions, while the opposite holds true for older children. For instance, among urban boys, a 10 percentage point rise in adult employment is associated with a decrease in the employment rate of 10-year-olds by approximately 5 percentage points. Conversely, for 15-year-olds, this is linked to an increase in their employment rate by around 15 percentage points.

In rural areas, there is no observable reduction in labour supply among children in response to increases in local labour demand (column 1). However, children become more responsive to the state of the local labour market as they age. For instance, there is no response in participation among rural children aged 10, while for those aged 15, a 10 percentage point rise in adult employment is associated with a participation increase ranging between 12 and 13 percentage points. Although participation rates for young rural children remain unchanged with stronger local labour demand, significant adjustments occur at the intensive margin. Column 7 indicates that a 10 percentage point rise in adult employment leads to a reduction of approximately 3.2 hours of work among rural boys aged 10 and an increase of about 7.9 hours for children aged 15. This is accompanied by a substantial rise in their school attendance during better economic times, indicating that young rural children increasingly opt for schooling without abandoning work. Conversely, older children increase their labour market participation and decrease school attendance when labour market conditions improve.

Wage and income data reveal interesting patterns. Household income increases for all children during better times, with a decreasing effect on income as children age. Wages, particularly in rural areas, show an increase for children of all ages, with a more pronounced effect for older children. However, caution is warranted in drawing conclusions about the effect of local labour market conditions on wages due to high standard errors. The differential effects across age groups may stem from changes in labour market constraints (household income) and opportunities (market wages) or, alternatively, from residual variation attributed to preferences. While household income appears less responsive to changes in local labour demand as children grow older, suggesting market forces play a role, it is challenging to assert significantly different effects across age groups. This suggests that residual variation attributed to preferences may be a contributing factor. The results imply that parents tend to shield younger children from work if given the opportunity, with the response changing around age 12–13, after which children's behaviour aligns more closely with adults.

The table reports results of an OLS regression of each variable (in the top row) on the employment to population ratio of individuals aged 25–30 in the

Table 5.2 Local labour demand and children's time use—no controls

(1)	(2)	(3)	(4)	(5)	(6)	(7)	(8)	(9)
Work	School	Work & school	Idle	Work & No school	school & No work	weekly Work hours	log Household income	log wages
				RURAL				
				Males				
0.956*** (0.181)	0.106 (0.152)	0.685*** (0.163)	−0.379*** (0.093)	0.270** (0.131)	−0.576*** (0.168)	27.292*** (6.443)	−0.418 (0.538)	1.483* (0.755)
				Females				
0.446*** (0.134)	0.077 (0.130)	0.404*** (0.114)	−0.115 (0.117)	0.043 (0.069)	−0.332** (0.158)	11.629*** (3.798)	0.404 (0.508)	1.333 (1.166)
				URBAN				
				Males				
0.233*** (0.086)	0.078 (0.067)	0.181*** (0.069)	−0.129** (0.051)	0.053 (0.051)	−0.104 (0.087)	5.368* (3.047)	2.186*** (0.370)	2.002*** (0.509)
				Females				
−0.028 (0.057)	0.018 (0.062)	0.007 (0.047)	0.014 (0.049)	−0.033 (0.032)	0.012 (0.073)	−4.471* (2.423)	1.988*** (0.368)	3.283*** (0.763)

Table 5.3 Local labour demand and children's time use—controls separately by age

	(1)	(2)	(3)	(4)	(5)	(6)	(7)	(8)	(9)
	Work	**School**	**Work & school**	**Idle**	**Work & no school**	**School & no work**	**Weekly work hours**	**Log household income**	**Log wages**
					RURAL				
					Males				
10	0.459	0.610**	1.317***	0.254*	−0.861***	−0.710***	−31.944***	1.320**	4.294***
	(0.283)	(0.258)	(0.243)	(0.147)	(0.218)	(0.269)	(11.507)	(0.660)	(1.618)
11	0.783***	0.718***	1.429***	−0.069	−0.646***	−0.713***	−12.972	1.411**	4.453***
	(0.272)	(0.239)	(0.240)	(0.145)	(0.204)	(0.253)	(11.111)	(0.639)	(1.381)
12	1.114***	0.233	1.202***	−0.137	−0.092	−0.972***	10.130	1.512**	5.724***
	(0.292)	(0.222)	(0.255)	(0.136)	(0.196)	(0.273)	(11.047)	(0.650)	(1.339)
13	1.129***	−0.206	0.576**	−0.341**	0.550***	−0.786***	33.777***	1.121*	5.080***
	(0.279)	(0.238)	(0.237)	(0.145)	(0.205)	(0.267)	(10.831)	(0.629)	(1.240)
14	1.453***	−0.854***	0.136	−0.454***	1.316***	−0.998***	68.396***	1.502**	5.186***
	(0.276)	(0.250)	(0.256)	(0.138)	(0.217)	(0.257)	(11.008)	(0.656)	(1.214)
15	1.380***	−1.052***	−0.279	−0.599***	1.655***	−0.777***	79.031***	0.993	5.302***
	(0.287)	(0.299)	(0.277)	(0.143)	(0.262)	(0.274)	(12.432)	(0.642)	(1.165)

					Females				
10	0.001***	1.342***	0.905***	−0.434**	−0.903***	0.432	−20.350***	2.154***	3.794*
	(0.212)	(0.268)	(0.164)	(0.202)	(0.155)	(0.287)	(7.403)	(0.647)	(2.129)
11	−0.053	0.967***	0.644***	−0.269	−0.697***	0.323	−16.566**	2.129***	3.298*
	(0.217)	(0.233)	(0.170)	(0.197)	(0.146)	(0.272)	(7.150)	(0.627)	(1.717)
12	0.411*	0.613***	0.641***	−0.384**	−0.230*	−0.028	3.824	2.055***	6.568***
	(0.217)	(0.210)	(0.182)	(0.192)	(0.131)	(0.262)	(6.660)	(0.622)	(1.518)
13	0.683***	0.245	0.447***	−0.476**	0.235*	−0.206	22.510***	2.259***	4.372***
	(0.215)	(0.236)	(0.170)	(0.219)	(0.132)	(0.272)	(6.885)	(0.610)	(1.533)
14	1.038***	−0.432	0.227	−0.379*	0.811***	−0.659**	40.081***	1.972***	4.342***
	(0.225)	(0.262)	(0.184)	(0.221)	(0.155)	(0.294)	(7.399)	(0.642)	(1.407)
15	1.234***	−0.684**	0.015	−0.532**	1.217***	−0.700**	58.156***	1.991***	3.727***
	(0.225)	(0.266)	(0.180)	(0.217)	(0.174)	(0.278)	(8.307)	(0.625)	(1.339)
					URBAN				
					Males				
10	−0.544***	0.514***	0.000	0.031	−0.545***	0.514***	−34.426***	2.289***	1.672*
	(0.106)	(0.086)	(0.082)	(0.060)	(0.063)	(0.119)	(3.943)	(0.314)	(1.008)
11	−0.408***	0.565***	0.042	−0.117*	−0.450***	0.526***	−29.097***	2.283***	0.864
	(0.101)	(0.085)	(0.083)	(0.062)	(0.061)	(0.114)	(3.709)	(0.309)	(1.007)
12	−0.094	0.376***	0.190**	−0.091	−0.286***	0.186*	−15.534***	2.117***	1.083
	(0.105)	(0.082)	(0.084)	(0.059)	(0.061)	(0.112)	(3.826)	(0.319)	(0.689)
13	0.238**	0.103	0.223**	−0.117**	0.014	−0.120	4.801	1.896***	2.023***
	(0.108)	(0.083)	(0.092)	(0.057)	(0.060)	(0.115)	(3.766)	(0.324)	(0.703)
14	0.942***	−0.320***	0.464***	−0.158**	0.478***	−0.784***	38.809***	1.871***	2.354***
	(0.114)	(0.090)	(0.087)	(0.062)	(0.070)	(0.116)	(4.501)	(0.318)	(0.602)
15	1.575***	−0.857***	0.459***	−0.260***	1.115***	−1.314***	77.247***	1.810***	2.681***
	(0.141)	(0.116)	(0.100)	(0.065)	(0.097)	(0.153)	(6.118)	(0.320)	(0.590)

Continued

Table 5.3 *Continued*

	(1)	(2)	(3)	(4)	(5)	(6)	(7)	(8)	(9)
	Work	**School**	**Work & school**	**Idle**	**Work & no school**	**School & no work**	**Weekly work hours**	**Log household income**	**Log wages**
					Females				
10	−0.415***	0.464***	−0.042	−0.092	−0.371***	0.506***	−26.367***	2.284***	1.829
	(0.076)	(0.087)	(0.058)	(0.064)	(0.042)	(0.104)	(3.137)	(0.327)	(2.038)
11	−0.327***	0.497***	0.014	−0.159**	−0.339***	0.484***	−22.155***	2.132***	2.211*
	(0.075)	(0.084)	(0.059)	(0.062)	(0.042)	(0.103)	(3.082)	(0.330)	(1.152)
12	−0.207***	0.242***	0.039	0.003	−0.244***	0.202**	−16.123***	1.916***	1.945*
	(0.073)	(0.073)	(0.059)	(0.059)	(0.038)	(0.092)	(2.911)	(0.328)	(1.065)
13	0.058	−0.018	0.071	0.033	−0.012	−0.093	−1.582	1.895***	3.445***
	(0.076)	(0.075)	(0.063)	(0.061)	(0.038)	(0.097)	(3.036)	(0.330)	(0.853)
14	0.375***	−0.416***	0.128*	0.167**	0.250***	−0.545***	15.908***	1.633***	4.082***
	(0.085)	(0.093)	(0.066)	(0.069)	(0.048)	(0.115)	(3.588)	(0.332)	(0.782)
15	0.700***	−0.782***	0.112	0.191***	0.592***	−0.895***	34.865***	1.476***	3.917***
	(0.111)	(0.109)	(0.080)	(0.070)	(0.067)	(0.137)	(4.951)	(0.334)	(0.763)

area or residence (rural or urban part of each state) and year (Equation (5.1)). All regressions control for state, year, and age effects and interactions of decade dummies (1980s, 1990s, and 2000s) with state dummies. Standard errors clustered by state and year.

5.2 Industrial Structure and Child Labour

To the extent that children possess a comparative advantage in specific industries, the prevalence of child labour in the population can vary depending on the mix of industries. This aspect is a potentially significant, yet often overlooked, factor contributing to the ongoing decline in child labour. If children are primarily engaged in low-productivity industries with outdated production technologies due to the unskilled nature of their work or because child labour legislation encourages them to specialize in informal occupations, changes in the industry composition resulting from technological advancements or shifts in consumer preferences could be a key driver behind the observed decrease in child labour associated with economic growth.

It is important to acknowledge that children may adjust their occupational choices in response to changes in employment opportunities. This is especially relevant when child labour is motivated by extreme poverty, and children are compelled to work solely to ensure their household attains a subsistence level of consumption, as discussed by Basu and Van in 1998. In such cases, changes in the industry mix might not necessarily lead to alterations in child labour rates.

Manacorda and Rosati (2011) address the question of whether sector-specific labour demand contributes to the varying prevalence of working children across Brazilian states. Unlike existing research on Brazil, this study explores long-term trends in child labour by utilizing data from the 1980, 1991, and 2000 population censuses. This approach offers two significant advantages compared to the more commonly used data from the PNAD. Firstly, starting in 1980, the census provides a detailed breakdown at the three-digit level for economic activity sectors. This granularity enables to thoroughly examine how changes in the industrial structure contribute to shifts in the incidence of child labour. Secondly, the exceptionally large sample sizes (ranging from 0.8 to 1.3 million children per year) allow us to derive highly precise estimates of child employment by industry and state, a level of precision not achievable using typical household survey data.

For this analysis, Manacorda and Rosati utilize micro data from the IPUMS version of the Brazilian Population census (Minnesota Population Center 2007) covering the years 1980, 1991, and 2000. The dataset contains information on labour market participation for individuals aged 10 or above. The sample sizes are substantial, increasing from approximately 5.8 million observations in 1980 to over 10 million observations in 2000. Children, defined as those aged 10–15, constitute around 12% of the sample.

Work activity, encompassing both paid and unpaid economic work but excluding non-economic activities like household chores, refers to the week before the census week. In our discussion, we interchangeably use terms such as 'child labour', 'work', or 'labour force participation' to describe children's engagement in economic activities, whether inside or outside their homes.

For individuals engaged in work, the census captures the sector of activity at the three-digit level. To account for changes in activity classification over time, we standardized the classification, resulting in 105 three-digit industrial categories consistently defined throughout the observation period.

An examination of census data reveals a noteworthy decline in the nationwide incidence of child labour from 1980 to 2000. The prevalence drops from 23% to 11% for boys and from 10% to 6% for girls. Rural boys, particularly in states with initially higher child labour rates, experience more significant reductions, indicating regional convergence. Conversely, there is no substantial change over time in the propensity of rural girls to work, likely reflecting their generally lower inclination to work compared to boys. In urban areas, where child labour is less prevalent than in rural settings, we observe a rapid convergence in child labour rates across states for both boys and girls.

Table 5.4, reproduced from Manacorda and Rosati (2001), presents the top 10 industries with the highest child labour intensity, measured by the ratio of child (ages 10–15) to adult (ages 16–60) workers. The figures represent nationwide averages across three periods and are disaggregated for males and females in both rural and urban areas. Notably, in rural settings, the most child-intensive productions are linked to agriculture, with cotton cultivation leading, followed by tobacco, corn, coffee, manioc root, sugar cane, rice, and various undefined agricultural activities. These sectors employ a disproportionate number of children compared to other areas of the economy. For instance, while the average ratio of male children to male adult workers in rural areas is approximately 0.11, in the cotton industry, this ratio rises to 0.16, indicating a 50% higher concentration of child labour.

Generally, the industries in Table 5.4 involve labour-intensive cultivations, where manual harvesting is common, explaining the higher representation of children. Additional data analysis (not reported) reveals a positive correlation between child labour intensity and the proportion of unskilled

Table 5.4 Child-intensive industries

Boys		Girls	
Rural:		Rural:	
Herbaceous cotton	.157	Herbaceous cotton	.235
Tobacco	.142	Coffee	.204
Corn	.135	Tobacco	.179
Other activities	.133	Corn	.167
Manioc root	.132	Transf. non-metallic miner.	.165
Undefined crops	.127	Lumber	.162
Coffee	.120	Domestic services	.157
Sugar cane	.119	Undefined crops	.148
Rice	.116	Cocoa beans	.141
Paper commerce	.110	Horti/floriculture	.140
Average	.110	Average	.137
Urban:		Urban:	
Herbaceous cotton	.099	Herbaceous cotton	.134
Horticulture	.098	Tobacco	.114
Domestic services	.094	Domestic services	.111
Personal services	.093	Coffee	.102
Footwear	.090	Undefined crops	.089
Tobacco	.090	Footwear	.088
Sugar cane	.089	Soybeans	.087
Supermarkets	.086	Horti/floriculture	.079
Coffee	.085	Sugar cane	.074
Paper commerce	.085	Manioc root	.068
Average	.033	Average	.041

Note. The table reports the ratio of children to adults employed in the top 10 child intensive industries separately by sex and area. For example, row 1, column 1, shows that in rural areas there are 15.7 male children employed in cotton for every 100 adult males employed in that industry. The bottom row reports the ratio of employed children to adults in the economy as a whole. Transf. non-metallic miner. p transformation of non-metallic minerals.

adult workers in each industry. This suggests that children tend to have a comparative advantage in productions with lower skill requirements.

The right-hand-side panel of Table 5.4 outlines results for girls. Surprisingly, the employment of rural girls relative to adult females is even higher than that observed for boys relative to their adult counterparts (0.14 versus 0.11). This is partly due to adult women being less likely to participate in the labour market than adult men. Importantly, most productions intensive in boys' employment also exhibit high intensity in girls' employment, indicating a high substitutability between rural boys and girls in production. An exception is the domestic services sector, a significant source of employment for girls but not for boys. Social norms, along with girls' comparative advantage in household chores and the associated acquisition of valuable domestic skills, likely explain their predominant employment in the paid domestic service sector.

Examining urban children in the bottom panel of Table 5.1, we find that, even in urban areas, sectors with high child employment proportions relative to adults are linked to agricultural (cotton, tobacco, sugar cane), horticultural, and floricultural production. Interestingly, while the majority (80%) of child workers in urban areas receive pay, over 50% of those in agriculture are unpaid, suggesting that these children may be working on household-owned plots of land. Beyond agriculture, highly child-labour-intensive sectors in urban Brazil include domestic services, paper trade, and footwear. These informal sectors are less likely to enforce child-labour regulations. Particularly, the footwear industry, a major export sector for Brazil, often involves subcontracted production in sweatshops under hazardous conditions (US Department of Labour 1998).

In order to identify the possible role of changes in the industry structure in determining the reduction of child labour observed in Brazil, the authors use a simple modified version of the traditional shift-share decomposition that is borrowed from Lewis (2004).

In particular, they decompose the change in child labour in several components: between, within, unskilled employment, population and residual. The between component is the one of interest as it measures the share of the change in child labour that can be attributed to the varying industrial structure. The within component express instead the change due to the average reduction in the overall use of child labour, holding the industrial structure constant.

In order to ascertain the role of these different factors in explaining the incidence of child labour, Manacorda and Rosati regress each single element of the decomposition on the share of working children in each state and year. In order to control for macroeconomic changes that affect all states similarly or permanent differences across states, they include in the regressions state and time fixed effects. These regressions provide a measure of the average contribution of different factors in explaining the differential evolution of child labour across different states. Table 5.5, also reproduced from Manacorda and Rosati, presents the results of the estimates.

The ‘between’ term explains 21% of the variations in rural boys’ employment (row 1, col. 1). This indicates that roughly one-fifth of the divergent trends in the proportion of working boys across states can be attributed to differential shifts in their industry mix. In simpler terms, states witnessing larger declines in child labour intensity also experience greater declines in child-intensive industries.

Table 5.5 Decomposing changes in child labour

	Boys						Girls					
	Between	Within	Unskilled Employment	Aggregate Employment	Pop.	Residual	Between	Within	Unskilled Employment	Aggregate Employment	Pop.	Residual
	(1)	(2)	(3)	(4)	(5)	(6)	(7)	(8)	(9)	(10)	(11)	(12)
Rural	.209***	.600***	−.006	.123***	.043	.032	.231***	.371**	.049	.314*	.024	.011
	(.069)	(.142)	(.056)	(.030)	(.104)	(.150)	(.047)	(.102)	(.036)	(.129)	(.108)	(.226)
Urban	−.022	.489***	.133***	.023*	.071**	.306***	.062***	.512***	.046**	.014	.027	.339***
	(.019)	(.065)	(.022)	(.012)	(.028)	(.050)	(.019)	(.107)	(.019)	(.021)	(.021)	(.065)

Note. The table reports OLS estimates of Equation (5.1). Each cell corresponds to a different regression. Standard errors in parentheses. All regressions weighted by cell size. Number of observations: 78. Pop. p population.
* Significant at the 10% level.
** Significant at the 5% level.
*** Significant at the 1% level.

The 'within' changes (columns 2 and 8 of Table 5.2) play a predominant role. These changes result from the differential shift in child labour incidence relative to unskilled adult labour across various industries within each state and basically reflect the overall tendency to the reduction of use of child labour in production. For rural boys, differences in adult employment (column 4 of Table 5.5) contribute to 12% of the disparities in trends in child labour incidence across Brazilian regions. The positive and significant coefficient implies, in line with what discussed in the first part of this chapter, that stronger labour demand is associated with increased child employment. Columns 5 and 6 indicate that changes in the adult-to-child population ratio are not systematically linked to lower or higher child labour, and the residual component shows no significant effect. This suggests that the approximation of evaluating changes at the year and state means effectively captures the data trends.

In general, the results hold true for urban boys and girls, whether in urban or rural areas. A few exceptions are notable: firstly, rural girls exhibit greater responsiveness to changes in local labour demand, with changes in adult female employment accounting for approximately 31% of female child labour. This is coherent with the well-known phenomenon that female labour supply is more responsive to demand shifts than male labour supply, a characteristic observed in adults. Secondly, population changes play a small and generally insignificant role, except for urban boys. In urban areas, an increase in the share of children in the population (a decline in the share of adults) is associated with lower child labour. This supports the idea of a market for salaried boys' labour in urban areas but not in rural areas. Changes in population-driven labour supply depress wages and reduce the incentives for children to work. Finally, the demand for skills, as indicated by the employment of low-educated adult workers, only affects children's employment in urban areas and not in rural areas.

5.3 Conclusion

In this chapter we have seen how also the demand side is important in determining the evolution of child labour. Although the majority of children work in family farms of business, both the stance of labour market and the structure of production have a role to play.

In particular, cyclical movements in the local adult labour market appear to have an impact on the number of children employed. Such effects, at least for the case of Brazil, are differentiated by the level of household income, area of residence and by age. These findings are consistent with the complex interactions that exists when income effects (due to the better labour stance for adults) are combined with changes in the opportunity cost of children's time (due to increased wages also for children): a theme that is constantly recurring both in the theoretical and in the empirical parts of this book and that is of particular relevance for policy design.

Also, the presence of relatively child-labour-intensive industries affects the evolution of child labour. As the productive structure of the economy changes, and child intensive industries become less relevant, child labour decreases. The transformation of the Brazilian economy, characterized by a decline of the importance of relatively child intensive industries, explains about 20% of the reduction of child labour observed in the country. An important role in this context can be played by international trade. As the country moves up along the so-called 'value-added ladder', the industries that are relatively child-labour-intensive are likely to lose importance, and this will contribute to the reduction of child labour. We shall come back to the role international trade in Chapter 9 from a theoretical point of view, and Chapter 10 from the empirical one.

6

Health Effects of Child Labour

Evidence

In Chapter 2, we mentioned the possibility that work by school-age children could affect their health either while they are still children, or in adult life. If the former were true, it would follow that parents can affect the children's well-being not only through their current consumption and future human capital, c_2 and h, but also through the amount (or the type) of work that they are required to carry out at a young age. If the latter were true, parents would be affecting their children's future earnings not only through the amount of h, but also through the probability that h is used for a long time (hence, other things being equal, that the rate at which h is remunerated, ω, is high). In the theoretical analysis, we assumed for simplicity that neither of these effects was present. If that assumption is not warranted, the amount of time worked (or type of work done) will affect the child's utility not only through c_2 and h, as in the model of Chapter 1, but also through the child's present and future health status. The net effect is thus ambiguous.

If we further allow for the possibility that c_2 affects the marginal product of child labour (the child's ability to carry out physical work), the relationship between work and utility becomes even more complicated for two reasons. First, because it is efficient, hence in the common interest of parents and children, that the additional income generated by the children's work is allocated disproportionately to the children's consumption. Second, because work may increase a child's bargaining power. If some children work, and some do not (because they are too young to work, or because they go to school), the amount consumed by the former will then definitely increase, because both household income and their share of this income do. But the amount consumed by children who do not work may increase or decrease, because their share of household income will decrease (Pitt, Rosenzweig, and Hassan 1990). The policy implication is in any case that the government can affect the children's present and future health not only by spending on sanitation and health (see Chapters 3 and 5), but also either by using taxes and subsidies to modify the marginal effect of child work on family income or by forbidding certain forms of child work.

The Economics of Child Labour. Second Edition. Alessandro Cigno and Furio C. Rosati, Oxford University Press.
 DOI: 10.1093/oso/9780198903000.003.0007

It is thus important to establish empirically whether the direct health effect of working at a young age is indeed negative and whether it is the amount or the type of work carried out that is detrimental to health. International conventions define activities that children should not be allowed to carry out in terms of the consequences of such activities, rather than on the basis of the characteristics of the activity itself. For example, categories of child labour to be abolished under the provisions of International Labour Office Conventions 138 and 182 include *hazardous work*, defined as 'labour that jeopardises the physical, mental or moral well-being of a child' (ILO 2002). The ILO estimates that there are 79 million children worldwide engaged in hazardous work, of which nearly two-thirds are under the age of 15 (ILO 2021). These estimates are extrapolated from data on the prevalence of child workers in activities considered to be *potentially* damaging to child well-being.[1] There is remarkably little evidence on the *actual* health effects of child work.

A recent review (Ibrahim et al., 2019) indicates that child labourers are likely to be subject to a large number of bad health outcomes, both physical and psychological. However, they conclude that 'Most of the current literature about child labor follow a cross-sectional design, which although can reflect the health status of working children, it cannot establish cause–effect associations. This in turn affects strategies and policies that target child labor' (Ibrahim et al. 2019, p. 25). To our knowledge, there are no works that try to establish the causal effect relationship in the literature.

To some extent, the lack of empirical evidence is not a major obstacle to policy formation. There can be little doubt that children working with dangerous materials, such as asbestos or molten glass, in unhealthy environments, such as mines or quarries, or long hours in sweatshop conditions place their health in serious jeopardy. There is little doubt also about the wretchedness of children engaging in such activities even though it is difficult to accumulate evidence on the health effects, not least because such child labour is usually illegal. However, the vast majority of child work consists of agricultural work, usually within a family context. The best available estimate is that 70% of all child workers worldwide are in the agricultural sector (ILO 2021).

The health consequences of such work are not obvious. On the one hand, the toll of heavy labour on young bodies, use of dangerous tools and

[1] All children aged 5–17 working in designated hazardous industries and/or hazardous occupations and/or that entails 43 hours or more per week are considered by the ILO to be engaged in hazardous work.

machinery, contact with fertilizers and pesticides, sheer exhaustion, and, in the long term, forgone schooling, may all impact negatively on health (see Ibrahim et al. 2019. On the other hand, work in the open air under the supervision of parents might not be considered a particularly unhealthy environment. In addition, in very poor societies, the produce of the child's work may be crucial to the maintenance of its own sustenance and health.

Establishing the health consequences of child work empirically is not easy for a number of reasons. First, because work and health are jointly determined. This is particularly true in poor countries, and even more so among children in poor countries. Second, because common unobservables (e.g., preferences and genetic health endowments), influencing both health and the decision to work, may give rise to an endogeneity problem. Third, because of two-way causal relationships. While work conditions and experiences can impact on health, a sick child is simply incapable of work. Physical work consumes energy required to fend off infection, but disease itself depletes the stock of energy and can leave a child incapable of work (Dasgupta 1993: 401–436). A health shock may derive from a workplace accident or be the accumulated effect of past work experience. Given any of these circumstances, the contemporaneous correlation between child work and health reveals little of the true impact of the former on the latter. Unobservable heterogeneity, simultaneity, and relationships that operate with a lag obscure any causal impact of child work on health.

The present chapter aims to establish whether there is a negative impact of work during childhood on health, controlling for observable and unobservable confounding factors. As mentioned, hardly any research has produced evidence on this. Part of the analysis presented here was subsequently to the first edition of this book published in O'Donnell, Rosati, and van Doorslaer (2005) and Rosati and Straub (2007). The analysis uses of a particularly rich two-wave panel data set, the 1992/1993 and 1997/1998 *Vietnam Living Standards Surveys*, and of the retrospective information contained in the 2000 *Guatemalan National Survey on Living Conditions* (NSLC). The panel nature of the Vietnamese data, and the availability of good instrumental variables, make it possible to correct for potential endogeneity arising from both unobservable heterogeneity and simultaneity. The Guatemala survey contains information on adult health, and retrospective information about age of entry in the labour market. Used in combination with a sub-sample of siblings selected from the main sample, such retrospective information makes it possible to identify the long-term effect of working during childhood on health in adult life.

6.1 Child Work and Health

Occupational hazards jeopardize health. The risks faced by working children may be greater than those confronted by adult workers. Physiological and psychological immaturities make children more vulnerable to abuse and to given health risks. Children are more prone to injury through accidents and more sensitive to noise, heat, and toxicity (Bequele and Myers 1995; Forastieri 1997; ILO 1998; Fassa et al. 2000). The physical strain of work on growing bones and joints can lead to stunting and spinal injury (ILO 2002: 12). All these risks are higher for poorly fed children, whose physiology has already been weakened through malnourishment (2002: 12). Physical work depletes a child's stock of energy. Overexertive work exhausts the energy stock below the minimum required to sustain physical growth and combat infection (Dasgupta 1993: 401–436).

Agriculture, the dominant sector of child employment, is an industry with a very poor record of safety, with 1 in 8 child workers suffering illness or injury (Ashagrie 1998: table 6). A child working on a farm is exposed to dangerous tools and machinery, to chemicals, to water-, soil-and animal-borne infection, to heavy lifting and poor posture, as well as to heatstroke and sheer exhaustion. The difficulty of regulating child work environments that are invariably informal and small-scale, and often illegal, further raises the health risks faced by child workers (Fassa et al. 2000). Most child work is undertaken within the family unit. Perhaps surprisingly, this setting generally accounts for a disproportionately high percentage of all working children with health problems (O'Donnell, Rosati, and van Doorslaer 2002).

Health gains from child work are not inconceivable, but these benefits are indirect (coming through parental expenditure for the child's nutrition and medical care). There is evidence that a child's labour can make an important contribution to the household's living standard (Bhalotra 2003), and consequently to the health of all its members (Steckel 1995; Smith 1999). There is also a theoretical argument that a disproportionate amount of resources will be allocated to maintaining the strength and health of the most productive members (Pitt, Rosenzweig, and Hassan 1990). This implies that a working child can be expected to receive a disproportionate share of the income he or she produces.[2]

While many of the health risks of childwork threaten immediate damage to health, others are likely to develop over many years and might only

[2] At the aggregate level, these arguments have less force. A large supply of child labour will reduce market wages and may leave the economy at a low-level equilibrium with low wages, low education levels, and poor health (Basu 1999).

become manifest in adulthood. Exposure to pesticides, chemicals, dusts, and carcinogenic agents increases the risks of developing bronchial complaints, cancers, and a wide variety of diseases (Forastieri 1997; ILO 1998; Fassa et al. 2000). Individuals working in childhood are doubly vulnerable to chronic health problems—they are exposed to risk factors for longer periods and the biological process of rapid cell growth reduces the latency period of some diseases (Fassa et al. 2000). Childwork may also have a long-term impact on health through forgone education, and subsequently reduced lifetime earnings and constrained knowledge of health production mechanisms. Evidence on the trade-off between childwork and schooling is mixed but, on balance, supports the crowding-out hypothesis (Rosenzweig and Evenson 1977; Psacharopoulos 1997; Grootaert and Patrinos 1999; Cigno and Rosati 2002).

6.2 Vietnam

O'Donnell, Rosati, and van Doorslaer make use of a two-wave panel for 1992–1993 and 1997–1998 carried out within the Vietnam Living Standards Survey (VLSS). The survey has detailed information on work activity for all household members aged six and above, as well as self-reported and anthropometric indicators of health. Work and health are primarily reported by the child itself but can be reported by a parent on behalf of young children. Commune surveys, which can be matched to household records, provide information on health care, as well as potential instruments for child work in the form of indicators of the local economy, labour market, and school quality. In addition to these data advantages, Vietnam offers an interesting context. Child work activity is substantial and exhibited a significant decline between the two waves of the survey, which span a period of economic transition and rapid growth.

6.2.1 Sample Description

In 1992–1993, the VLSS interviewed a nationally representative (self-weighting) sample of 4,800 households. In 1997–1998, 4,305 (89.6%) of the original households were reinterviewed and a supplementary sample was taken to give a cross-section sample of 5,999 households. To facilitate disaggregate analysis, disproportionate sampling by region was adopted in the 1997–1998 cross-section and for this reason, 96 of the original households were deliberately dropped from follow-up. No attempt was made to trace households moving out of a commune, and this probably accounts for the majority of the 400 households lost in the follow-up process.

Glewwe et al. (2002a) find the panel households to be broadly nationally representative. Attrition through children moving out of households does not appear to be a major problem either. Edmonds and Turk (2004) report that of 6,003 children aged 0–10 years in the first wave, 92% were still in the household by the second wave. Of the missing 8%, the vast majority (78%) left the household when their parents moved home. There is some child attrition that is directly related to the two variables of central interest here—health and work—but the numbers are not large.

Of all the children aged 0–10 years at the first wave, 0.8% had died and 0.4% had moved out of the household to enter employment by the time of the second wave. Being a household survey, the VLSS does not sample street children and is unlikely to pick up all illegal forms of child work. The prevalence of child work, in general, and health-damaging work, in particular, is likely to be underestimated by the data. This is less of a problem with respect to estimation of the health effects of child work in rural areas.

A child is defined as a person aged 6–15 years, and in the definition of work is included not only paid work outside the household, but also any unpaid work on the household farm or business, at any time in the past twelve months. The proportion of children working in Vietnam fell from roughly a third of the age group in 1992–1993 to a quarter in 1997–1998 (Table 6.1). This decline can be explained primarily by the impressive improvement in living standards that Vietnamese households experienced (Edmonds 2002; Edmonds and Turk 2004). Work participation is strongly correlated with age. One in ten children aged 6–11 years works (1997–1998), but the ratio rises to almost one in two among children aged 12–15 years (Table 6.1).

The figures in Table 6.1 indicate little or no difference between the proportion of boys and of girls working, but this understates gender differences since household chores, a prevalently female activity, are not included in the definition of work. The exclusion is deliberate in order to reduce the heterogeneity of work captured by a binary indicator of participation and avoid dilution of any health effect through inclusion of work likely to be least threatening to health.[3] To completely ignore household chores, however, would

[3] There is also a pragmatic reason for the omission. The data on household chores refer only to the previous seven days (not twelve months). The question is: 'During the past 7 days have you done any other work for your family at home. For example, cleaning the house, preparing, meals, washing the family's clothes....' Subsequent questions ask the number of days such work was done and for how many hours each day.

Table 6.1 Work participation rates of children aged 6–15 years, Vietnam, 1992–1993 and 1997–1998

	Rural		Urban		Total	
	1992–	1997–8	1992–	1997–8	1992–	1997–8
All	0.3747	0.2876	0.1630	0.0687	0.3395	0.2499
	0.0163	*0.0164*	*0.0310*	*0.0162*	*0.0145*	*0.0141*
Male	0.3646	0.2903	0.1599	0.0635	0.3317	0.2522
	0.0180	*0.0198*	*0.0348*	*0.0170*	*0.0161*	*0.0170*
Female	0.3852	0.2846	0.1660	0.0739	0.3476	0.2475
	0.0175	*0.0159*	*0.0309*	*0.0204*	*0.0154*	*0.0138*
Age 6–11	0.2012	0.1221	0.0575	0.0152	0.1782	0.1051
	0.0176	*0.0129*	*0.0217*	*0.0087*	*0.0153*	*0.0110*
Age 12–15	0.6742	0.5147	0.3249	0.1283	0.6126	0.4417
	0.0225	*0.0234*	*0.0523*	*0.0273*	*0.0202*	*0.0206*
Sample size	5,069	6,274	1,008	1,484	6,077	7,758

Note: Standard error appears in italic.

be ill advised since the distinction between work in the household business or farm, and household chores, is often arbitrary. In the estimated models of health, a separate dummy was used to indicate engagement in household chores for at least seven hours per week, but never found this to be significant and do not report the results.

Child work is much more prevalent in rural areas, and the rate of decrease has been greater there than in the cities. By 1997–1998, the participation rate was more than four times greater in rural than in urban areas (Table 6.1). The data offer no plausible instruments for child work in urban areas. Commune surveys were not conducted in these areas and household land holdings are obviously of limited relevance to child work decisions in towns and cities. The analysis is restricted to the rural sample, which covers the vast majority of child work undertaken in the country. In rural Vietnam, child work is predominantly (93%) in household-based agriculture (Table 6.2). As already noted, this is the dominant form of child work worldwide.

Work for a household business is the second most popular form of child work. Relatively few work for pay outside the household (Table 6.2). The domination of household-based agriculture is mainly a reflection of the general structure of the Vietnamese economy, but also the outcome of legislation and cultural factors. As an early signatory to the International Convention on the Rights of the Child (1990) and ILO Convention on the Worst Forms of Child Labour (2000), Vietnam has enacted legislation that restricts the conditions under which a child, at various ages, can work (Edmonds and Turk

Table 6.2 Work type, hours, and job tenure of working children aged 6–15 years in rural Vietnam, 1992–1993 and 1997–1998

	Proportion of working children in:				Mean	Mean	sample
	Paid	Household		School	hours of work	months in	size
	work	Agriculture	Business		per week	current job	
1992–3	0.0845	0.9044	0.1420	0.6030	18.95	26.14	1894
	0.0122	*0.0122*	*0.0204*	*0.0215*	*0.724*	*0.696*	
1997–8	0.0650	0.9332	0.1100	0.7185	16.87	24.65	1487
	0.0087	*0.0120*	*0.0184*	*0.0247*	*0.897*	*0.757*	

Note: The primary objective is to determine the health consequences of this type of work. The 1998 sample consists of VLSS panel and cross-section supplementary observations. Sample weight applied for 1998; the 1993 survey is self-weighting. Standard error of estimate of population proportion appears in italics, adjusted for stratification and cluster sampling.

2004). In law, opportunities for a child to work outside the household unit are more constrained than work on behalf of the household. The latter is legal provided it is not 'harmful, dangerous or exploitative' (2004: 15). Child work on behalf of the household has deep cultural roots and is often considered to have positive effects on the development of the child.

A majority of working children in Vietnam also attend school, the percentage doing so increasing from 60% in 1992–1993 to over 70% in 1997–1998 (Table 6.2). This is made possible by the low level of compulsory school hours (Edmonds and Turk 2004). Enrolment rates are much lower among children doing paid work outside the household. Among rural working children, the average number of hours worked was around 17 hours per week in 1997–1998, and the average length of employment (in the current main job) around two years. Due to an inconsistency of measurement, work hours cannot be compared across waves. In the first wave, respondents were asked to report total hours worked in agriculture. In the second wave, hours specific to each particular type of agricultural activity were reported. Aggregating the latter probably gives a more accurate, but a higher, estimate of total hours, such that the fall in average hours shown in the table understates the real decline. Given this inconsistency, we do not use the hours data from both waves, necessary to estimate the contemporaneous impact on health, but test for a long-term effect through the relationship between health at the second wave and hours worked at the first wave.

O'Donnell, Rosati, and van Doorslaer examine three indicators of health: the weight-for-age z-score, height growth, and reported illness or injury. The z-score is a child's weight (or height) expressed in number of standard deviations from the mean weight (or height) of children of the same age and gender in a well-nourished population. The (WHO-recommended) reference population is that of the USA. Anthropometric indicators, such as z-scores and height growth, measure most directly nutritional status. However, they are also good proxies for morbidity and survival probability (Waterlow et al. 1977; Martorell and Ho 1984; Fogel 1993; de Onis and Habicht 1996; World Health Organization 1995).

In effect, the distinction between nutritional and health status is somewhat tenuous. Malnourishment weakens defences against infection. Disease reduces the absorption of nutrients, draws down the body's stock of energy, and can lead to malnourishment (Dasgupta 1993: 405–408; Steckel 1995: 1910). Work may affect weight and growth directly through the consumption of energy and indirectly through morbidity. Both effects are of interest. The anthropometric indicators are used here to understand the consequences of child work for both nutritional and health status. Height growth is used as a proxy for long-term health and nutritional experience. It reflects the difference between the accumulated intake of nutrients and use of energy in work and fighting disease (Steckel 1995: 1910).

The long-term consequences of child work are examined through the relationship between work at the first survey and subsequent annual average growth in height between the waves. To estimate the contemporaneous relationship between child work and health, we need an indicator of short-term health/nutritional status. BMI is a long-term indicator. The weight-for-height z-score would be an obvious choice, but it is available in the data set only up to the age of 11 years. So, we use the weight for-age z-score, and control for height in the regression analysis.

The anthropometric indicators show marked improvements in the average nutritional and health status of Vietnamese children. In 1992–1993, the mean height-for-age z-score of rural children was a little less than 2 (Table 6.3), a conventional threshold used to define stunted growth. By 1997–1998, the mean z-score for this population had increased to 1.7. Trends in the weight-for age z-score tell the same story. Descriptive statistics indicate that working children tend to be smaller, and this difference appears to have increased over time.

Anthropometric indicators have the advantage of objectivity. The disadvantages, for present purposes, are that the measures are more closely correlated with health at younger ages and might be rather insensitive to some work-related health problems, such as injury. For these reasons, we examine the relation of child work to morbidity, as reported by the child himself or by a parent on behalf of a young child. There is evidence that self-reported health is closely correlated with underlying morbidity and that,

Table 6.3 Health indicators of children aged 6–15 years by work status, rural Vietnam, 1992–1993 and 1997–1998

	Weight-for-age z-score		Height-for-age z-score		Proportion reporting illness/ injury in past 4 weeks	
	Mean	SE	Mean	SE	Mean	SE
1992–3						
All	−1.86	*0.022*	−2.06	*0.040*	0.1969	*0.0117*
Not working	−1.86	*0.026*	−1.89	*0.038*	0.2012	*0.0112*
Working	−1.85	*0.026*	−2.08	*0.042*	*0.1948*	*0.0139*
1997–8						
All	−1.67	*0.021*	−1.70	*0.036*	0.3379	*0.0130*
Not working	−1.65	*0.023*	−1.50	*0.033*	0.3370	*0.0120*
Working	−1.72	*0.029*	−1.86	*0.044*	0.3186	*0.0197*

Note: SE = standard error adjusted for stratification and cluster sampling.

even after controlling for clinically measured physiology, it is a good predictor of future mortality (Kaplan and Camacho 1983; Idler and Benyamini 1997). This evidence refers to a general self-assessment of health status. The question available in the VLSS refers to experience of illness or injury in the previous four weeks. There are concerns about the reliability of such measures. Their subjectivity most probably reduces the signal to noise ratio. This would not be particularly problematic if reporting differences were random, but there is evidence, particularly from developing countries, that it is correlated with variables, such as income, which are potential determinants of true health (Strauss and Thomas 1998; Sadana, Mathers, Lopez, et al. 2000). For present purposes, this is not necessarily problematic.

In the regression analysis, we control for factors potentially correlated with both work status and reported morbidity. It does not matter whether the control variables are determinants of true health or reporting behaviour. If work status is correlated with reporting behaviour through unobservables, this is reason to treat work as endogenous, as we do. The crucial issue is whether a child's health is reported differently *because* the child is working. Then, there is no way to identify the work effect on true health separately from that on reporting behaviour. When health-related benefits are available to non-workers, reporting is expected to differ with work status. It is not immediately obvious that a child should report its health differently because he or she is working. One possibility is that an illness becomes apparent only through interference with work activities. Then, use of self-reported morbidity would give an overestimate of the impact of work on morbidity. On the other hand, if the prevalence of health problems among child workers leads to their acceptance as the norm, then use of self-reported morbidity will give an underestimate of the impact of work on ill health. These possibilities require that the estimated relationship between work and reported illness be interpreted cautiously, but there is no reason to dismiss it as uninformative of the impact of child work on morbidity. Unfortunately, the illness question was changed between survey waves. In the first wave, individuals were asked whether they had experienced any illness or injury in the previous four weeks and were given a few example conditions. In the second wave, respondents were asked explicitly whether they had experienced each one of nine illnesses and/or an injury in the previous four weeks. This form of questioning is expected to reduce noise in responses. There is evidence that it makes individuals more likely to report illness (Kooiker 1995.) This is evident in the data. The proportion of children reporting illness or injury apparently increased from a fifth in 1992–1993 to a third in 1997–1998, which is inconsistent with improvement in child health indicated by the anthropometrics. Given this inconsistency, we do not use the self-reported morbidity data from both waves but examine the long-term relationship between child work at the first wave and illness at the second wave. Although the reference period is only four weeks, illness propensity over one month will be a decreasing function of longer-term health status. To the extent that child work has a sustained negative impact on health status, this should be reflected in a positive relationship between past work and current illness propensity.

Both child work status and health status are strongly correlated with living standards. Child work participation falls as household consumption per capita rises, such that participation among the poorest quintile of children was more than twice that of the richest quintile in 1997–1998. Child height and weight both rise with household consumption. Inequality is less apparent in the distribution of reported morbidity, an indication of the discrepancies in reporting behaviour discussed above.

6.2.2 Contemporaneous versus Longer-Term Work–Health Relationships

As usual, the main statistical issue is endogeneity, which may arise from both unobservable heterogeneity and simultaneity. In a short-term context, unobservable heterogeneity refers to the joint dependence of both measured (transient) health and work activity on unobservable (permanent) health endowments and preferences. Assuming that health is positively associated with labour market productivity, ceteris paribus, the inherently healthiest individuals are most likely to be available for employment and to be appointed. This *healthy worker selection effect* would tend to induce a positive statistical relationship between child health and work status. Other sources of unobservable heterogeneity may bias the relationship in the opposite direction. The more altruistic parents are vis-à-vis their child, the more they will invest in the health of the child and strive to keep the child from working. Such a *preference effect* would create a negative statistical relationship between child health and work status. Endogeneity can also arise through reverse causality—current work activity depends directly on the individual's transient health and nutritional status. A temporary bout of illness can leave the individual incapable of work. This will tend to induce a positive correlation between health/nutrition and work status. The authors use a number of estimation strategies to deal with these endogeneity problems. Instruments are described and justified in Section 7.4.3.

The longer-term health consequences of child work are examined through the relationship between childhood work at the time of the first survey and two indicators of subsequent health experience (reported illness four to five years later, and average annual growth in height between waves). Restricting attention to the longer-term health consequences of work eliminates the reverse causality problem. Health shocks cannot impact on past work. Lagged work status may still be endogenous, due to unobservable factors that impinge on work and health status in all periods. The impact of child work at the first wave on the probability of illness at the second is estimated through the bivariate probit system.

6.2.3 Definition of Variables

At the individual level, the regressors are basic demographics (*age*, *female*, and *ethnic minority*). Over the age range considered, growth spurts and the onset of puberty will result in highly non-linear relationships of weight and height to age, which can be expected to differ by gender. For each model, we search for the most suitably flexible functional form for the age effect. In gender-pooled estimates, we interact a gender dummy with polynomials in age. In addition, all models have been estimated separately by gender. With respect to the health–work relationship, the results are generally consistent across genders. We concentrate on the pooled estimates and present disaggregated results only when important gender differences emerge. At the household level, we control for household composition (*# infants*, *# kids*,

 # adults, dad in household), mother's age and education (*mum's age, mum has diploma*) and housing/hygiene conditions (*drinking water OK, sanitation OK, house walls*). Living standards are proxied by the logarithm of the value of household consumption per capita (*hhold consumption*). Controlling for living standards deals with an important confounding factor but also takes out any positive indirect effect from child work to health through the household income. We are testing for a negative effect of child work on health, not estimating the total effect through all possible pathways. This needs to be kept in mind in drawing policy conclusions from the results. For each model, exogeneity of household consumption is tested and relaxed where necessary and feasible. Household consumption is an important determinant of child nutritional intake and medical care. As a further proxy for nutrition, we include the (log) quantity of household rice consumption per capita (*rice consumption*). Nutrition should increase with rice consumption but not linearly. Where it is a staple food, as in Vietnam, rice is essential to the sustenance of malnourished children. But a rice-dominated diet is not a nutritious one. To better capture nutritional intake, we experimented with the disaggregation of household consumption into food and non-food expenditures but it made no difference to the results.

Commune-level survey data allow control for the availability of medical facilities and personnel (*doctor/pharmacy in commune, distance to hospital, most births at home*) and services provided by the local health centre, including child growth and nutrition-specific interventions, such as mothers' health/nutrition education programmes and the provision of oral rehydration salts (*child health exam, child growth chart, mum health education, oral rehydration, nutrition education*). Medical interventions, such as oral rehydration salts, affect the nature of the relationship between nutrition and health. Controlling for such services increases the health information content of residual variation in the anthropometrics. Our initial specification included a much longer list of medicines and health services, including the availability of iron supplements and vitamin A. Many were not significant. The weight-for-age z-score equation is estimated in differences. Not all of the commune health services variables are available in both waves and so a restricted set are used to estimate this equation.

School attendance is deliberately left out of the empirical specification to avoid yet another potentially endogenous regressor. Consequently, the estimated effect of child work on health includes any indirect effect operating through schooling. We expect the contemporaneous effect of schooling on health during childhood to be small. In the longer term, an indirect schooling effect is more plausible, but the five-year period we examine, spanning into early adulthood for only part of the sample, is unlikely to be sufficient to pick up much of the impact that education has on health.

The instruments include three types of variables—household land holdings, indicators of the commune economy/labour market, and indicators of school quality. Household agricultural land is a plausible determinant of both child work and household living standards and, controlling for all else, there seems no reason for child health to be influenced by land possessions. There is widespread evidence of child work activity increasing with the size of household land holdings (Rosenzweig and Everson 1977; Cigno and Rosati 2002; Bhalotra and Heady 2003). This may operate through a positive effect on the productivity of child workers in the presence of labour and land market imperfections (Bhalotra and Heady 2003).

Using the VLSS, Edmonds and Pavcnik (2001) find that the propensity for a child to work in Vietnam increases slightly if the household has any land but, conditional on this, is decreasing with the size of the land holding. As full income is not controlled, the latter result may be explained by a wealth effect, strengthened by credit market imperfections, outweighing the productivity effect (Bhalotra and Heady 2003). Glewwe et al. (2002b), also using the VLSS, argue that land holdings are a valid instrument for household consumption as a determinant of child health, proxied by height-for-age z-scores. Land markets are underdeveloped in Vietnam and simply do not exist in many rural areas. To a large extent, agricultural land is controlled by the government and allocated to households. There is thus little opportunity for a household to adjust its land holdings in response to the sickness of a child (Glewwe et al. 2002b: 16). When estimating differences, we use total household agricultural land holdings (*land*), which are measured consistently across waves. For estimation of lagged relationships, where we need instruments at wave 1 only, we use land that has been allocated to the household or which it has for long-term use (*any allocated land, allocated land size*). This should be an even more exogenous source of variation in household wealth and farm productivity.

The remaining instruments are defined at the commune level. Edmonds and Pavcnik (2001) find the commune relative price of rice (*rice price*) to be a substantial determinant of child work activity in Vietnam. According to their estimates, the rise in the price of rice, as a result of market liberalization, was a major factor contributing to the fall in child work activity between 1992–1993 and 1997–1998. Since much of this effect operated through household earnings opportunities, the rice price should be a determinant of household living standards, as well as child work. Controlling for all regressors, including total household expenditure and the quantity of rice consumed, the rice price is assumed to have no independent influence on child health. Living standards and child work will be influenced by the condition of the economy and labour market at the commune level, which we proxy by indicators of work-related migration to and from the commune (*immigration*, *emigration*, *migrant ratio*).

The quality of schooling on offer is a potentially important determinant of child work. As a proxy for school quality, we use the year in which the commune primary school was built (*school year*) and, for the estimation of longer-term relationships, the pupil–teacher ratio in the nearest secondary school (*pupil–teacher*), which is available for wave 1 only. For each model, the relevance of the instruments is checked through tests of significance in first-stage regressions. For linear estimators, overidentification restrictions are tested formally (Wooldridge 2002: 122–124). For the bivariate probit, overidentification is checked, somewhat informally, by tests of exclusion of each instrument from the illness equation conditional on the assumption that the remaining instruments are valid. Sensitivity of the estimates to dropping variables from the instrument set is also checked and reported on.

For each dependent variable, we test down from a very general specification, sequentially removing variables of low significance, to arrive at the most appropriate empirical model. In the main tables 7.4–7.6), we present, for each dependent variable, the work coefficients for a variety of estimators and specifications. In the baseline specification, work activity is represented through a dummy for any work in the past year. We experiment with effects from paid work outside the household (*paid work*), household chores for at least seven hours in the past week (*hhold chores*), number of months in the current job (*job tenure*), and, for the longer-term relationships, total hours of work in the past year (*work hours*). These effects are reported when significant.

6.2.4 Results

We now present, separately for the short and the long term, the Vietnam estimates of the health effects of child work.

6.2.4.1 Contemporaneous Work–Health Relationship

Estimates of the contemporaneous relationship between child work status and weight-for-age *z*-score (*waz*) are presented in Table 6.4. The sample consists of children within the 6–17 years age range in both waves. *z*-scores are only computable up to the age of 17. We control for height (third degree polynomial) and interpret coefficients as reflecting relationships with thinness, or wasting. Pooled OLS gives a significantly positive relationship between child work participation and current *waz*. The possibility that this reflects selection of the stronger kids into work is supported by the FD-OLS results, which show no relationship between child work status and *waz*.[4]

The coefficient of (log) household consumption changes from positive and significant under pooled OLS, to negative and marginally significant under FD-OLS. The direction of change suggests that fixed unobservables raise both household expenditure and child weight. The negative FD-OLS estimate is surprising and might reflect simultaneity bias. To deal with this, along with any remaining endogeneity of child work, we proceed to FD-2SLS. The instrument set consists of *land*, *rice price*, *immigration*, *emigration*, and *school year*. Their relevance to the determination of child work and household consumption is confirmed by significant rejection of exclusion restrictions on the respective reduced form regressions (see Table 6.4, column 3). In the case of child work, IV significance is only at the 7% level, and the R_2 is low, which could indicate a weak instruments problem. Overidentification is not rejected at the 5% level but is on the margin at the 10% significance level (Table 6.4, column 3).

The exclusion of each instrument from the structural equation are also tested, while relying on the remaining instruments for identification. In each case, the exclusion condition cannot be rejected. The Hausman (1978) F-test rejects joint exogeneity of child work status and household per capita consumption. On an individual basis, examining the *t*-statistics on the respective reduced-form residuals, only the exogeneity of household consumption is rejected (Wooldridge 2002: 118–122). As with FD-OLS, the FD-2SLS estimate of the child work effect is insignificantly different from zero (Table 6.4, column 3). The FD-OLS estimate of a negative relationship between household consumption and child weight becomes positive and significant when estimated by FD-2SLS. The direction of change is as expected in the case that the medical needs of a low-weight, sick child force a household to increase expenditure financed by dissaving and/or raising labour supply. Estimation by FD-2SLS greatly increases the magnitude of the estimate of the household consumption effect, which corresponds to an elasticity of 0.39 at the sample mean.

The FD-2SLS estimates are robust to dropping variables from the instrument set, with the exception that exclusion of *rice price* reduces the magnitude of the coefficients on the endogenous variables and leaves the household

[4] Splitting the sample by gender does not alter this conclusion. The work coefficient is negative for boys and positive for girls, but in neither case does it remotely approach significance.

Table 6.4 Weight-for-age z-score against current child work activity (sample: 6–17 years in both waves)

	Pooled OLS		First difference OLS		First difference 2SLS			
					Work and household consumption instrumented		Household consumption only instrumented	
					Full IV set[a]	Full IV set less rice price	Full IV set less school year	
Child in work	0.0359**	(0.0147)	–0.0001	(0.0144)	0.0863 (0.3318)	–0.0302 (0.2778)	0.0147 (0.0218)	0.0077 (0.0215)
Child in paid work								0.0876** (0.0390)
(log) Hhold consumption	0.0649***	(0.0232)	–0.0428*	(0.0246)	0.6643** (0.3294)	0.2780 (0.4067)	0.6424** (0.3132)	0.6714** (0.3237)
Sample size	5572		2786		2542	2593	2582	2582
R^2	0.6419		0.5526		0.4068	0.5210	0.4203	0.4099
F-test of joint significance	160.93	(p = .000)	69.12	(p = .000)	42.07 (p = .000)	52.92 (p = .000)	44.24 (p = .000)	43.36 (p = .000)
Hausman test of exogeneity[b]			Work		t = –0.26 (p = .795)	t = 0.02 (p = .998)		
			Hhold consumption		t = –2.52 (p = .013)	t = –0.59 (p = .556)	t = –2.72 (p = .008)	t = –2.79 (p = .006)
			Work and hhold consumption		$F(2, 105)$ = 3.77 (p = .026)	$F(2, 107)$ = 0.31 (p = .737)		

Reduced forms:	Work	$R^2 = 0.0736$	$R^2 = 0.0733$		
R^2		$F(5, 105) = 2.09$	$F(4, 107) = 3.03$		
F-test of IV		$(p = .072)$	$(p = .206)$		
significance	Hhold consumption	$R^2 = 0.2845$	$R^2 = 0.2784$	$R^2 = 0.2831$	$R^2 = 0.2837$
		$F(5, 105) = 2.35$	$F(4, 107) = 1.95$	$F(4, 107) = 2.80$	$F(4, 107) = 2.77$
		$(p = .046)$	$(p = .107)$	$(p = .029)$	$(p = .031)$
Overidentification[c]		X^2 (3) = 6.16	X^2 (2) = 1.02	X^2 (3) = 5.90	X^2 (3) = 5.57
		$(p = .104)$	$(p = .602)$	$(p = .116)$	$(p = .135)$

Note: Cluster adjusted robust standard errors in parentheses. *, ** and *** denote significance at 10%, 5%, and 1% respectively; p = denotes p-value.

[a] *land, rice price, emigration, immigration, school year.*

[b] t-test of individual significance and F test of joint significance of reduced form residuals in augmented structural equation (Hausman 1978; Wooldridge 2002: 118–122).

[c] Overidentification test robust t. heteroskedasticity (Wooldrige 2002: 122–124).

consumption effect insignificantly different from zero (Table 6.4, column 4). The work effect remains insignificant. Without the rice price in the instrument set, exogeneity is not rejected for household consumption as well as child work. The remaining instruments perform better with respect to the overidentification test but are weaker. Given that exogeneity of child work is not rejected in any case, we estimate treating only household consumption as endogenous and returning *rice price* to the IV set but dropping *school year* since this is not a plausible determinant of household living standards (Table 6.4, column 5). The household consumption effect is robust to the assumption that work status is exogenous. Without instrumentation, the work effect is estimated more precisely, but it remains insignificantly different from zero.

There is no evidence to support a contemporaneous negative impact of child work on weight for age. The same conclusion emerges using two alternative health indicators—body mass index and reported illness.[5] The lack of a work participation effect may mask differential effects by type and tenure of work. We test this by including, in turn and in addition to work participation, *hhold chores*, *paid work*, and *job tenure*. Given the change in measurement of hours in agricultural work between waves, it is not possible to test for a contemporaneous health effect from hours of work. *Hhold chores* and *job tenure* are never significant. Irrespective of the estimator, the coefficient on *paid work* is positive and significant. In first differences, exogeneity of *paid work*, as well as any work participation, is not rejected.

In the final column of Table 6.4, we give FD-2SLS estimates with household consumption only instrumented and *paid work* included. While non-paid work within the household environment has no significant impact on child weight, children working for pay are significantly heavier. Given that selection effects have been eliminated through differencing and there is no indication of remaining endogeneity in the work variables, the analysis supports a causal relationship. Working for pay makes the child heavier and, by extension, healthier. This is not the effect one might expect and it should certainly be interpreted with caution.

Failure to detect simultaneity in the relationship between child work and weight is a little surprising. If *paid work* is instrumented, the effect remains positive but is no longer significant. Significance is lost also if the sample is

[5] Body mass index is weight divided by the square of height. In estimating the contemporaneous impact on illness, we try to deal with the change in the illness question through flexible time effects. Correcting for both unobservable heterogeneity and simultaneity through instrumentation, the illness propensity is *lower* for working children (10% significance) but the estimate is not robust to the instrument set.

split by gender, but the estimated coefficient is roughly the same for boys and girls.

On the other hand, it is not implausible that working for pay may benefit the child nutritionally. As explained at the outset of this chapter, work may in fact increase a child's claim on household resources. At least in the short term, it is thus possible that the nutritional and health benefits of a child engaging in paid work are positive. Of course, in the longer term there may be legitimate concerns about the health consequences of sustained exposure to workplace risks. We now turn to estimates of such longer-term effects.

6.2.4.2 Longer-Term Work–Health Relationship

Estimates of the relationship between illness propensity in 1997–1998 and child work activity up to five years earlier are presented in Table 6.5. The sample consists of wave 2 observations of children that were aged 6–15 years at wave 1. The gender-pooled univariate probit estimates (column 1) indicate a positive but insignificant relationship between current illness and past child work. The relationship increases substantially in magnitude and significance in moving to the bivariate probit model (Table 6.5, column 2). This is consistent with a *healthy worker selection effect.* The univariate model does not allow for the fact that the inherently more healthy individuals are more likely to have worked in the past. The negative correlation between the work and illness equation error terms is also consistent with selection into work on the basis of unobserved health endowments. This correlation is significant only at the 11% level, but the magnitude of the correlation and the difference between the estimates support the bivariate probit model.

The bivariate probit is identified through the exclusion of *any allocated land, allocated land size, rice price, emigration, migrant ratio, pupil–teacher ratio,* and *school year* from the illness equation. We confirm the significance of the instruments in the work equation (results not reported) and check the validity of the identification restrictions by testing the exclusion of each of the instruments from the illness equation under the assumption that the remaining instruments are valid. The exclusion restriction is not rejected in any case. The estimates are fairly robust to variations on the identification strategy. Dropping household land holdings from the model, and so relying principally on commune-level factors for identification, increases the work coefficient from 0.5140 to 0.6370 and raises its significance. The correlation of the errors also increases in magnitude and becomes significant at the 5% level. Omitting the commune-level factors has the opposite effect, reducing the magnitude and significance of both the work coefficient and the error

Table 6.5 Illness/injury in 1997–1998 against child work activity in 1992–1993 (sample: 6–15 years in 1992–1993)

	Males and females ($N = 3370$)			Males ($N = 1803$)			Females ($N = 1567$)		
	Univariate probit	Bivariate probit	Bivariate probit	Univariate probit	Bivariate probit	Univariate probit	Univariate probit	Bivariate probit	Bivariate probit
Child work in 1992-3	0.0987	0.5140**	0.3472	0.0422	0.2926	−0.2952*	0.1632*	0.7351**	0.9112***
	(0.0715)	(0.2582)	(0.3086)	(0.0948)	(0.3459)	(0.1665)	(0.0866)	(0.3238)	(0.3434)
Job tenure in 1992-3 (months)			0.0140			0.0255**			−0.0058
			(0.0088)			(0.0112)			(0.0042)
Job tenure squared (/100)			−0.0241*			−0.0348**			
			(0.0129)			(0.0158)			
Correlation of errors (rho)		−0.2639	−0.2536		−0.1592			−0.3677	−0.4009
		(0.1579)	(0.1647)		(0.2083)			(0.1989)	(0.1979)
Wald test of rho = 0		2.54	2.17		0.5647			2.81	3.24
		($p = 0.1113$)	($p = 0.1409$)		(0.4524)			($p = 0.0935$)	($p = 0.0717$)
Log-likelihood	−1950.5	−3366.0	−3363.7	−1039.2	−1792.13	−1036.6	−894.4	−1538.9	−1538.0
LR test of pooling across gender	40.46	75.77							
	($p = 0.0000$)	($p = 0,3273$)							

Note: Cluster adjusted robust standard errors in parentheses. *, **, and *** denote significance at 10%, 5%, and 1% respectively. p = denotes p-value.

correlation. Dropping the school quality variables reduces the work coefficient to 0.4739, with significance preserved at 1%. Dropping the commune rice price and migration indicators gives a work coefficient of 0.4896, not significant at 10%.

Besides the significant work effect, illness propensity is greater for ethnic minorities and less if the child's mother has a school diploma. Safe drinking water and satisfactory sanitation also significantly reduce the probability of illness. Illness is greater in communes where more than half of women give birth at home and less where there is a pharmacy in the commune, a child growth chart in the health centre, where there was a mothers' health education programme within a year of the first survey, and where the commune has received food relief within the past year. These estimates make sense and suggest that the reported illness measure is reflecting variation in underlying health and its determinants.

Other regressors capture reporting behaviour. Illness is more likely to be reported when the question is answered by the subject (*self report* = 1) rather than by a parent on behalf of a young child. The propensity to report illness is greater where the commune health centre conducts a child health exam. Most likely, such examinations make families aware of child health problems, which are subsequently reported. The one counter-intuitive result is the positive and significant effect of both current and past household consumption. This may reflect reporting behaviour and/or endogeneity. In developing countries, strong pro-rich inequalities in objective indicators of health, such as infant mortality rates, are often not apparent in more subjective measures, such as reported morbidity. The better off may be more aware of their health problems and have higher expectations of health. These differences will be reflected in reported illness, for any given level of true health. As argued in Section 7.3, such reporting behaviour need not bias our estimates of the child work effect on illness. The control variables are intended to pick up variation in both true health and reporting behaviour. There is a problem only if any remaining variation in reporting behaviour is determined by work status itself.

If the positive household consumption coefficient reflects endogeneity, there is a problem, since this could contaminate the work effect. We test exogeneity by the two-step method of Rivers and Vuong (1988), which is a test of the significance of reduced-form (OLS) residuals in a probit containing all the regressors of the structural model. We test the exogeneity of past work participation, as well as that of current and past household consumption. The instruments are as defined for the bivariate probit. Exogeneity of all three variables is not rejected (χ^2 (3) 4.94, p 0.1765). On an individual basis, the *z*-ratios on the reduced form residuals indicate marginal rejection of exogeneity of lagged consumption (z 1.68, p 0.094) but not of current consumption (z 0.52).

Maximum likelihood estimation allowing for the potential endogeneity of both current and past household consumption, in addition to that of work status, is likely to prove difficult.[6] Given it is the work effect that is of central interest, we simply check whether the estimate of this parameter appears to be contaminated by any endogeneity of consumption. Since we are treating work as endogenous, we can drop household consumption from the model and avoid omitted variables bias in the coefficient of interest. The bivariate probit work coefficient is robust to dropping either or both household consumption variables, varying between 0.5129 and 0.5332, and remaining significant at 5%.

A further alternative is to replace the value of total household consumption in the model with the value of food consumption alone. Since the latter does not include expenditures on health care and medicines, it should be less endogenous to sickness. Food expenditures are the least discretionary component of the household budget and should be less sensitive to unobservable household preferences that are correlated with both child work and health investment decisions. The Rivers and Vuong test gives no indication of any endogeneity of current food expenditure, and exogeneity of lagged food expenditure is not rejected even at the 15% significance level (z-ratio 1.38, p 0.166). Replacing total household consumption with food consumption raises the work coefficient in the bivariate probit from 0.5140 to 0.5711, with significance preserved at the 5% level. These sensitivity checks suggest that the positive and significant effect of past child work on illness propensity is not an artefact of endogeneity bias deriving from household consumption.

Representation of child work activity through a simple participation dummy obscures any variation in the work effect with the intensity, nature, and tenure of work. Conditional on participation, hours of work at wave 1 have no significant effect on illness propensity at wave 2. In contrast to the result for weight for age, there is no significant difference between the illness effects for children working within the household and those working outside the household for pay. Illness propensity does rise non-linearly with the length of time an individual worked as a child. We estimate a bivariate probit for illness and past work status with a quadratic in past *job tenure*, in addition

[6] A two-stage conditional maximum likelihood procedure (Rivers and Vuong 1988) would not be consistent due to the binary nature of one of the potentially endogenous variables (work).

to work participation, included in the illness equation (Table 6.5, column 3). The assumed exogeneity of past *job tenure* is tested and not rejected. With *job tenure* included, the participation effect falls in magnitude and loses individual significance, but participation and tenure are jointly significant ($\chi^2(3)$ 7.81, p 0.0502). Illness propensity is increasing with time in work up to a period of twenty-nine months, which corresponds to the 67th percentile of distribution for those in work.

The relation of illness propensity to past work activity differs by gender. For males, there is evidence of a job tenure effect, while for females it is participation itself that is most important. Failure to reject error independence at any reasonable level of significance in the bivariate probit for males suggests a univariate probit is adequate (Table 6.5, columns 4 and 5). This is confirmed by a Rivers and Vuong test that does not reject exogeneity of work participation and job tenure in a univariate probit. The participation effect is negative and significant at 10%, while illness propensity rises significantly with job tenure until a turning point at 36 months, equivalent to the 75th percentile of the distribution for males in work (column 6). For females, there is a positive and significant impact of past work participation on illness propensity irrespective of the model and specification adopted. The magnitude and significance of the effect rise in moving from the univariate to bivariate probit and the latter is supported by rejection (10%) of zero error correlation. The tenure effect is negative but not significant.

The explanation of these gender differences in the work–illness relationship most likely lies in the nature of work undertaken and the differential burden of other activities. Our definition of work does not include household chores. Among the children working at wave 1, one-third of girls were also performing household chores for at least seven hours per week, while only 13% of boys were doing so. Given the greater energy that girls are exerting in the performance of household chores, the marginal burden of entering work is probably greater than that experienced by boys. Working girls are more likely to be withdrawn from school than working boys, suggesting that the intensity and nature of work undertaken by girls is more onerous.[7] For boys, work participation itself does not appear to endanger health but the risk of illness increases, up to a point, the longer they are exposed to workplace health hazards.

There is no evidence of any significant relationship between child work and subsequent growth in height (Table 6.6). The OLS estimate is slightly

[7] Among non-working children there is no difference in school participation rates by gender. For working children, the school participation rate is 70% for boys but only 65% for girls.

positive, but not significantly different from zero (column 1). Joint exogeneity of work and initial height is rejected (at the 5% level). On an individual basis, only the exogeneity of initial height is rejected (column 2). Instrumenting both work and initial height, the work effect remains insignificantly different from zero (column 2). The instruments are the same as those used for past work in the determination of illness. These are significant determinants of work but are not jointly significant in the reduced form for initial height. It is difficult to find a plausible instrument for initial height in an equation for subsequent growth in height.[8] One solution is to drop initial height from the

Table 6.6 Average annual growth in height 1992/1993–1997/1998 against child work status in 1992–1993 (sample: 6–15 years in 1992/1993)

	OLS	2SLS—Work and height instrumented	2SLS—Height dropped and work instrumented
Child worked in 1992/3	0.0293 (.0478)	0.0110 (0.4682)	−0.9941 (0.6998)
Height in 1992/3	−0.0764*** (.0048)	−0.193*** (0.0698)	
Sample size	3,164	2,870	2,870
R^2	0.6158	0.4048	0.4866
F-test of joint significance	127.01 ($p = 0.0000$)	110.19 ($p = 0.0000$)	96.95 ($p = 0.0000$)
Hausman test of exogeneity	Work	$t = 0.00$ ($p = 0.998$)	$t = 1.31$ ($p = 0.194$)
	Height	$t = 3.07$ ($p = 0.003$)	
	Work and height	$F(2.94 = 4.71$ ($p = 0.0113$)	
Reduced form: R^2	Work	$R^2 = 0.3709$ $F(7.94) = 7.82$ ($p = 0.0000$)	$R^2 = 0.3709$ $F(2.94) = 5.48$ ($p = 0.0056$)
F-test of IV significance	Height	$R^2 = 0.7929$ $F(7.94) = 1.41$ ($p = 0.2125$)	
Overidentification		$X^2(5) = 6.54$ ($p = 0.2571$)	$X^2(1) = 4.39$ ($p = 0.0361$)

Note: Cluster adjusted robust standard errors in parentheses. *, **, and *** denote significance at 10%, 5%, and 1% respectively. p = denotes p-value.

[8] One possibility would be to use mother's age and education, on the grounds that these may influence growth in early, but not later, childhood. Tests did not support this hypothesis.

model and allow for omitted variable bias by instrumenting work. This is implemented using only the school quality variables as instruments.

The other variables, such as the indicators of economic conditions and wealth, may have explanatory power for height and so become relevant regressors in the growth equation once initial height is dropped. This is confirmed by rejection of overidentification with the full instrument set. Following this strategy, the work coefficient switches sign, rises in magnitude, but remains insignificant (Table 6.6, column 3). The exogeneity of work is not rejected.

Estimating by OLS with initial height omitted gives a negative work effect significant at 10% but, despite the result of the exogeneity test, one suspects this reflects OV bias—initially taller children are more likely to work and have less potential to grow. Exogeneity of initial household consumption is not rejected. But, even if this variable is instrumented, along with initial work and height, there is no change in the result that the effect of work is not significant.[9] This holds for both males and females.

The lack of a work participation effect does not mask any significant effects of work hours, work outside the household environment, or job tenure (results not presented). While childhood work appears to raise vulnerability to subsequent illness, the health impact is not sufficiently strong to impede the growth of the child. This is consistent with evidence from rural Ghana showing differences in morbidity, but not in growth, between children enrolled and children not enrolled in school (Fentiman et al. 2001).

6.3 Guatemala

We have seen that child work can have immediate and delayed health effects. We now try to assess whether the delayed effects extend as far as adult life. The retrospective information on the age at which adults begun to work contained in the Guatemala survey permits the formulation of a relatively simple empirical test. The test consists in assessing whether having worked as a child has an impact on current health status. However, the interpretation of a possible correlation as a causal relationship poses several problems.

[9] The change in household consumption is left out of the model to avoid any possible simultaneity. This does not appear to introduce any OV bias. The correlation between initial child work status and subsequent change in household consumption, conditional on all other regressors, is not significantly different from zero. Including the change in household consumption in the model has little or no impact on the work coefficient.

6.3.1 Econometric Issues in the Estimation of the Effect of Childhood Work on Adult Health

According to Behrman and Wolfe (1989), the reduced-form determinants of an adult's health generally fall into four categories: observed indicators of earlier childhood and environment, unobserved household-specific indicators, observed individual-specific indicators (e.g., gender, age), unobserved individual-specific effect and the price structure. The main concern to be addressed is that the impossibility of controlling for a set of potentially relevant variables in the estimates may generate spurious results. We can identify two sets of unobservables that are relevant to our problem at both the individual and household level.

As mentioned earlier in this chapter, one possible source of bias is the so-called 'healthy worker effect'. All else equal, and assuming that health is positively related to labour productivity, healthier individuals are more likely to be selected for work. Hence, a negative effect of work on health could be confounded by the fact that unobservable individual characteristics are not taken into account. This effect may account for the measured positive (or weakly negative) relationship in simple correlation analysis between working children and health status. Since it obviously depends on the genetically given characteristics of the individual, we call this the unobservable 'individual effect'.

A second source of bias depends on the fact that our data do not contain information on the household characteristics of the adult during his childhood: correlation between these unobserved characteristics and adult health outcomes might lead to biased estimates. Consider, for example, the relationship between the income of the household where the individual under observation was born, the work performed during childhood, and the current (adult) health status of the individual. Poor households, invest less in health and education and are more likely to send their children to work. A negative correlation between child work and adult health might be spurious as it might reflect (also) the low level of the unobserved investment in health during childhood.

Ideally, we would like to ensure that our conclusion about the relationship between child labour and health is not distorted by unobservables. One possible way to achieve this is to find a valid instrument that is uncorrelated with the unobservable term but highly correlated with the endogenous explanatory variable. However, as explained in Bound, Jaeger, and Baker (1995), and Staiger and Stock (1997), the validity of the instruments depends highly on the correlation between the instruments and the endogenous explanatory variable. The weaker the correlation, the closer the IV estimator is to the standard OLS result. Another stream of the literature—see for example Imbens and Angrist (1994)—uses experimental or quasi-experimental data to handle the endogeneity problem. The variable of interest is considered under these circumstances as a treatment. Assuming that treatment is assigned completely at random, hence uncorrelated with the unobserved characteristics of the individual, the estimation results are unbiased. Under these conditions, the random assignment can be considered as a valid instrument.

In our case, the use of any of these approaches appears to be precluded. As the data set did not contain information on possible good instruments for either unobservable individual characteristics, or unobserved past household characteristics., Rosati and Straub (2007) decided to follow a different route, similar to the methodology chosen by Ashenfelter and Krueger (1994) to measure the return to schooling. To overcome the problems linked to unobservables, those authors used a sample of twins. Rosati and Straub use a self-constructed sample of siblings from the Guatemalan NSLC to analyse the long-run impact of child labour on health. To control for unobservable household-specific characteristics, we transform the data in a panel structure and estimate the model by conditional fixed effects. In this way, the household effects are taken care of by the fixed effects, and the estimated coefficient can be considered as unbiased by the unobserved past household characteristics.

Since the data set is not restricted to monozygotic, genetically identical, twins as in the case of Ashenfelter and Krueger, there is still the problem that the coefficient of interest to us might be contaminated by individual-specific characteristics. Were that the case, the estimator would be biased according to the formula

$$E(b_2) = \beta_2 + \beta_3\gamma_2, \tag{6.1}$$

where $E(b_2)$ is the estimated coefficient of the effect of child labour on adult health, β_2 is the unbiased impact, β_3 is the effect of the unobservable variable on health, and γ_2 is the correlation between the unobservable individual specific characteristic and child labour. The question is the sign of γ_2. As there is no rationale for assuming that less healthy, hence weaker, children are sent to work—and there certainly is no evidence, even anecdotal, pointing in that direction—we cannot assume that γ_2 is negative. There is more support, both theoretical and empirical, for assuming that the correlation between the unobservable genetic health endowment and child labour is positive (i.e., that healthier children are more likely to be selected to work).[10] Hence, it seems reasonable to assume that, if biased, our estimator will underestimate the true impact of child labour on health.

6.3.2 Sample Description

The Guatemalan National Survey on Living Conditions (NSLC) of the year 2000 provides information on household composition, education, migration, economic activities, and health indicators. The two main variables of interest are the health status and the age of entry into the labour market. As the true health status is not observable, we use a self-reported health indicator taking value 1 if the person reports having had bad health in the last month, 0 otherwise. This might cause a measurement error in the dependent variable. If the measurement error is systematically related to one or more of the explanatory variables, the estimator will be biased. However, epidemiological studies show that self-reported health indicators seem to be good predictors of bad health status and mortality. Over a nine-year period, individuals reporting a health problem have a death rate three times greater than that of individuals reporting good health (Kaplan and Camacho 1983).

Child labour is defined as a dummy taking value 1 if the person entered the labour market before the age of 15, value 0 otherwise. Around 67% of the individuals in the sub-sample reported having worked during childhood; 25% declared they had health problems (see Table 6.7). The average age of the individuals in the sub-sample was about 24. The average age of labour market entry was 13. The majority (52%) were rural residents, and only 22% were born in an urban area. Forty-two per cent were women. Fourteen per cent had some education. Almost 80% reported being employed in the week preceding the interview; 43% reported having suffered from an individual shock and 31% from a collective shock during the six months prior to the interview.

6.3.4 The Logit Model

In this subsection, we present the estimates obtained by a standard logit regression. The dependent variable is the self-reported health index. The

[10] This is the well-known healthier work effect, which, however, has not found overwhelming empirical support.

Table 6.7 Summary statistics

Variable	Obs.	Mean	Std. dev.	Min.	Max.
Age	3,409	23.96	9.09	16	85
Gender	3,409	0.42	0.50	0	1
Labour market entry	3,407	12.94	4.04	6	45
Child labour	3,409	0.66	0.47	0	1
Self-reported health index	3,409	0.25	0.43	0	1
Collective shock	3,409	0.31	0.46	0	1
Individual shock	3,409	0.43	0.49	0	1
Education	3,409	0.14	0.35	0	1
Employed last week	3,409	0.79	0.40	0	1
Worked last week	3,409	0.70	0.45	0	1
Born urban	3,324	0.22	0.41	0	1
Rural resident	3,409	0.52	0.50	0	1
Income	3,399	6.44	1.08	2.52	9.11

Source: Guatemalan NSLC.

independent variable is the dummy indicating whether the individual was a child labourer.[11]

The control variables include the education of the parents as an indicator of the childhood environment of the current adult,[12] a dummy for an urban birthplace to control for the price structure of health services in earlier childhood, and one for each Guatemalan state to control for geographical differences. The other controls are individual-specific characteristics like age, gender, education, and current household characteristics like income, individual and collective shocks,[13] a dummy for rural residency, and a dummy for indoor plumbing. Education is a dummy taking value 0 if the individual has nothing less than completed primary education, 1 otherwise.[14] The inclusion of income and education allows us to distinguish the direct effects of child labour from the indirect ones it might have through higher earnings or reduced educational achievement.

[11] We also run regressions replacing the dummy for child labour with the actual age of labour market entry in both the standard logit and conditional logit set-up. These results confirm the negative impact of early labour market entry on health (although with varying levels of significance). However, since using the age of labour market entry as a proxy for child labour assumes that the effect is linear and independent of being an adult or not, we consider these results not as sound as the ones presented in this section.

[12] As we have very few observations in some groups we aggregated the variable in three categories. No education, preparatory school, and adult's education are grouped together and indicate the lowest level of education. Primary school constitutes the second category. Secondary, higher, and postgraduate education are combined to indicate the highest level of education. The reference category in the estimates is the lowest level of education.

[13] For the precise definition of these variables see Chapter 8.

[14] We also experimented with various different cut-off points, but this had no significant effect on the results.

Table 6.8 Logit estimates

	(1)	(2)	(3)	(4)
Child labour	.161	.159	.151	.148
	(.096)*	(.097)*	(.097)	(.097)
Born urban	.069	.073	.079	.079
	(.119)	(.119)	(.12)	(.119)
Father primary school	.11	.096	.111	.11
	(.1)	(.101)	(.108)	(.108)
Father higher education	.428	.404	.414	.409
	(.174)**	(.176)**	(.176)**	(.176)**
Mother primary school	–.118	–.118	–.104	–.106
	(.104)	(.104)	(.105)	(.105)
Mother higher education	.113	.102	.109	.108
	(.188)	(.192)	(.192)	(.192)
Age	.017	.017	.017	.017
	(.004)***	(.004)***	(.005)***	(.005)***
Rural resident	–.181	–.157	–.161	–.161
	(.102)	(.181)	(.181)	(.181)
Gender	.251	.254	.244	.237
	(.084)***	(.084)***	(.085)***	(.087)***
Water	.013	.035	.05	.051
	(.107)	(.108)	(.109)	(.109)
Individual shock	.378	.282	.281	.281
	(.085)***	(.09)***	(.09)***	(.09)***
Collective shock	—	.331	.333	.334
		(.094)***	(.094)***	(.094)***
Income	—	.101	.108	.109
		(.175)	(.176)	(.176)
Education	—	—	.144	.143
			(.129)	(.129)
Worked last week	—	—	—	–.037
				(.093)
Controls	—	—	—	—
Obs.	3248	3246	3246	3246
Log likelihood	−1765.253	−1757.343	−1756.727	−1756.644
X^2 statistic	95.817	108.27	109.501	109.666

Note: Standard errors in brackets. The results of several further controls are not depicted.

Table 6.8 shows the results. The coefficient of the child labour dummy has the expected positive sign in all model specifications, but the coefficient is never highly significant (the p-values are all around 0.10). As neither education nor household income is significant, the main effect of child labour on health appears to be direct, rather than indirect. Age, gender, and individual and collective shocks are highly significant. As was to be expected, age is positively associated with bad health. Women are more likely to experience bad health. Individual and collective shocks also increase the probability of bad health. The finding that having a father with higher education has a detrimental effect on health is puzzling. The mother's education has no significant effect.

7.3.5 The Conditional-Fixed-Effects Logit Model

The results obtained by the logit model suffer from the defect that we do not control for unobserved heterogeneity. There are several ways in which one can address the problem in a cross-section analysis. If there is a suitable proxy for the unobserved effect, one can estimate an equation by the logit model described before. If there are suitable instruments for the explanatory variables, one can apply instrumental variable methods. As none of these strategies appears to be feasible in the present case, however, we resorted to using a sub-sample of adult siblings. If siblings have a common household-specific background, we can hope to capture the effect of this unobservable characteristic through the information contained in the sub-sample.

The sub-sample was selected in two stages. First, we selected all persons aged 16 or more. Second, we selected all households that included siblings.[15] In some cases, we found more than one set of siblings in the same household. Since each household member was required to declare his or her relationship to the household head, we dealt with the problem of multiple sets by considering the offspring of the household head, and that of each sibling of the household head, as a different 'household'. Table 6.9 shows the frequency

Table 6.9 Household composition

No. of siblings	No. of households	Observations in the sample
2	935	1,870
3	339	1,017
4	96	384
5	21	105
6	2	12
7	3	21
All	1,396	3,409

Source: Guatemaian NSLC.

[15] The latter was only possible in the case where the siblings lived in the same household at the time of the interview. This might pose a section problem, but as our estimates are based on within-household variation rather than on between-household variation we do not think this might be a serious problem.

distribution of the number of siblings in each set. The sub-sample is clearly not representative of Guatemalan society. As we shall control for the unobservable common household background of each set of siblings, and other relevant factors, however, the estimates should not be affected by the selection criteria.

After identifying the sets of siblings, we transformed the data in a panel by defining Y_{ij} (the dependent variable), X_{ij} (the independent variables) as observable characteristics of person *j* in household *i* (i.e., sibling *j* in the set *i*). Assuming that the unobserved household-specific effect is constant within siblings, we are able to control for this effect by using the Conditional-Fixed-Effects Logit Estimator.[16]

While not contaminated by the household-specific effect, the estimator will still be influenced by the individual-specific effect. Since correlation between the unobservable individual-specific effect and child labour is assumed to be nonnegative, we can however interpret our estimator as a lower bound of the true impact. The results of the Conditional-Fixed-Effect estimation are reported in Table 6.10.

The estimate of the β vector gives us the effect of each element of x_t on the logodds ratio. Unfortunately, we cannot estimate partial effects on the response probabilities unless we plug in a value α_i, and we cannot estimate average partial effects because that would require specifying the distribution of α_i.

All 'households' (sets of siblings) that have the same value of the dichotomous dependent variable health status are automatically eliminated from the sample. Any variable that takes the same value for all siblings belonging to the same 'household' is also dropped. The omitted variables represent common household-specific characteristics. Of the remaining variables, gender and age remain highly significant. As in the last subsection, the effect of child labour on health appears to operate directly, rather than indirectly through education.

[16] Unconditional-Fixed-Effects and Random-Effects estimation methods are not applicable in our framework. Random-Effect estimation requires the additional assumption that the unobserved error terms, *αi* (for household-specific effect) and *dj* (for individual-specific effect) are uncorrelated with the explanatory variables. Since it is hard to assume that unobserved household and individual-specific effects are uncorrelated with child labour, we will employ the Fixed-Effect estimation techniques. Although the name suggests it, fixed effect does not necessary mean that the unobserved effect is non-random. In our application, it rather means that we allow for arbitrary correlation between the unobserved effect and the observed variables (see Wooldridge 2002). As shown by Andersen (1970) and Chamberlain (1980), however, the Unconditional-Fixed-Effects Estimator is not able to control for the household-specific effect under general circumstances, because of the incidental parameter problem described by Neyman and Scott (1948).

Table 6.10 Conditional-Fixed-Effects logit

	(1)	(2)	(3)	(4)
Child labour	.369	.369	.363	.348
	(.188)**	(.188)**	(.184**)	(.185*)
Born urban	.04	.04	.04	.06
	(.29)	(.291)	(.291)	(.291)
Father primary school	1.596	1.596	1.603	1.699
	(1.116)	(1.116)	(1.115)	(1.12)
Mother primary school	.33	.33	.326	.275
	(.847)	(.847)	(.847)	(.845)
Mother higher education	.863	.865	.857	.73
	(1.659)	(1.659)	(1.659)	(1.655)
Age	.025	.025	.025	.027
	(.014)*	(.014)*	(.0.14)*	(.014)*
Rural resident	—	—	—	—
Gender	.394	.394	.387	.358
	(.135)***	(.135)***	(.137)***	(.139)***
Water	—	—	—	—
Individual shock	—	—	—	—
Collective shock	—	—	—	—
Income	—	—	—	—
Education	—	—	.081	.078
			(.271)	(.271)
Worked last week	—	—	—	-.192
				(.161)
Controls	—	—	—	—
Obs.	1080	1078	1078	1078
Log likelihood	-381.684	-380.953	-380.908	-380.192
X^2 statistic	16.923	16.999	17.089	18.521

Note: Standard errors in brackets. The results of several further controls are not depicted.

Notice that, once the household unobservables are taken into account, the effect of child labour on health becomes highly significant and of a relevant magnitude. Since the coefficient of child labour is equivalent to the log-odds ratios, our results predict an over 40% increase in the probability of having health problems as an adult if the person worked as a child. This is a substantial effect. Since our result is a lower bound, the 'true causal effect' could be even larger. Another interesting point is that, in contrast with received wisdom, our results indicate that the unobserved household-specific effect generates a downward bias in the coefficient. The point estimates reported in Table 6.8 (the logit estimates) are in fact lower and less significant than those estimated by the Conditional-Fixed-Effects Logit.

6.4 Concluding Remarks

Does work during childhood have a negative impact on health? We tried to answer this question by looking for possible short- and long-term effects during childhood, and for even longer-term effects in adult life. We also tried to distinguish the effects of different types of work.

The evidence from rural Vietnam suggests that work has no negative short-term effect on childhood health. It also shows that children doing paid work are significantly heavier than their contemporaries who are either working for the household, or not working. Assuming that health is an increasing function of weight for this age group, the dominant form of child work—unpaid agricultural work for the household—appears to have no short-term impact on health. Paid work may even be beneficial to nutrition and health. The most likely pathway for this effect is through the direction of household nutritional resources to the child earner. Health does appear to determine the selection of children for work. Controlling for a large range of covariates, the simple cross-section relationship between child work status and weight for age is significantly positive. Differencing out fixed individual and local factors, the relation weakens and becomes insignificant, suggesting that the initial positive relationship is attributable to selection of the inherently stronger and healthier children into work. The absence of a contemporaneous negative impact of child agricultural work on health is robust to a variety of estimators, identification strategies, specifications, and health indicators.

In the longer term, child work appears to have negative health repercussions. Individuals working during childhood are significantly more likely to report illness up to five years later. This is true after controlling for an extensive range of individual, household, and community-level covariates and for common unobservable determinants of past work and current illness. The result is robust to different empirical specifications and identification strategies, and is consistent with evidence from Brazil showing that self-reported health in adulthood is lower, the younger the age at entry to the workforce (Giuffrida, Iunes, and Saredo 2001, Kassouf, Mckee, and Mossialos 2001). We add to this evidence and strengthen it by correcting for any correlation through unobservables. The nature of the effect differs by gender. For females, work participation appears to provoke illness in the long term. For males, there is no work participation effect, but illness propensity increases with the period of time spent in childhood work. While childhood work raises the risk of future illness, the health impact is not sufficiently large to impede the growth of the child.

The analysis of the Guatemalan data reveals that adult health is influenced by the age of entry into the labour market. Using a sample of Guatemalan siblings, and thus controlling for unobserved household characteristics, we have shown that having worked as a child increases by about 40% the probability of reporting a bad health status. There are two general pathways through which this effect may operate. First, it may be that a child suffers a workplace accident with long-term consequences for health. Second, it may be that there is a latency period in the development of work-related health problems (for example, of conditions that are the cumulative effects of sustained exposure to chemicals, poor posture, or heavy lifting). The evidence that male illness propensity is increasing with past job tenure is consistent with the latent development of health problems. This justifies public concern for children working over extended periods (ILO 2002).

Some caveats are in order. The data at our disposal have led us to focus on the most common form of child labour, agricultural work. That was made explicit in the case of Vietnam, but was implicit also in that of Guatemala, because the data show that the vast majority of children in that country work in agriculture today (and this was even more true twenty years ago). Although work in agriculture is the most commonly practised form of child labour, it is, however, fair to say that it is unlikely to be more damaging than some of the work undertaken by children in large urban centres.

It must be kept in mind, furthermore, that we have also uncovered evidence of a positive effect of paid work. As we control for total household consumption, this effect appears to operate through a reallocation of household resources in favour of working children. That is indeed the theoretical prediction of Pitt, Rosenzweig, and Hassan (1990). If the reallocation in favour of working children is at the expense of others, however, this may still be bad for other children in the family. There is empirical support for this hypothesis. Using data on calorie intakes from rural Indonesia, Ralston (1997) found the intra-household calorie allocation to be positively related to children's labour contributions, and morbidity to be negatively related to calorie intake. On the other hand, child work raises household resources. If household income increases more than the share of non-working children decreases, the net effect on non-working children could be positive. The available evidence suggests that it is not. A study of rural Guatemala, Immink and Payongayong (1999), does in fact find that, while participation of school-age children in farm production does not appear to reduce their own growth and development, its effect on the growth of younger siblings is negative.

The international community wants better evidence on the health consequences of different types of child work in order to identify hazardous work, make effective its prohibition, and offer rehabilitation to children withdrawn from such activities (ILO 2002: 12). Our finding of significantly negative health effects of child work strengthens the case for policies that reduce children's work engagement. Our finding that this is true also of the bulk of child economic activity, agricultural work, does not make the task politically any easier.

7

Child Labour, Fertility, and Gender

Evidence

The theoretical analysis in Chapters 1 and 2 shows how child labour and fertility are jointly determined as part of the parents' optimizing strategy. Therefore, changes in fertility behaviour determined by some exogenous change are likely to affect child labour as well. Similarly, changes in child labour determined by some exogenous change are likely to affect fertility behaviour as well. In this chapter, we first discuss the evidence about the linkage between child labour and fertility, and then some of factors that might have led to their changes.

The seminal paper of Rosenzweig and Evenson (1997) builds a time allocation model that takes into consideration the economic contribution of children to household income. Consistently with the theory developed in Chapters 1 and 2, the econometric model shows that changes in exogenous variables like child and adult wages, and the amount of land available for cultivation, push fertility and child labour in the same direction. What increases the supply of child labour increases also fertility. They test the model using data for India at district level, and a reduced form approach that takes into account the endogeneity of some of the explanatory variables. The results confirm that an increase in the value of children's time in productive activities also raises the desired number of children by the households.

Similar results are obtained in a different context by Dupas, Falezan, Mabeu, and Rossi (2023), who look at the effects of seasonal migration in West Africa. They exploit the existence of migration networks between today's Bourkina Faso as sending region and Côte d'Ivoire and Niger as receiving regions, established because of forced migration during the French colonial era. Such networks still exist today and allow the households involved to diversify their income sources, in particular to rely more on wage income through remittances and less on agriculture. As a consequence, their demand for labour in the household farm is reduced. This leads to a reduction in fertility and in the need of child labour. Dupas, Falezan, Mabeu, and

The Economics of Child Labour. Second Edition. Alessandro Cigno and Furio C. Rosati, Oxford University Press.
 DOI: 10.1093/oso/9780198903000.003.0008

Rossi (2023), therefore, provide additional evidence of the comovement of fertility and child labour due to the fact that fertility decisions are affected, at least in part, by the economic strategy of the household. Unfortunately, we have no evidence on exogenous positive shocks on fertility, that would allow us to assess whether an increase in fertility due to an exogenous shock does change the economic strategy of the household, making them, for example, rely more on labour intensive activities.

Shanan (2023) examines the link between fertility and child labour in the USA from a different point of view. Although referred to a now highly developed country, the period studied is sufficiently distant in time to be able to say that the USA was not so different, then, from one of today's middle development countries like Mexico or Brazil. The author focuses on the fertility effects of restrictions on child labour by studying the effects of the introduction of compulsory schooling law and child labour restrictions in the period between 1880 and 1930. In 1900, 12% of children aged 10–15 worked in urban areas and 22% in rural areas. Following Massachusetts that enacted the first compulsory school law, by 1920 all states had enacted similar laws. Moreover, several states introduced legislation regulating the minimum age for working. The minimum age at which it was possible for children to work, given by the intersection of compulsory schooling law with labour regulations, varied across states and over time across and within states. Limiting the possibility for children to contribute to household income increases the cost of quantity of children with respect to their quality and might induce a reduction in fertility. The estimates, in fact, indicate that women exposed to higher minimum age of entry in the labour market for their children, reduced substantially the number of births, a reduction that according to the Shanan's preferred estimates explain about 10% of the decrease in fertility observed in the period considered in the study.

7.1 The Impact of Fertility on Child Labour

We now turn to the discussion of how the endogeneity of fertility might affect child labour estimates. Given the backward-induction structure of the household decision model (see Chapters 1 and 2), and given that children are not born all at the same time, the effect of realized fertility on labour supply decisions cannot be properly determined without taking into account the endogeneity of the number of children present in the household. The issue is recognized and modelled in a variety of different ways in the empirical literature on adult labour supply, and the results generally show strong evidence of the endogeneity of fertility.[1] In the empirical literature on child labour, by contrast, the issue has not been addressed. Several papers include controls for the number and ages of children in models of child labour and schooling,[2] but these variables are treated as if they are exogenous.

It is reasonable to expect that important sources of heterogeneity, affecting both fertility and child activity decisions, are not observable. In addition to unobserved preferences, the data typically offer poor proxies for income, wealth, and returns and costs of education and child labour. Therefore, econometric models of children's activity that treat the number of children as exogenous may provide biased estimates of the effect of these variables. While endogeneity bias is to be expected, the direction and magnitude of such effects is not clear. In the literature on adult labour supply, Angrist (2001) finds that the effect of children on female labour supply when endogeneity is accounted for is just over half as large as the effect when fertility is treated exogenously. Lundberg and Rose (2002), on the other hand, find evidence that the effect of children on male labour supply is substantially larger when endogeneity is taken into account.

Deb and Rosati (2004) depart from the practice of estimating a structural model by a linear instrumental-variables approach. Instead, they develop a structural econometric model of fertility and children's activities that respects important features of the data. The first is that survey data typically show a substantial fraction of children neither attending school nor participating in work activities. We saw that to be true, for example, of the data used in earlier chapters. Deb and Rosati (2004) show that reportedly idle children are different from children reported working or attending school. This highlights the importance of modelling child activities as a multinomial process. Since the linearization of children's activities requires that the multinomial variable be reduced to a binary variable, this has substantive and statistical consequences. The second feature is that fertility can take only a small number of integer values; hence it is a count process. Linearizing it leads to substantially inefficient estimates with poor finite sample properties. Consequently, the number of children in the household is better modelled as a Poisson process, and children's activities as a multinomial logit process.

Latent factors are incorporated into the equations for the number of children, and for children's activities, to allow for unobserved influences on fertility to affect children's activities. The latent factor structure has three

[1] See, for example, Moffitt (1984), Hotz and Miller (1988), Angrist and Evans (1998), Angrist (2001), Francesconi (2002), Gong and van Soest (2002), and .

[2] See among the earlier studies Jensen and Nielsen (1997), Ravallion and Wodon (2000), Ray (2000), Deb and Rosati (2002), and Maitra and Ray (2002).

advantages over alternative ways of generating correlated errors. First, it can be used to combine sets of any marginal distributions into an appropriate joint distribution. Secondly, correlated errors have a natural interpretation as proxies for unobserved covariates since they enter the equations in the same way as observed covariates. The factor loadings can therefore be interpreted in much the same way as coefficients on observed covariates. Thirdly, the approach provides a parsimonious representation of error correlations in models with large numbers of equations. Deb and Rosati (2004) apply maximum simulated likelihood (MSL) techniques to estimate the parameters of the models. As no closed-form solutions exist, simulation is used to evaluate integral expressions in the likelihood function of the model.[3]

This approach bears similarities to those adopted in a number of other microeconometric papers. In a fertility context, Olsen and Farkas (1989) examine the effect of childbirth on the hazard of dropping out of school, while Carrasco (2001) examines the effect of childbirth on labour force participation of women in a panel data context. In other contexts, Bingley and Walker (2001) examine the effect of duration of husbands' unemployment on wives' discrete labour supply choices, Jensen (1990) examines the effect of contraceptive use on duration between births, and Pitt et al. (1990) study the effect of endogenous health status of infant children on their mothers' main daily activity.

The econometric models used in all these studies share a number of statistical features. One is that both treatment and outcome processes are non-normal and non-linear: multinomial, count, discrete, or censored. Another is that the treatment is endogenous. Yet another is that the investigator often has good a priori reasons for choosing a particular (and incontrovertible) marginal model for both treatments and outcomes. But, the transition from given marginal distributions to a joint model for treatment and outcome continues to be a methodological challenge, because multivariate distributions are typically non- normal. In some cases (e.g. in count and duration models), the marginal models have no (or very restrictive) tractable multivariate counterparts. In others, treatment and outcome belong to different statistical families (e.g., treatment is multinomial, and the outcome is a hazard rate), as a consequence of which analytically tractable multivariate distributions often do not exist.

[3] MSL using pseudo-random draws can be computationally very expensive if the number of observations and parameters is large, and a large number of draws is required to reduce the simulation error to acceptable levels. For computational efficiency, Deb and Rosati (2004) thus adapt an acceleration technique that uses quasi-random draws based on Halton sequences (Bhat 2001, Train 2003).

Reliable estimates of the effects of realized fertility on child labour are very important for policy purposes. Consider, for example, the introduction of a subsidy for school attendance. This will reduce the cost of attending school, but also the cost of raising children. While the direct objective is to increase school attendance, the policy might thus have the (possibly undesirable) effect of also increasing fertility. If there is a significant effect of fertility on child labour and schooling, this policy would have an effect on schooling not only directly, but also indirectly through fertility. Correct information on the effects of realized fertility on child labour is needed also to assess the importance of cross-sectoral policies. For example, policies aimed at modifying fertility behaviour, such as those that improve the children's survival probabilities (see Chapter 2), will have unintended consequences for the supply of child labour and school attendance.

The theory suggests that the econometric model should have a recursive structure, with the number of children entering the equation for the children's activities.[4] Decisions regarding the latter may be assumed to be made when the children are of school age. Deb and Rosati (2004) model only the activities of the youngest child in each family. In families where all the children are seven years of age or older, the youngest of these children can be taken to be the 'marginal' child. In the case of families where some (but not all) of the children are less than seven years old, it is assumed that the survival of the youngest children is uncertain. Where decisions concerning children's activities are concerned, the 'marginal' child is then taken to be the youngest child aged at least seven. Assuming that the youngest child in the relevant age group is also the least entrenched in a possibly undesirable activity (working or being idle), he or she may be taken to be also the target of social policy.[5]

As only 0.71% of children are reported working and attending school, it is assumed that a child can only do one of the following: attend school, work, or do nothing (children working and attending school at the same time are classified as working). These activities are modelled as a multinomial logit process conditional on the number of children. In what follows, we describe the data and define the variables used in the estimation.

The data set is a sub-sample of households drawn from the 1994 Human Development of India survey. The sub-sample includes only households with at least one child between the ages of 7 and 15. The sub-sample consists of

[4] A recursive structure is required for logical coherency also in models with discrete and count outcomes; see Maddala (1986), and Blundell and Smith (1994).

[5] This choice is not without statistical consequences. One may wish to model the activities of each of the children in the relevant age group, thus absolving the analyst of making a choice of which child to consider. Since the activities of all children within the family share the same unobserved heterogeneity, however, the model is considerably more complicated to programme and estimate than the one described.

12,830 observations. Summary statistics for the variables used in the analysis are presented in Table 7.1

The explanatory variables common to the fertility and the children's activities equations include two proxies for full household income: a dummy for the household being poor (belonging to the lowest income quintile), and the number of appliances in the household. Two other dummies, showing whether the household owns land and whether the household owns livestock, may also be thought of as proxies for full household income, but they are also proxies for returns to work. The costs of education are proxied by three variables: two dummies indicating the presence of primary and secondary schools in the village, and the village-level average monetary cost of school

Table 7.1 Summary statistics

Variable	Definition	Mean	Std. dev.
School	= 1 if child is in school	0.703	0.457
Work	= 1 if child is working	0.086	0.280
Idle	= 1 if child is neither in school nor working	0.211	0.408
Number of children	number of children	3.374	1.336
Child is female	= 1 if female	0.449	0.497
Child's age	age in years/10	0.977	0.252
Mother's education	education of mother	1.374	0.816
Father's education	education of father	1.993	1.321
Primary school in village	= 1 if primary school is in the village	0.457	0.498
Secondary school in village	= 1 if secondary school is in the village	0.441	0.497
Cost of education	village mean of education cost in Rs./1,000	0.660	0.577
Household is poor	= 1 if household income is in lowest quintile	0.559	0.497
Household owns land	= 1 if household owns land	0.669	0.471
Household owns livestock	= 1 if household owns livestock	0.693	0.461
Number of appliances	number of appliances in household	0.912	1.168
Household is Hindu	= 1 if Hindu	0.836	0.370
Household is Muslim	= 1 if Muslim	0.106	0.307
Household is Christian	= 1 if Christian	0.024	0.153
Household is in low social class	= 1 if scheduled caste or tribe	0.370	0.483
First child is male	= 1 if first child was male	0.669	0.470
Mother's age	age of mother in years/10	3.663	0.881
Father's age	age of father in years/10	4.136	1.130
Mortality rate in village	village mean of child mortality rate	0.082	0.029

Notes: Income quintiles are defined over urban and rural populations, although the sample consists of only rural households.
Education costs include expenditures on exams, fees, books, stationery, and uniforms.

attendance. The other household-level variables are the education levels of the parents, and dummies for religion and caste. A full set of state dummies is used to control for geographical heterogeneity. Two child-specific explanatory variables, age and gender of the child, are included in the multinomial logit equations for the child's activities but excluded from the fertility equation.

A dummy variable for the gender of the first-born child, the ages of the parents, and the village-level mortality rate are used as instruments for the fertility equation. It is assumed, in other words, that these variables directly affect the number of children in the family, but do not directly affect the chosen activity of the youngest (eligible) child. The gender of the eldest child controls specifically for the well-known preference for male children in India. The ages of the parents control for the possibility that the observed number of children may not reflect completed fertility, or that there may be cohort effects in fertility. The village-level mortality rate is used as a proxy for the effects of expected child mortality on fertility decisions (see Chapter 2). This choice of instruments is obviously open to discussion, but informal checks suggest that the instruments are valid in a statistical sense.[6] To check the robustness of the results to the choice of instruments, the models were also estimated with subsets of these instruments. The results of these checks are described below, after the discussion of the main results.

7.2 Estimates

Table 7.2 reports the estimated parameters of the truncated-Poisson fertility model. The ages of the parents have positive effects on the number of children, supporting the view that fertility may be incomplete for younger parents, or that there may be cohort effects. Households where the eldest child is male are found to have fewer children (parents need not look any further for a son). This supports the claim of a gender bias in India. Households with more- educated mothers are found to have fewer children. By contrast, households with better-educated fathers have more children. Religion and caste have large and statistically significant effects on fertility.

The dummies for land and livestock ownership are not statistically significant, possibly because they are proxies for both full household income and the marginal return to child work. The cost of education proxies are not significant either, possibly because they are crude aggregate proxies that do not

[6] There are no formal tests for validity of overidentification restrictions in the context of non-linear models such as the present one.

Table 7.2 Truncated Poisson model for number of children

	Parameter
First child is male	−0.060[a]
	(0.013)
Mother's age	0.085[a]
	(0.008)
Father's age	0.048[a]
	(0.007)
Village mortality rate	−0.627[b]
	(0.371)
Mother's education	−0.069[a]
	(0.009)
Father's education	0.010[a]
	(0.005)
Primary school present	−0.031
	(0.020)
Secondary school present	−0.018
	(0.020)
Cost of education	0.017
	(0.011)
Household is poor	−0.099[a]
	(0.012)
Household owns land	0.002
	(0.013)
Household owns livestock	0.047[a]
	(0.013)
Number of appliances	−0.000
	(0.005)
Household head is Hindu	−0.094[a]
	(0.036)
Household head is Muslim	0.140[a]
	(0.040)
Household head is Christian	−0.265[a]
	(0.055)
Household head is low caste	0.041[a]
	(0.012)

[a] The estimate is statistically significant at the 5% level.
[b] The estimate is statistically significant at the 10% level.
Notes: The model is estimated jointly with multinomial logit equations for a child's activities.
Asymptotic standard errors are in parentheses.

capture differences in the actual costs of education within households. The negative coefficient on the village survival rate indicates that an exogenous reduction in mortality reduces the number of births but may increase the number of surviving children.

Parameter estimates and the marginal effects of the multinomial logit model for a child's activities are reported in Table 7.3. In order to evaluate the statistical and substantive impact of the endogeneity of fertility, these estimates should be compared with those obtained treating fertility as exogenous, reported in Table 7.4. The coefficient of the number of children in the equation for idle children is statistically significant and of roughly the same magnitude in the two cases, but the coefficient on work, negative and statistically insignificant in the exogenous case, is positive and statistically significant when endogeneity is taken into account.

The effects of realized fertility are thus different according to whether its endogeneity is considered or not. Although the effect on the probability of being idle is the same in either case, the probability of attending school in the case where endogeneity is allowed for is twice as large as in the case where fertility is assumed exogenous. The finding that the effect of fertility on the probability of work changes sign and becomes statistically significant when endogeneity of fertility is taken into account indicates that the number of children and the allocation of these children's time are closely linked.

The factor loading parameter, λ, is not statistically significant in the idle equation, but it is negative and highly significant in the work equation. A negative value of λ is indicative of a negative correlation between the unobserved components of the choice of work (relative to schooling) and the unobserved components of fertility choice. This is consistent with the a priori belief that the most likely sources of common unobserved heterogeneity between fertility and choice of the child's activities are household-level costs of education, returns to education, and unobserved components of full income. It is also consistent with the finding in Lundberg and Rose (2002) of a negative correlation between the errors of the fertility and female labour supply equations.

The marginal effects show that the youngest child is about two percentage points less likely to attend school, 1 percentage point more likely to work, and 1 percentage point more likely to be idle in households with more children. The presence of a primary school raises the probability of attending school by about 4 percentage points, reduces the probability of being idle by 4 percentage points, and has no effect on child labour. Land ownership increases school attendance by 2.4 percentage points and decreases the probability of being idle by less than 2 percentage points.

The effect of fertility on the likelihood of school attendance is twice as large when the endogeneity of fertility is taken into account than when it is not. If fertility is assumed exogenous, a child belonging to a large household is less likely to work than a child belonging to a small household, but this effect

Table 7.3 Multinomial logit model for a child's activities

	Parameters		Marginal effects		
	Work	Idle	School	Work	Idle
Number of children	0.208[a]	0.110[a]	-0.019[a]	0.008[a]	0.011[a]
	(0.083)	(0.033)	(0.004)	(0.004)	(0.004)
Child is female	1.263[a]	0.719[a]	-0.126[a]	0.054[a]	0.072[a]
	(0.103)	(0.051)	(0.008)	(0.005)	(0.006)
Child's age	-0.920	-9.720[a]	1.041[a]	0.016	-1.056[a]
	(1.552)	(1.019)	(0.137)	(0.065)	(0.118)
Child's age squared	2.519[a]	4.161[a]	-0.526[a]	0.086[a]	0.440[a]
	(0.730)	(0.490)	(0.064)	(0.031)	(0.057)
Mother's education	-0.759[a]	-0.687[a]	0.100[a]	-0.029[a]	0.071[a]
	(0.119)	(0.080)	(0.009)	(0.005)	(0.008)
Father's education	-0.419[a]	-0.461[a]	0.064[a]	-0.016[a]	-0.048[a]
	(0.053)	(0.029)	(0.004)	(0.002)	(0.003)
Primary school present	-0.087	-0.353[a]	0.039[a]	-0.002	-0.038[a]
	(0.159)	(0.089)	(0.012)	(0.007)	(0.010)
Secondary school present	-0.295[b]	-0.527[a]	0.065[a]	-0.010	-0.055[a]
	(0.161)	(0.092)	(0.012)	(0.007)	(0.010)
Cost of education	0.185[a]	0.201[a]	-0.028[a]	0.007[b]	0.021[a]
	(0.082)	(0.053)	(0.007)	(0.004)	(0.006)
Household is poor	0.005	0.105[b]	-0.011	-0.000	0.011[b]
	(0.095)	(0.060)	(0.008)	(0.004)	(0.006)
Household owns land	-0.159	-0.170[a]	0.024[a]	-0.006	-0.018[a]
	(0.100)	(0.060)	(0.008)	(0.004)	(0.007)
Household owns livestock	0.025	-0.135[a]	0.013[b]	0.002	-0.015[a]
	(0.100)	(0.060)	(0.008)	(0.004)	(0.006)
Number of appliances	-0.414[a]	-0.406[a]	0.058[a]	-0.016[a]	-0.042[a]
	(0.054)	(0.035)	(0.005)	(0.003)	(0.004)
Household head is Hindu	-0.518[b]	0.171	0.006	-0.027[b]	0.021
	(0.276)	(0.208)	(0.025)	(0.015)	(0.020)
Household head is Muslim	-0.027	0.900[a]	-0.119[a]	-0.008	0.127[a]
	(0.314)	(0.221)	(0.038)	(0.012)	(0.038)
Household head is Christian	-1.373[a]	0.069	0.025	-0.037[a]	0.013
	(0.529)	(0.366)	(0.043)	(0.009)	(0.042)
Household head is low caste	0.274[a]	0.338[a]	-0.047[a]	0.010[a]	0.036[a]
	(0.087)	(0.055)	(0.007)	(0.004)	(0.007)
λ	-1.256[a]	-0.096			
	(0.407)	(0.164)			

[a] The estimate is statistically significant at the 5% level.
[b] The estimate is statistically significant at the 10% level.
Notes: The model is estimated jointly with a truncated Poisson equation for fertility. Asymptotic standard errors are in parentheses.

Table 7.4 Multinomial logit model for a child's activities assuming exogeneity of fertility

	Parameters		Marginal effects		
	Work	Idle	School	Work	Idle
Number of children	−0.026	0.093[a]	−0.009[a]	−0.003[b]	0.012[a]
	(0.031)	(0.020)	(0.003)	(0.002)	(0.002)
Child is female	1.162[a]	0.720[a]	−0.134[a]	0.062[a]	0.072[a]
	(0.075)	(0.051)	(0.007)	(0.005)	(0.006)
Child's age	−0.675	−9.721[a]	1.106[a]	0.116	−1.221[a]
	(1.382)	(1.013)	(0.141)	(0.092)	(0.120)
Child's age squared	2.207[a]	4.171[a]	−0.565[a]	0.072[b]	0.493[a]
	(0.623)	(0.487)	(0.065)	(0.038)	(0.061)
Mother's education	−0.720[a]	−0.692[a]	0.110[a]	−0.034[a]	0.076[a]
	(0.102)	(0.080)	(0.011)	(0.006)	(0.010)
Father's education	−0.383[a]	−0.461[a]	0.069[a]	−0.017[a]	−0.052[a]
	(0.043)	(0.029)	(0.004)	(0.003)	(0.004)
Primary school present	−0.103	−0.348[a]	0.043[a]	−0.001	−0.042[a]
	(0.142)	(0.089)	(0.013)	(0.009)	(0.011)
Secondary school present	−0.295[a]	−0.523[a]	0.072[a]	−0.010	−0.061[a]
	(0.144)	(0.092)	(0.013)	(0.009)	(0.011)
Cost of education	0.171[a]	0.201[a]	−0.030[a]	0.008	0.023[a]
	(0.072)	(0.053)	(0.007)	(0.005)	(0.006)
Household is poor	−0.054	0.099[b]	−0.008	−0.005	0.013[b]
	(0.083)	(0.059)	(0.008)	(0.005)	(0.007)
Household owns land	−0.155[b]	−0.172[a]	0.026[a]	−0.007	−0.019[a]
	(0.090)	(0.060)	(0.008)	(0.006)	(0.008)
Household owns livestock	0.048	−0.129[a]	0.012	0.005	−0.017[a]
	(0.089)	(0.059)	(0.009)	(0.006)	(0.007)
Number of appliances	−0.382[a]	−0.406[a]	0.063[a]	−0.018[a]	−0.045[a]
	(0.045)	(0.035)	(0.005)	(0.003)	(0.004)
Household head is Hindu	−0.410[b]	0.121	0.006	−0.028b	0.022
	(0.248)	(0.205)	(0.027)	(0.016)	(0.026)
Household head is Muslim	0.196	0.854[a]	−0.104[a]	−0.001	0.105[a]
	(0.276)	(0.218)	(0.029)	(0.017)	(0.027)
Household head is Christian	−1.273[a]	−0.011	0.061	−0.081[a]	0.019
	(0.479)	(0.364)	(0.050)	(0.029)	(0.047)
Household head is low caste	0.280[a]	0.337[a]	−0.050[a]	0.012[a]	0.038[a]
	(0.078)	(0.054)	(0.008)	(0.005)	(0.008)

[a] The estimate is statistically significant at the 5% level.
[b] The estimate is statistically significant at the 10% level.
Note: Asymptotic standard errors are in parenthesis.

is on the margin of significance. By contrast, if endogeneity of fertility is taken into account, a child is significantly more likely to work in a large than in a small household, and the size of the effect is more than double that found in the exogenous case. The effect of fertility on the likelihood that the child is idle appears robust to whether fertility is assumed exogenous or not. Consequently, accounting for endogeneity does make a substantial qualitative and quantitative difference.

Accounting for the endogeneity of fertility has little impact on the effects of other exogenous covariates on a child's activities. The effects have the signs predicted by the theory set out in Chapters 1 and 2 and are of plausible magnitudes. Girls are more likely than boys to work and to be idle. This may simply be a consequence of the fact that the work of girls is more likely to be regarded and reported as work than that of boys. Children of better-educated parents, and especially of better-educated mothers, are more likely to attend school. The presence of a primary or secondary school in the village increases school attendance and reduces the probability that a child works or is idle. The same is true of the village-level cost of education. Ownership of both land and livestock increases the probability of attending school but leaves the probability of working almost unchanged. Families owning land or livestock are less likely to have idle children. The number of appliances appears, on the other hand, also to reduce the probability that a child works.

8

Social Norms and Family Rules

The benefit that a person derives from taking an action may depend on the actions taken by others. If it is not possible for a person to control what others do, it is then in that person's interest to coordinate her or his actions with those of others as in the cooperative phase of the Nash-bargaining game we encountered in Section 2.2 of Chapter 2. If coordination is not possible for some reason, the game is said to be non-cooperative. In the two-person, non-cooperative game portrayed in Table 8.1, each player has two possible strategies: cooperate, denoted by **C**,[1] and defect (not cooperate), denoted by **D**. The first number in the (**I**, **J**) cell, where **I**, **J**= **C**, **D**, is the pay-off, or utility, to the row player, if he plays **I** and the column player plays **J**. The second number is the pay-off to the column player, if she plays **J** and the row player plays **I**. A non-cooperative Nash equilibrium (Nash equilibrium for short) is a strategy pair, such that neither player has any interest in changing strategy. If $T > R > P > S$, the Nash-equilibrium is (**D**, **D**).

A game with this pay-off structure is called a Prisoner's Dilemma, because of the story that goes with it.[2] Two persons are suspected of a serious crime, but there is not enough evidence to convict them. The two are arrested on trumped-up charges and kept in separate cells where they cannot communicate with each other. The police or the investigating magistrate (according to legal system) promise each prisoner in turn a light sentence, yielding utility P, in return for a confession to have taken part in the serious crime together with the other, and threaten a heavy sentence, yielding utility $S < P$, if the prisoner to whom the offer is made does not confess, and the other does. Both prisoners will confess (defect) and thus incriminate each other. This equilibrium is inefficient because each player gets P, but would get $R > P$ if neither of them confessed (if they cooperated).

Prisoner's dilemma-type situations arise in many walks of life. In the business sphere, the remedy is often a legally enforceable contract setting out what each party should do. There are ambits, however, where a contract is

[1] That is only a manner of speech because, by assumption, the players cannot actually cooperate. What is meant is that the strategy denoted by **C** is the one each player would choose if cooperation were possible.

[2] See Rapoport and Chammah (1965).

The Economics of Child Labour. Second Edition. Alessandro Cigno and Furio C. Rosati, Oxford University Press.
 DOI: 10.1093/oso/9780198903000.003.0009

Table 8.1 The Prisoner's Dilemma

	C	D
C	*R*, *R*	*S*, *T*
D	*T*, *S*	*P*, *P*

either not drawn up because it would cost too much, or would not be legally enforceable.[3] We came across an example of the latter in Chapter 1 (resulting in the Baland–Robinson problem), and of the former in Chapter 2 (resulting in opportunistic bargaining). If a mutually beneficial contract exists but is not implementable, we say that there is a 'hold-up problem'. In the present chapter, we show that the problem may be overcome by a family rule, or a social norm, that it is in the interest of every member of a family or society to obey, and have others obey. By endogenizing such rules and norms, the present chapter bridges the gap between the economic approach, according to which individuals make choices subject only to the law of the land, and the sociological approach, according to which there are no choices to be made (because everything is socially determined).[4] In the first section, we examine family rules. In the second, we look at social norms.

8.1 Family Rules

In the game portrayed by Table 8.1, the efficient allocation would be implemented by a legally enforceable contract stipulating that each party must play **C**. In the context examined in Chapter 1, the contract would concern a loan by the parents to their school-age children. As already said there, however, such a contract is not legally implementable. That would not be a problem if the parents were sufficiently rich and altruistic to want, and be able to, give their children the efficient amount of education as a present. It is a problem in a majority of cases, however, especially in a developing country, because parents are too poor to do that without borrowing from the credit market, and to save for their own old age at the same time. As we saw in Chapter 1, the resource allocation is then inefficient, because the constraint that parents cannot take money away from their grown-up children prevents the former from borrowing on behalf of the latter. As we saw in Chapter 2, if that entails

[3] This happens also in the business sphere when it is difficult to demonstrate before a court of law that a party did not comply with the contract.

[4] See Duesenberry (1960).

that child labour is inefficiently high, and the net cost of a school-age child inefficiently low, fertility will be inefficiently high.

The problem would be less severe, or disappear altogether, if a family rule obliging working-age family members to make transfers to their own school-age children and retirement-age parents were in force. Following Cigno (1993, 2000, 2006), we now show that such a rule may be self-enforcing and renegotiation-proof.[5] Let the life cycle consist of three periods, labelled $t = 0, 1, 2$. A person is an infant in Period 0, an adult in Period 1, old in Period 2. These periods of life coincide with Stages 1, 2, and 3 of the decision process examined in Chapters 1 and 2 of the present book. As in those chapters, adults can produce income, and reproduce. Infants and the old can do neither. Compared with those chapters, the model is simplified by assuming zero infant mortality.

Parents deterministically choose how many children n to have by bearing a fixed cost p (corresponding to $p_0 + bp_1$ of Chapter 2) for each child, subject to

$$0 \leq n \leq n^m, \tag{8.1}$$

where n^m is a physiological maximum. Let c_t denote a person's consumption in period t. In the basic version of the model, people derive utility only from their own lifetime consumption. A person's lifetime utility is given by

$$U = u_0(c_0) + u_1(c_1) + u_2(c_2), \tag{8.2}$$

where $u_t(.)$ is a concave function. The model's purpose is to demonstrate that, although completely selfish, people may give something to others, because it is in their own interest that everybody should.

8.1.1 Family Rules as Nash Equilibria

In any given period, a family consists of individuals at three different points of the life-cycle. That is important, because it provides an opportunity for mutually beneficial deals. Differences of sex and other personal characteristics also provide scope for such deals, but we abstract from those to concentrate on the intergenerational dimension. We shall thus assume asexual reproduction and refer to each family member as 'she'. Let us now imagine that a family rule requires every adult member to (i) give at least z units of the numeraire

[5] Analogous results are obtained by Guttman (2001).

good to each of her children, if she has any, and (ii) at least x to her parent, conditionally on the latter having complied with the rule in her turn a period earlier. The conditionality attached to (ii) makes it in every adult's interest to punish transgressors. How will adult family members respond?

The rule faces an adult with a choice of two strategies. One is to disregard the rule and provide for old age by saving (lending to the market, or buying assets) as predicted by standard microeconomic theory. This is called the *go-it-alone* strategy. Given that children yield no direct utility, in period 1, a go-it-aloner sets $n = 0$. Given the adult wage rate w and interest factor r, and normalizing an adult's time endowment to 1, she will then choose how much to save, s, so as to maximize her own utility over what is left of her life, $u_1(w - s) + u_2(rs)$. We shall assume that she has no net assets, but can buy assets or lend to the credit market as much as she likes. Having no other way of providing for her old age, a go-it-aloner chooses s positive. There is thus no possibility that she will be credit rationed. From the first-order conditions for the maximization of utility, we find that a go-it-aloner saves to the point where the Marginal Rate of Substitution of c_1 for c_2 equals the interest factor,

$$\frac{u_1'(w - s)}{u_2'(rs)} = r. \tag{8.3}$$

The value of s chosen by a go-it-aloner is thus an increasing function, $s(r, w)$, of r and w.

The pay-off of the go-it-alone strategy, equal to the maximized value of $u_1(w - s) + u_2(rs)$,

$$v(r, w) := u_1(w - s(r, w)) + u_2(rs(r, w)), \tag{8.4}$$

also is a function of r and w. In view of (8.3), the effects of r or w on the pay-off of this strategy are given by the partial derivatives of $v(r, w)$,

$$v_r(r, w) = s(r, w)\, u_2'(rs(r, w)) \tag{8.5}$$

and

$$v_w(r, w) = r[1 + s_w(r, w)]\, u_2'(rs(r, w)), \tag{8.6}$$

both positive because $s_w(r, w)$ is.

The alternative is to obey the rule. This is called the *comply* strategy. Children do not yield direct utility. If they also comply when they become adults, however, they yield indirect utility, because each of them will pay x to her parent. We will show in a moment that, if a certain condition is satisfied, a complier's child will indeed comply, and that the marginal return to having children is higher than the marginal return to saving. Compliers then have children, but do not save. Being selfish, a complier gives her children and parent only the minimum that the rule requires, namely z to the former, and x to the latter. In period 1, a complier then chooses n so as to maximize $u_1(w - x - (p + z)n) + u_2(xn)$, subject to (8.1). The first-order conditions for this constrained maximization tell us that a complier will have children to the point where her Marginal Rate of Substitution of c_1 for c_2 is equal to the Marginal Return of children,

$$\frac{u_1'(w - x - zn)}{u_2'(xn)} = \frac{x}{p + z}, \tag{8.7}$$

or, if that value of n violates the second constraint in (8.1), up to the physiological maximum n^m.[6] Assuming an interior solution (i.e., that parents stop having children before they reach the physiological maximum) the value of n chosen by a complier is the one that solves (8.7).

The pay-off of the comply strategy, obtained substituting this value of n into the maximand, is a function of w, z and x,

$$v^*(w, z, x) := u_1(w - x - (p + z)n) + u_2(xn). \tag{8.8}$$

The effects of w, z or x on this pay-off are

$$v_w^*(w, z, x) = u_1'(w - x - (p + z)n), \tag{8.9}$$

$$v_z^*(w, z, x) = -nu_1'(w - x - (p + z)n) \tag{8.10}$$

and

$$v_x^*(w, z, x) = -u_1(w - x - (p + z)n) + nu_2'(xn) = u_2'(xn)\left[-\frac{x}{p + z} + n\right]. \tag{8.11}$$

That of w is clearly positive, and that of z clearly negative. In view of (8.7), the effect of x may be positive, zero or negative depending on whether the

[6] The first constraint in (8.1) is never binding, because a complier needs children to survive in old age.

number of children n is higher than, equal to, or lower than the Marginal Return of children, $\frac{x}{p+z}$.

If the pay-off of the comply strategy is at least as large as the pay-off of the go-it-alone strategy,

$$v^{*}(w,z,x) \geq v(r,w), \tag{8.12}$$

a family rule prescribing (z,x) is a Nash equilibrium.[7] If that is the case, the rule is self-enforcing. The best an adult can do, given that her children will comply with the rule, is to do the same. Given that complying has a fixed cost, represented by the amount x that a complier must pay to her own parent irrespective of how many children she chooses to have, a necessary condition for (8.12) to hold true is that

$$\frac{x}{p+z} > r. \tag{8.13}$$

Were it not so, there would in fact be no way of recovering the fixed cost of complying. Given that the marginal return to children is strictly larger than the marginal return to conventional assets, we can then conclude that compliers will not lend to the market. This justifies the assumption that their s is equal to zero.

While making it disadvantageous for compliers to lend to the market, (8.13) makes it advantageous for them to borrow from the market in order to finance additional births. But there are limits to this arbitrage operation: first, because n cannot be larger than n^m; second, because there is no legal mechanism through which entitlements arising from an informal, typically unwritten, family arrangement can be transferred to a third person. Consequently, a complier's entitlement to receive x from each of her children cannot be used as collateral to obtain credit from the market. In conclusion, go-it-aloners do not want to borrow. Compliers would like to borrow, but they cannot.[8]

Figure 8.1 illustrates the properties of the set of family rules that are supported by a Nash equilibrium. Any point on the solid concave-to-the-origin curve through point (z^*, x^*) satisfies (8.12) as an equation. Any point inside it satisfies (8.12) as an inequality. We shall refer to this curve as the Nash frontier. Any rule prescribing a combination of z and x on or inside this frontier

[7] Cigno (1993) demonstrates that this equilibrium is sub-game perfect.

[8] Nothing of substance changes if we allow compliers to borrow without collateral up to some positive amount smaller than xn.

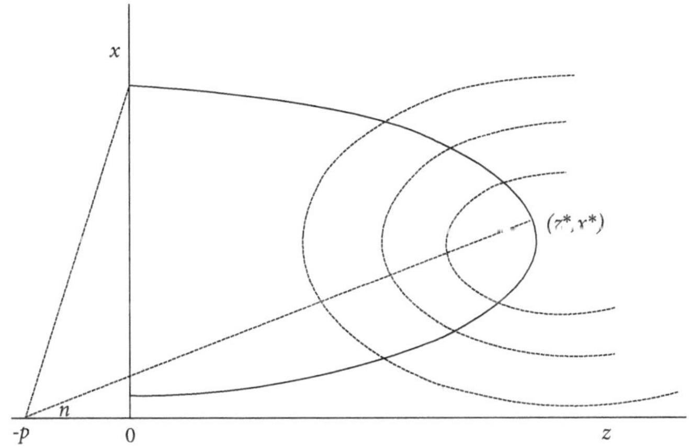

Figure 8.1 The Nash frontier and the family constitution

is a possible Nash equilibrium, and thus potentially self-enforcing. Why has this curve the shape shown in Figure 8.1?

The line joining point $(-p, 0)$ to any point of the frontier has slope $\frac{x}{p+z}$. The slope of the frontier is given by

$$\frac{dx}{dz} = -\frac{v_z^*(w, z, x)}{v_x^*(w, z, x)}. \tag{8.14}$$

In view of (8.10) and (8.11), this slope may be negative, zero or positive, depending on whether n is greater than, equal to, or lower than $\frac{x}{p+z}$. The frontier is thus downward-sloping anywhere above the line with slope $\frac{x}{p+z} = n$, vertical at the point where the frontier crosses that line, and upward-sloping anywhere below it. Given (8.12), the largest possible values of z and x that a family rule can prescribe are thus z^* and x^*. Since young children cannot make transfers to their parents, z cannot be negative. It can be zero, however, because agents are past childhood, and have already received z from their own parents. Being selfish, an adult would thus be happy to subscribe to a family rule that, in period 1 of her life, did not oblige her to make each of her children a positive transfer in addition to paying p. By contrast, an adult would not countenance a rule that did not entitle her to receive transfers from her children in period 2. Given (8.12), the smallest possible value of z that a family rule can prescribe is thus zero, but the lowest possible value of x is positive.

Given that $v_r(r, w)$ is positive in view of (8.5), a rise in r would shift the frontier inwards. Intuitively, that is because r is the opportunity-cost of investing in children. An exogenous rise in the interest factor (or in the availability of attractive investment opportunities other than children) would thus make the set of self-enforcing family rules smaller. For r sufficiently large, no family rule will be self-enforcing. By contrast, a rise in w would shift the frontier outwards. Why? In view of (8.6) and (8.9), $v_w^*(w,z,x)$ and $v_w(r,w)$ are both positive. In view of (8.13), however, compliers save more, and thus consume less, than go-it-aloners. The marginal utility of current consumption is thus higher for the former than for the latter, and $v_w^*(w,z,x)$ consequently larger than $v_w(r,w)$. An exogenous rise in the wage rate would thus enlarge the set of self-enforcing family rules.

Let us now consider the effects of an actuarially fair pension scheme exacting a contribution T in period 1, and paying a benefit Tr in period 2.[9] In the presence of such a scheme, the pay-off of the go-it-alone strategy is

$$v(r,w,T) := \max_s u_1(w-s-T) + u_2((s+T)r), \tag{8.15}$$

and that of the comply strategy

$$v^*(r,w,x,z,T) := \max_n u_1(w-x-(p+z)n-T) + u_2(xn+Tr).$$

The former is the same as it would be without the scheme, because

$$v_T(r,w,T) = -u_1'(w-s-T) + ru_2'((s+T)r)$$

is equal to zero in view of (8.3). The latter, by contrast, is smaller $\frac{x}{p+z}$, because

$$v_T^*(w,x,z,T) = -u_1'(w-x-(p+z)n-T) + ru_2'(xn+Tr) \tag{8.16}$$

is negative in light of (8.7) and (8.13). The policy thus shifts the Nash frontier inwards. Intuitively, that is because the policy hurts only compliers, who are obliged to participate in a scheme offering a marginal return r that is lower than the marginal return $\frac{x}{p+z}$ offered by the family-based scheme.

It is thus clear that an improvement in investment alternatives to having children, or the introduction or expansion of a public pension scheme, would lower the share of the adult population who comply with a family rule, and raise the share of those who go it alone in the market. Since go-it-aloners have no children, a rise in the interest factor r, or easier access to financial markets, is thus predicted to reduce the fertility rate. Evidence of that is found

[9] In the absence of uncertainty, it would be more correct to say 'fair' rather than actuarially fair, but the expression is standard.

by Cigno and Rosati (1992), Filoso and Papagni (2015), and others. Since compliers have children, but do not save, while go-it-aloners do the opposite, an increase in pension coverage (meaning by that either an increase in T, or an increase in the share of the population that is included in the scheme, which in a developing country is typically small) would reduce the fertility rate. The effect on the saving rate is ambiguous. Given that pension benefits satisfy at least in part the demand for old-age consumption, savers will in fact save less. Given that the share of savers (equal to the share of compliers) in the adult population rises, however, the saving rate may rise or fall. This result conflicts with the prediction of standard life-cycle theory, that an actuarially fair pension system reduces s by T.[10]

8.1.2 Family Constitutions

Given that an infinite number of (x, z) pairs may satisfy (8.12), which will prevail? Cigno (2005, 2006) offers a criterion akin to the renegotiation-proofness concept developed by Bernheim and Ray (1989), and Maskin and Farrell (1989). At any date, the adult members of a family are at liberty to propose a new rule. Will future adults take any notice? Not if (i) the old rule satisfies (8.12), and (ii) there is no other rule also satisfying (8.12) that makes future generations better-off. In other words, a rule is renegotiation-proof if, in addition to being a Nash equilibrium, it is not Pareto-dominated by any other rule that is itself a Nash equilibrium. If the existing rule is undominated, the only way an adult can offer her children a better deal, and not lose in the bargain, is in fact to pay her parent less than the existing rule requires, in other words to disobey the existing rule. But that would make her liable to punishment at the hands of her own children. The latter would in fact be better-off upholding the existing rule, which entitles them to pay nothing to their parent, than acquiescing to the proposed new one. Once established, a rule satisfying the double requirement of being a Nash equilibrium, and undominated by any other constitution itself a Nash equilibrium, is thus unamendable. It is then the family-level analogue of what, at the political level, is called a *constitution*, the fundamental law that constrains all future decisions.[11]

[10] A comprehensive examination of the nexus between public pensions and family decisions is provided by Cigno and Werding (2007); see also Fenge and Scheubel (2017).

[11] A political constitution is difficult to amend because it has very stringent revision clauses (qualified majority voting, approval by a constitutional court deputed to ensure that any change is consistent with the spirit of the original constitution, etc.) built into it. As a family constitution cannot rely on any such clause, it must be so constructed that it will never be in any generation's interest to amend it; see Cigno (2005).

At any given date, the adults of the day are only interested in c_1 and c_2, but their children are interested also in c_0. A rule prescribing x and z given w is then renegotiation-proof if it maximizes lifetime utility

$$U(x, z, w) = u_0(z) + u_1(w - x - (p + z)n) + u_2(xn), \qquad (8.17)$$

subject to (8.12). Using the first-order conditions, we then find

$$\frac{u_0'(z)}{u_1'(w - x - (p + z)n)} = n - \lambda \frac{v_z^*(w, x, z, T)}{u_1'(w - x - (p + z)n)} \qquad (8.18)$$

and

$$\frac{u_1'(w - x - (p + z)n)}{u_2'(xn)} = n - \lambda \frac{v_x^*(w, x, z, T)}{u_2'(xn)} = \frac{x}{p + z}, \qquad (8.19)$$

where λ is the Lagrange-multiplier of (8.12).

If the Nash constraint is not binding ($\lambda = 0$), the constitution then satisfies

$$\frac{u_0'(z)}{u_1'(w - x - (p + z)n)} = n = \frac{u_1'(w - x - (p + z)n)}{u_2(xn)} = \frac{x}{p + z}. \qquad (8.20)$$

It thus equalizes the Marginal Rate of Substitution of present for future consumption across generations, and sets their common value equal to that of the marginal return of children and the number of children.[12] In this case, the $(n, c_0, c_1.c_2)$ allocation brought about by the constitution is efficient (it is a Pareto optimum). Otherwise ($\lambda > 0$), in view of (8.11) and (8.10), the marginal return of children is still equal to the number of children, and their common value is still equated to the adults' Marginal Rate of Substitution of present for future consumption. But, the children's Marginal Rate of Substitution is now smaller than the number of children, and thus smaller than the adults' Marginal Rate of Substitution. In this case, the constitution still gives rise to a Pareto improvement, but this improvement is not large enough to achieve efficiency (the allocation is a constrained Pareto optimum).

In Figure 8.1, the dashed curves with slope

$$\frac{dx}{dz} = \frac{u_0'(z) - nu_1'(w - x - (p + z)n)}{u_1'(w - x - (p + z)n) - nu_2'(xn)}. \qquad (8.21)$$

are the contours of the $U(.,., w)$ function. In view of (8.7), the denominator of (8.21) is equal to zero for $\frac{x}{p+z}$ equal to n, positive for $\frac{x}{p+z}$ greater than n,

[12] This property is reminiscent of the 'golden rule of accumulation'; see Phelps (1961).

negative for $\frac{x}{p+z}$ smaller than n. Along the straight line with slope equal to n, the contour is thus vertical. Above that line, the denominator is positive, but the numerator may be positive, zero, or negative depending on whether $\frac{u_0'(z)}{u_1'(w-x-(p+z)n)}$, the children's MRS, is greater than, equal to, or smaller than n. Therefore, off the line with slope equal to n, the contours may be either upward or downward sloping. Given diminishing marginal rates of substitution, however, they will be upward-sloping for $\frac{x}{p+z}$ sufficiently greater than n, and downward-sloping for $\frac{x}{p+z}$ sufficiently smaller than n, as pictured in Figure 8.1. In light of (8.19), we know that the (x, z) combination which maximizes $U(x, z, w)$ given w is represented by a point on the straight line with slope equal to n. If this (x, z) combination does not violate the Nash constraint (8.12), the point representing that combination lies inside the frontier. The allocation induced by the constitution is a Pareto optimum. Otherwise, the point in question lies outside the frontier and is thus unattainable. In that case, the constitution prescribes (x^*, z^*), and the allocation induced by it is a constrained Pareto optimum. At that point, the frontier and the contour are both vertical.

Therefore, anywhere inside the frontier. The solution is a point on the line through points $(-p, 0)$ and (x^*, z^*). The $U(.,., w)$ function may reach its maximum inside or on the Nash frontier. In the first case, the (8.12) constraint is not binding, and the constitution satisfies (8.20). The allocation induced by the constitution is a Pareto optimum. In the second case, illustrated in Figure 8.1, the free maximum cannot be reached. The constrained maximum is at point (z^*, x^+), where the frontier is tangent to a contour of $U(.,., w)$. The allocation induced by the constitution is then a constrained Pareto optimum.

We saw in Chapter 1 that, if the constraint preventing transfers by elderly parents to grown-up children to be negative,

$$mn \geq 0,$$

is binding, child labour may be inefficiently high even if parents are altruistic towards their children as assumed there. If a self-enforcing family rule requiring adults to pay at least a positive amount x to their elderly parents exists, the constraint becomes

$$mn \geq -xn,$$

obviously less stringent than it would be without the rule. Even in the more complex framework envisaged in Chapter 1, a self-enforcing family rule may thus induce a Pareto improvement. If the rule is renegotiation-proof (if it is a constitution), the constraint ceases to be binding. Even within that framework, therefore, the allocation induced by a constitution is a Pareto optimum. The Baland–Robinson problem disappears.

A direct test of the family constitution hypothesis is carried out in Cigno et al. (2006). Using Italian micro-data, the authors find that credit-rationed parents are more likely than unrationed ones to make money transfers to their children. This rejects the hypothesis that such transfers are altruistically motivated, because credit-rationing makes people poorer, and poorer people are less likely to make presents. It rejects also the hypothesis that transfers are payment for unobserved services received, because poor people are less likely than rich people to buy services from their children, or from anyone else. The finding is consistent, by contrast, with the hypothesis that transfers are mandated by a family constitution. Lowenstein and Daatland (2006), and Klimaviciute et al. (2017) also find that the family constitution hypothesis is not rejected by cross-national data.

8.1.3 Altruism, Uncertainty, and Personal Services

Rosati (1996), Cigno and Rosati (2000), and Cigno (2006) consider various possible extensions of the basic constitution model. Allowing for uncertainty (in particular about the survival of children, that in a developing country context is far from certain), turns the prediction that compliers do not save into a prediction that they save less than go-it-aloners, because risk-averse compliers may then save to some an extent for precautionary reasons. Allowing for descending altruism ($\beta > 0$) entails that not only compliers, but also go-it-aloners may have children, albeit fewer than compliers do. The signs of the predicted effects of r, T and w on the fertility rate and on the saving rate remain the same. If we allow for the possibility that parents derive direct utility not only from market goods, but also from their own children's personal services, and assuming that the former are not perfect substitutes for the latter, a constitution will then entitle compliers to receive either a sum of money x, or a combination of money (or market goods) and personal services yielding the same utility as x.[13] By permitting agents to substitute personal services requiring their own time for money, this extension reduces the fixed cost of complying, and raises the marginal return to having children. It thus makes it more likely that a family constitution exists. The argument acquires special significance in a developing country context, where an elderly person may

[13] The same applies to the amount z that a parent must give each of her young children.

well need the assistance of grown-up children for security purposes, and in order to gain physical access to consumption and medical care.

While making the family constitution model more realistic, these extensions do not alter the prediction that introducing or extending a public pension system would reduce the fertility rate, and possibly raise the saving rate. The policy implications will be discussed in Section 9.1 of Chapter 9, and the empirical evidence regarding these effects in Section 10.5 of Chapter 10.

8.2 Social Norms

The approach followed in the last section to demonstrate the possible existence of a self-enforcing, renegotiation-proof rule rests on the assumption that currently working-age agents observed, when of school age, what currently retirement-age agents did when of working age. That is a reasonable assumption to make if the rule is supposed to apply to members of the same family, but not if it is supposed to apply to all members of a large and anonymous society. An analogous approach may be followed, however, if the society in question is sufficiently small for every member to know what everybody else is currently doing. Boyd and Richerson (1992, 2002), Kandori (1992), and others demonstrate that punishing defectors may be the winning strategy, and thus bring about cooperation, in a Prisoner's Dilemma type of game. Ellickson (1994) and Greif (2006) show that a social norm can be enforced by a variety of means, ranging from the threat of ostracism, to that of physical punishment.[14] Acemoglu and Wolitzky (2020) compare the merits of 'specialized enforcement' by the state, with those of 'community enforcement' by ordinary members of society, and derive conditions under which the former is better than the latter at sustaining cooperation.

The emergence of a social norm is often associated with an accident of history or geography, but the norm may persist even when those initial circumstances cease to be relevant, because the expected gain of developing a new norm is smaller than the cost. A pay-as-you-go public pension system introduced by referendum thanks to the vote of the first generation of pensioners, who most gain from it because they do not pay their full share of the cost, will not be revoked by subsequent generations, because the cost of those

[14] For evidence, see Kosse et al. (2020).

'inaugural gains' can never be recovered.[15] Norms may concern any aspect of life, including fertility behaviour,[16] but also social conduct.[17]

Alesina et al. (2013) find that the descendants of immigrants to the EU and the US whose ancestors used the plough are more likely to hold prejudices against women working outside the home than the descendants of immigrants whose ancestors did not experience that technological innovation.[18] That is all the more remarkable because it implies that the descendants of ancient plough users tend to marry among themselves (otherwise, they would blend with the rest of the population). Cigno (2022a) explains this empirical finding by demonstrating that a social norm requiring married men to take responsibility for income production, and married women to take responsibility for the care of the children, is self-enforcing and renegotiation-proof among the members of a plough using agrarian society. He also argues that it is in the interest of those of them who emigrate to a modern industrial society (where the plough is not a relevant factor), and of their descendants, to marry among themselves in order to keep the norm going.

The model is a simplified version of the one in Section 2.2 of Chapter 2. If a man or woman i does not marry, i's utility depends only on i's own consumption c_i,

$$u_i = c_i. \tag{8.22}$$

Normalizing time endowments to 1, i' budget constraint is

$$c_i = m_i + w_i. \tag{8.23}$$

If a man m and a woman f marry, they have a daughter, D, and a son, S (the decision to marry coincides with the decision to become parents). The utility of parent $i = f, m$ then depends not only on c_i, but also on the couple-specific public good represented by the sum of D and S's maximized lifetime utilities, v_D and v_S,[19]

$$U_i = c_i + \beta\,(v_D + v_S)\,, 0 < \beta < 1. \tag{8.24}$$

[15] See Boldrin and Rustichini (2000), and Cigno and Werding (2007).

[16] See, for example, Spolaore and Wacziarg (2021).

[17] See, for example, Tabellini (2008), and Guiso et al. (2016).

[18] Geography largely explains why the plough was introduced in some parts of the world and not in others; see Diamond (2005).

[19] The pain and health hazard a woman suffers in giving birth to a baby (see Section 2.2 of Chapter 2) are disregarded.

As D and S enter their parents' utility functions symmetrically, we are saying that parents do not have gender preferences. The maximized lifetime utility of child $K = D, S$ is a concave function of the amount of money, m_K, that the child receives from either or both parents, and of the child's future wage rate, w_K,

$$v_K = \ln(m_K + w_K). \tag{8.25}$$

People marry if their married utility is at least as large as their unmarried utility. Men and women are matched by their reservation utility, equal to their unmarried utility. In light of (8.22)–(8.23), if a woman called f is married to a man called m, it must then be the case that

$$u_i = m_i + w_i = R, i = f, m, \tag{8.26}$$

where R is their common reservation utility. Consequently,

$$w_m - w_f = m_f - m_m. \tag{8.27}$$

8.2.1 Primitive Economy

In a primitive agrarian economy wage rate or physical productivity differences may reflect gender difference even in the absence of gender discrimination. Given that the plough requires grip and upper-body strength, that are typical of men rather than of women, if this productivity enhancing implement is in use, the wage rate is w^H for men, and $w^L < w^H$ for women. Otherwise, the wage rate is w^L for both. We assume that half a unit of parental time ('attention') is needed to raise a child. If this time can be indifferently the father or the mother's, men have a comparative advantage in income (food) production, and women in child raising.[20] Each adult i is endowed with one unit of time and m_i units of some store of value ("money"), and commands a known wage rate w_i. If a woman called f marries a man called m, the couple's joint budget constraint is

[20] In terms of the model examined in Section 1.2 of Chapter 1, the assumption that mother and father are interchangeable where the care of the children is concerned implies that $t_0 = 0$. Setting $t = \frac{1}{2}$ implies that, if a spouse takes care of the children single-handed, he or she will have no time left for income production. Specialization will be complete.

$$c_f + c_m + m_D + m_S = m_f + m_m + (1 - \delta)\, w_f + \delta w_m, \tag{8.28}$$

where $0 < \delta < 1$ is the share of the child care time that is provided by the mother. The couple Nash-bargain over the division of the utility surplus generated by marriage.[21]

The Nash-bargaining equilibrium maximizes the product of f and m's gain over R,

$$N = FM, \tag{8.29}$$

where

$$F := U_f - R$$

and

$$M := U_m - R,$$

subject to (8.28). In light of (8.24), using (8.28) to eliminate c_m, we find that

$$F = c_f + \beta\,[\ln(m_D + w_D) + \ln(m_S + w_S)] - R$$

and

$$M = m_f + m_m + (1 - \delta)\, w_f + \delta w_m - c_f - m_D - m_S$$
$$+ \beta\,[\ln(m_D + w_D) + \ln(m_S + w_S)] - R.$$

For any given δ, the first-order conditions on the choice of c_f and m_K are, respectively,

$$F - M = 0 \tag{8.30}$$

and

$$M\left(\frac{\beta}{m_K + w_K}\right) + F\left(-1 + \frac{\beta}{m_K + w_K}\right) = 0. \tag{8.31}$$

[21] See Section 2.2 of Chapter 2.

Taken together, these conditions tell us that, in equilibrium, f and m consume the same amount,

$$c_i = c, i = f, m, \tag{8.32}$$

and give K the same amount of money,

$$m_K + w_K = 2\beta, K = D, S. \tag{8.33}$$

If the wage rate is w^L for all, D and S will then receive the amount of money. By contrast, if the male wage rate is w^H, and the female wage rate is $w^L < w^H$, S will get m_S, and D will get $m_D > m_S$. Given that a game analogous to that played by f and m was played, in their time, by f and m's respective parents, it will also be true that

$$m_i + w_i = 2\beta, i = f, m. \tag{8.34}$$

We now come to the choice of δ. Without the plough, the wage rate is w^L for everybody. As it is then a matter of indifference who looks after the children and who produces income, we may assume that f and m will take equal shares in both activities,[22] so that

$$\delta = \frac{1}{2}. \tag{8.35}$$

In light of (8.28), (8.32), (8.34), and (8.33), each spouse then consumes

$$c^{NP} := \frac{w^L}{2}, \tag{8.36}$$

and has the utility level,

$$U^{NP} := \frac{w^L}{2} + 2\beta \ln 2\beta. \tag{8.37}$$

With the plough, the wage rate is w^H for men, and w^L for women. In this case, the opportunity-cost of children is minimized by setting

$$\delta = 1.$$

[22] If they spun a coin instead, that would be true on average.

Each spouse then consumes

$$c^P := \frac{w^H}{2} \tag{8.38}$$

and has the utility level

$$U^P := \frac{w^H}{2} + 2\beta \ln 2\beta. \tag{8.39}$$

Clearly,

$$U^P > U^{NP}.$$

The reason why married utility is higher with than without the plough is not just that this implement raises men's productivity. It is also that, by postulating Nash bargaining, we have assumed that the couple's joint time endowment is efficiently allocated. In a plough economy, men then specialize in income production, leaving the care of the children entirely to women, whose time has a lower opportunity-cost. If men and women did not specialize, their common consumption level would be

$$\bar{c} := \frac{w^H + w^L}{4},$$

and their common utility level

$$\bar{U} := \frac{w^H + w^L}{4} + 2\beta \ln 2\beta,$$

higher than U^{NP}, but lower than U^P. This brings back to mind the hold-up problem we identified in Section 2.2 of Chapter 2.

If the equal-consumption agreement negotiated before marriage is not enshrined into a legally enforceable contract, after marriage, when the children are already born, the husband will be able to renegotiate the deal from a position of strength. Without a pre-marital contract, or equivalent guarantees, a woman will then refuse to specialize in child-raising activities, and the allocation will consequently be inefficient. We have seen that the dowry institution is a partial remedy to this problem, because it stops c_f falling below m_f, but it does not necessarily ensure that c_f will be equal to c_m, and has also other shortcomings (see Section 2.2 of Chapter 2). A better alternative would be for m to pay f her due, equal to c^P, in advance. At marriage, however, m has only got m_m. In light of (8.38), he can then pay her off only if

$$\frac{w^L}{2} \leq m_m. \tag{8.40}$$

That may or may not be the case. If not, another alternative to a legally enforceable pre-marital contract is a social norm saying that a wife must take care of her children, and a husband is obliged to give a wife as much consumption as he takes for himself. Such a norm is self-enforcing, because it is in every adult couple's interest that their son should be able to specialize in accordance with his personal comparative advantage, but their son-in-law should not be able to take advantage of their daughter. The community would thus implicitly threaten to punish a wife who insisted on doing paid work, or a husband who took more than his fair share of consumption. The norm is renegotiation-proof, because no other self-enforcing norm can do better.

8.2.2 Modern Economy

In a modern industrial economy, a high wage rate is the fruit of education and luck, rather than physical prowess. Let child K's future wage rate be w^H with probability $\pi(e_K)$, and w^L with probability $1 - \pi(e_K)$,[23] where e_K is the education that $K = D, S$ receives from f and m, and $\pi(.)$ a concave function. As the expected future wage rate,

$$E(w_K) = \pi(e_K)\, w^H + [1 - \pi(e_K)]\, w^L$$

is now the same for D and S, the two receive the same amount of money, and the same amount of education from their parents,

$$m_K = m \text{ and } e_k = e \text{ for } K = D, S.$$

The (f, m) couple's common budget constraint is now

$$c_f + c_m + 2(m + ep_e) = m_f + m_m + (1 - \delta)\, w_f + \delta w_m, \tag{8.41}$$

where p_e is the price of education. The utility of parent $i = f, m$ is now an expectation,

$$E(U_i) = c_i + \beta\, [E(v_D) + E(v_D)]\, , 0 < \beta < 1 \tag{8.42}$$

[23] In an industrial economy, w^H and w^L may well be higher than in an agrarian one, but we keep the same symbols to avoid introducing new notation.

where v_K is still determined by (8.25). Given that w_K is uncertain, however, v_K is uncertain too, but its expected value is the same for D and S, because both receive the same amount of education. Therefore,

$$E(v_K) = E(v) := \pi(e)\ln\left(m + w^H\right) + [1 - \pi(e)]\ln\left(m + w^L\right) \text{ for } K = D, S.$$

The Nash equilibrium now maximizes the product of f and m's expected gains from marriage,

$$E(F)\,E(M),$$

where

$$E(F) = c_f + 2\beta E(v) - R \tag{8.43}$$

and

$$E(M) = c_m + 2\beta E(v) - R, \tag{8.44}$$

subject to (8.41). Using the latter to eliminate c_m, the first-order conditions on c_f, e and m are, respectively,

$$E(M) - E(F) = 0, \tag{8.45}$$

$$E(M)\,2\beta\pi'(e)\left[\ln\left(m + w^H\right) - \ln\left(m + w^L\right)\right] + E(F)\left\{2\beta\pi'(e)\left[\ln\left(m + w^H\right) - \ln\left(m + w^L\right)\right] - 2ep_e\right\} = 0 \tag{8.46}$$

and

$$2E(M)\,\beta\left[\frac{\pi(e)}{m + w^H} + \frac{1 - \pi(e)}{m + w^L}\right] + 2E(F)\left\{\beta\left[\frac{\pi(e)}{m + w^H} + \frac{1 - \pi(e)}{m + w^L}\right] - 1\right\} = 0. \tag{8.47}$$

In light of (8.45), conditions (8.46)–(8.47) may be re-written as

$$\ln\left(m + w^H\right) - \ln\left(m + w^L\right) = \frac{ep_e}{2\beta\pi'(e)}$$

and[24]

$$\frac{\pi(e)}{m+w^H}+\frac{1-\pi(e)}{m+w^L}=\frac{1}{2\beta}.$$

This two-equation system determines the equilibrium values of e and m. Given those values, (8.45) tells us that, in equilibrium, the parents consume the same amount,

$$c_i = c, \text{ for } i = f, m.$$

Given e and m, the value of c can be calculated using either (8.43) or (8.44).

How is δ determined? When f and m play the Nash-bargaining game that we have just described, they know their own wage rates as well as their own money endowments. If w_f were different from w_m, the spouse with the higher wage rate would then specialize in income production, and the other in the care of the children, but that is not the case. As we said when we were examining the primitive economy, a game analogous to that played by f and m was played, in their time, by f and m's respective parents. As we have just established, f and m have thus the same money endowment, and consequently, if they are matched by their reservation utility, also the same wage rate. Therefore, the equilibrium value of δ is $\frac{1}{2}$. Such an economy is inefficient for two reasons. First, because all children receive the same amount of education, but only half of them expect to derive any benefit from it (remember that, under present assumptions, education raises expected utility only if the person receiving it will produce income when he or she becomes an adult). There is thus educational overinvestment. Second, because, as spouses are matched by their reservation utility, but persons with the same reservation utility have also the same wage rate, there is no scope for domestic division of labour. Consequently, the opportunity-cost of children is not minimized.

Now imagine that a social norm obliging men to specialize in income production, and women in raising children, is in force. Each couple will then give their daughter the amount of money $m_D = 2\beta$, but no education,[25] and their son the amounts of money and education, m_S and e_S, that solve

$$\ln\left(m_S+w^H\right)-\ln\left(m_S+w^L\right)=\frac{e_S p_e}{2\beta\pi'\left(e_S\right)}$$

[24] Assuming no compulsory education. Otherwise, e_D will be set equal to the legal minimum.

[25] That is on the assumption of no compulsory education. Otherwise, e_D will be set equal to the legal minimum.

and

$$\frac{\pi(e_S)}{m_S + w^H} + \frac{1 - \pi(e_S)}{m_S + w^L} = \frac{1}{2\beta}.$$

Given such a norm, all women have the same reservation utility,

$$R = 2\beta + w^L.$$

By contrast, men may have different reservation utilities, because they have all received the same amount of money and education from their parents, but their realized wage rates may differ as a result of chance. The matching will be random. Equity between and within couples will not be guaranteed.[26] As the opportunity-cost of children is minimized, however, the allocation will be efficient.

Having assumed that mothers and fathers are interchangeable where the care of the children is concerned, the same result would apply (with men in place of women) if the social norm said that women must specialize in income production, and men in raising children. Once established, either norm would be self-enforcing and renegotiation-proof. Which will be established? Here, history matters. There was a time when the now industrialized country was agrarian. If the country's geography is such that the plough was not in use, there was nothing to be gained from division of labour along gender lines, and no need for a social norm saying how tasks should be allocated between husband and wife. If the plough was in use, by contrast, allocative efficiency was ensured by a social norm saying that men should specialize in income production, and women in raising children. With industrialization, gender ceased to be relevant. Allocative efficiency would now be ensured if half the children received an education, and the other half did not, because only half the adult population produce income, and have thus a use for education. Which half? If children have different learning ability, and this ability is observable at an early age, the more able children should be educated, and the less able ones not educated. By assuming that, given the same amount of education, all children have the same probability of getting w^H, however, we are saying that learning ability is not observable ex ante.[27] Any criterion,

[26] A woman will consume more if she happens to be married to a high-wage man than if she happens to be married to a low-wage one, because the couple's income will be higher in the first than in the second case. In either case, the wife's consumption may be higher or lower than the husband's, because her reservation utility, and thus her bargaining power, may be higher or lower than his.

[27] In reality, there are ways of reducing uncertainty though appropriate tests, but such tests are best administered by, or on behalf of, the government, because parents tend to overestimate their own children's abilities.

however arbitrary, for deciding which half of the population should receive an education is thus equally valid.

Agreeing to a new social norm has a transactions cost, however, and this cost is higher in a modern industrial society where social and geographical mobility make it more difficult to have stable relations, than in a primitive society where people tend to live in the same place all their life. If no social norm was in force when a country was agrarian, it is thus unlikely that one will emerge when the country becomes industrial. By the same token, if a gendered norm was in force when a country was agrarian, it is unlikely that this norm will be changed when the country industrializes.[28] Does the same argument apply if a group of persons abiding by a gendered social norm emigrate from their ancestral seat to an industrial country? In the place of destination, the immigrants are part of a larger population, most of whom do not abide by the same or any other social norm. If the immigrants' children had the same probability of marrying among themselves, as of marrying with the children of other residents, after a few generations, there would not be a recognizable group of persons with a common interest in enforcing that ancient norm. That will not be the case, however, because the descendants of ancient plough users have an interest in marrying among themselves in order to benefit from their efficiency enhancing social norm. This theoretically explains the evidence found by Alesina et al. (2013).

8.2.3 Gender Discrimination

We sought to demonstrate that a social norm confining women to child raising activities may be self-enforcing and renegotiation-proof, and is also compatible with an equal distribution of the gain from marriage between husband and wife. This does not mean that, in reality, men have not taken advantage of their comparative advantage in the production of income in order to monopolize power within the family and in society at large, and used this power to appropriate more than their fair share of the benefits. It was important to demonstrate, however, that the gendered division of labour is efficient under certain circumstances, because we know from Becker (1971) that sheer discrimination, unequal treatment unjustified by efficiency considerations, is eventually wiped out by competition. It was important to

[28] All the more so, if we realistically admit that men and women are not perfectly substitutable in the care of children (for example, if a child needs at least a certain amount of specifically maternal time, t_0, as assumed in Section 1.2 of Chapter 1), in which case the existing norm is better than the alternative.

demonstrate that also because circumstances may change, and the gendered division of labour cease to be efficient.

The assumption underlying our analysis so far, that time allocation (between work and study in the case of a child, and between income production and care of the children in the case of an adult) does not yield direct utility is realistic at low levels of income and consumption, but not at high ones. As consumption rises above the subsistence level, education may in fact become a good in its own right, instead of just a means for improving one's earning prospects. Similarly, the time a parent spends with a child may become a good in its own right, rather than just a cost. The same may be said about the time a person spends doing paid work. Above a certain level of income, this time may be a source of satisfaction and personal development, rather than just a means to increase consumption.

Certain uses of time have thus the nature of luxury goods. At low income levels, the demand for these goods is derived from the demand for the goods that are produced thanks to the former. At high income levels, however, these goods yield direct utility. As per-capita income increases thanks to economic development, it may thus be expected that parents will start to educate their children of either sex beyond the point which would be justified by the maximization of expected future earnings criterion. It may also be expected that fathers will insist on spending more time with their children, and mothers on spending more time doing paid work, even in circumstances where the opportunity-cost minimization criterion would recommend specialization. According to this argument, therefore, gendered social norms will eventually loosen their grip. If they do not, it is because they have become part of a group's identity and, as such, embedded in its members' individual preferences,[29] or in the group's religion.

[29] See, on this, Akerlof and Kranton (2000) and Cigno (2022b).

9
Internal Policy

The reader who has worked his or her way through this book up to here will have realized that insufficient education, excessive child labour, excessive infant mortality and excessive fertility are different aspects of the same problem, economic underdevelopment. It is beyond the scope of the present book to provide a recipe for development, because that would require us to address government shortcomings, and go into the causes of credit and insurance market imperfections. Taking those shortcomings and imperfections as given, however, the present chapter pulls together the different strands of the theory presented in earlier chapters to determine the optimal mix of internal policy instruments at the government's disposal. The policies that are carried out in practice in developing countries with the deliberate purpose of curbing child labour will be assessed in Chapter 10. External and international policies will be the subject of Chapter 11.

9.1 Child Labour

In a widely influential article, Basu and Van (1998) argue that, if the labour market admits a multiplicity of equilibria, some with and some without child labour, a ban on the latter may be self-enforcing in the sense that, once an equilibrium without child labour is established, a ban is no longer required. The general idea, more fully developed in Basu (2002, 2011), is that, if more than one equilibrium exists, it may be possible to nudge the economy towards the socially more desirable one at (almost) no cost. That is a valuable result, because it implies that child labour can be eradicated without any need for coercion. However, the assumptions under which this result was originally demonstrated are rather extreme. One is that all child labour is observable, otherwise it could not be banned. The other is that the only alternative to working is for children to do nothing. We shall now outline the basic Basu–Van model with some minimal changes that make it comparable with the more general model examined in the final section of Chapter 1.

The Economics of Child Labour. Second Edition. Alessandro Cigno and Furio C. Rosati, Oxford University Press.
 DOI: 10.1093/oso/9780198903000.003.0010

There is a large number of identical firms demanding labour, and an equally large number of identical families supplying it. Firm owners are neither workers, nor parents of potential workers (therefore, profits do not end up in the latter's pockets). Adult labour, denoted by L_a, and child labour, denoted by L_c, are perfect substitutes in the production of the numeraire good ('income') at the constant rate $\gamma < 1$.[1] This allows us to conduct the analysis in terms of a single market for adult-equivalent labour,

$$L = L_a + \gamma L_c, 0 < \gamma < 1,$$

instead of two interrelated markets, one for adult and the other for child labour. The representative firm maximizes its profit,

$$\Pi = F(L_a + \gamma L_c) - wL_a - w_c L_c, \tag{9.1}$$

where w is the adult wage rate, w_c the child wage rate, and $F(.)$ the production function, increasing and concave. From the first-order conditions for an interior solution, we find

$$F'(L) = w \tag{9.2}$$

and $w_c = \gamma w$.

Each family consists of two adults, mother and father, and n school-age children. An adult is endowed with one unit of time, and a child with $0 < \gamma < 1$ units of adult-equivalent time. There are two critical values of w. One, denoted by $\overline{w}$, is the minimum adult wage rate that allows the entire family to survive if the adult members work full time, and the children do not work at all. The other, denoted by $\underline{w} < \overline{w}$,[2] is the minimum wage rate that would allow the entire family to survive if everybody, children included, worked full time. Clearly, $2\overline{w} = (2 + \gamma n)\underline{w}$ is equal to the subsistence level of family consumption. Parental preferences are assumed to be such, that the family will supply $L = 2$ units of adult labour if w is at least equal to $\overline{w}$, or $L = 2 + \gamma n$ units of adult-equivalent labour if w is lower than $\overline{w}$. At or above $\overline{w}$, no amount of the numeraire good could thus compensate the parents for even a very small amount of the child labour bad. If the wage rate falls below $\overline{w}$, child labour ceases to be a bad. Given such preferences, it is not possible to draw indifference curves, and no utility function exists.[3]

[1] We may think of γ as the ratio between the average child's, and the average adult's, human capital endownents.

[2] The original authors do not actually mention $\underline{w}$, but it matters.

[3] Above $\overline{w}$, preferences are 'lexicographic', meaning that alternative baskets of goods are ranked in order of preference like words in dictionary (where Albert comes before Bert, because the first letter of Albert

Figure 9.1 illustrates the possible equilibria. Having assumed equal numbers of families and firms, the quantity of adult-equivalent labour demanded by, and supplied to, the labour market is divided by that number. The labour supply schedule is represented by the broken **SS** curve. Below $\underline{w}$, there is no labour supply, because there are no workers. The demand for labour schedule is represented by a downward sloping line satisfying (9.2). If the line is **DD** as shown, the market has two possible equilibria. One is at point A, where the adult wage rate is w^A, higher than $\overline{w}$, and children do not work. The other is at point C, where the adult wage rate is w^C, lower than $\overline{w}$, and children work full time. If the equilibrium were initially at C, and child labour were banned, the only possible equilibrium would then be A. At that equilibrium, firms would have an interest in offering to employ children at a wage rate lower than γw^A, but parents would reject the offer because, for them, anything other than starvation is better than even a very small amount of child labour. The Basu–Van proposition thus applies. If the demand line were sufficiently more elastic than **DD**, however, there would be only one possible equilibrium, either A or C. In the first case, there would be no point in banning child labour, because there would be none. In the second, a child labour ban would cause starvation.

Even though a child cannot do as much work as an adult ($\gamma < 1$), the adult-equivalent labour force may be several times as large as the adult labour force because, as we saw in Chapter 2, in a developing country, n is typically large. A ban on child labour could thus reduce the supply of adult-equivalent labour, and consequently raise the equilibrium wage rate, by a substantial amount. That is not enough for the Basu–Van result to apply however. For it to apply, the demand for labour function must satisfy

$$\underline{w} \leq F'(2 + \gamma n) < \overline{w} \leq F'(2). \tag{9.3}$$

Given that the supply consists of two vertical segments, one ending and the other starting at $w = \overline{w}$, the demand for labour must be sufficiently elastic for the equilibrium wage rate to jump from below to above $\overline{w}$ as children are banned from the labour market. That is rather restrictive, because the properties of the demand function reflect those of the production function, which is exogenously given, and those of the supply function depend on the number of school-age children, which is predetermined. If the demand is more than unit-elastic as pictured, family income will decrease as child labour does.

comes in the alphabet before the first letter of Bert, even though the second letter of Albert comes after the second letter of Bert).

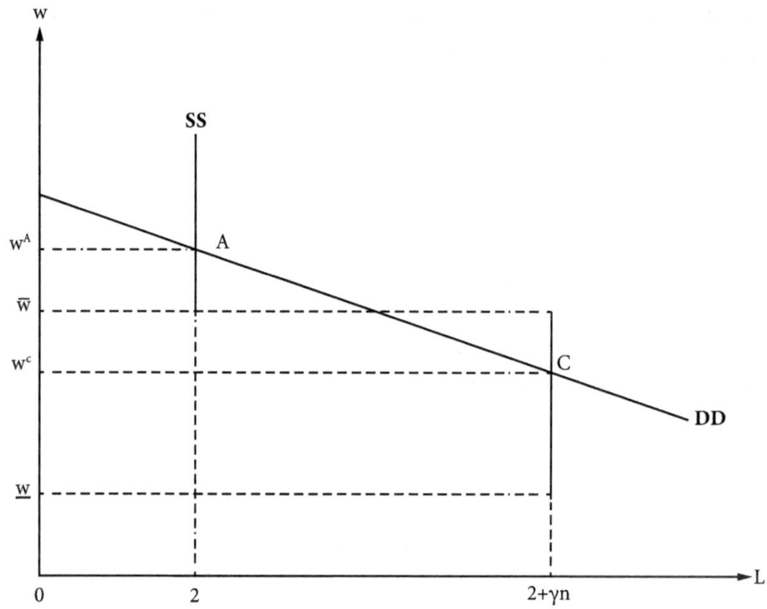

Figure 9.1 Child labour
Source: Cigno (2024)

9.2 Education vs Child Labour

Let us now consider a more conventional setting (a simplified version of the one described in Chapter 1),[4] where children have access to education, and education raises the expected future wage rate. There are two dates, indexed $t = 1, 2$. At date 1, the representative family consists of two adults and n school-age children as in Basu and Van. At date 2, the children have become adults, and their parents are dead.[5] Child labour is still a perfect substitute for adult labour in the production of the numeraire good. Additionally, we make the common assumption that parents regard their children's date 1 consumption as a perfect complement for their own. This simplification allows us to reason in terms of family consumption. The representative firm still maximizes (9.1). Therefore, (9.2) still holds. For comparability, we assume that the demand for labour function is the same as in the last section. If we retained the Basu–Van assumptions concerning parental preferences, the results derived in the last section would thus apply.

[4] The analysis that follows draws on Cigno (2024).

[5] Dates 1 and 2 correspond to stages 1 and 2 of the decision process envisaged in Chapters 1 and 2. Stage 3 disappears, because we now assume that parents do not live beyond date 2.

We saw in Chapter 1 that education may be inefficiently low, and child labour inefficiently high, because children cannot borrow from their parents or anyone else. As explained by Baland and Robinson (2000), that is because children cannot legally commit to pay the loan back when they become adults. In Chapter 8, we found that this problem goes away if a family constitution requires adults to make transfers to their young children and elderly parents. Even if such a constitution is in place, however, parents cannot borrow from the credit market on their children's behalf, because any credit they acquire towards their children by complying with the constitution cannot be legally transferred to a third party. The allocation is thus efficient at the family level, but not for the economy as a whole.

Chapter 1 also showed that education could be inefficiently low, and child labour inefficiently high, even if parents were not credit constrained, because education is a risky investment where individuals are concerned, but not necessarily where society as a whole is. As individuals are many, however, if individual risks are uncorrelated, education is a safe investment for society as a whole, because the average return is equal to the expected return. Given that the probability of an unfavourable educational outcome ($w_2 = w^U$) is conditional on the child's effort and ability, both of which are private information, we can realistically assume that parents cannot buy insurance ('moral hazard' and 'adverse selection' problems).[6] Therefore, risk-averse parents will invest less than the efficient amount for their children's education.

Dessy and Pallage (2001) identify yet another source of inefficiency. The difference between the skilled and the unskilled wage rate (the 'skill premium') depends on how much firms invest in skill-intensive technology, and parents invest in skill-enhancing education. Given that these decisions are taken independently of each other, there may thus be a coordination problem. Firms may not invest enough in technology because they do not expect skilled workers to be available in sufficient numbers, and parents may not invest enough in education because they do not expect the skilled wage rate to be high enough, for their investment to be worthwhile.

Suppose for simplicity that, at date 1, all workers (children and adults) are unskilled. The date-1 wage rate, denoted by w_1, is certain and the same for everybody. The date-2 wage rate, denoted by w_2, may not be the same for everybody. If a person does not receive an education, her or his wage rate will be equal to w^U for certain. If a person receives education e, her or his future wage rate is uncertain. It will be equal to $w^S > w^U$ with probability

[6] This applies not only in developing, but also in developed countries; see Cigno and Luporini (2009), Chatterjee and Ionescu (2012), and Gary-Bobo and Trannoy (2015).

$\pi(e)$, and w^U with probability $1 - \pi(e)$, where the function $\pi(.)$ is increasing and concave, with $\pi(0) = 0$. We shall refer to w^U as the unskilled, and w^S as the skilled wage rate. The probability of a favourable outcome ($w_2 = w^S$) depends not only on school attendance, but also on rest and homework. If a child comes to school without her homework done, or falls asleep during lessons, the child's educational results will not be as good as they otherwise would. We thus measure e as time not spent working.

An adult is endowed with one unit of time, and a child with γ units of adult-equivalent time. At date 1, the family then supplies 2 units of adult labour, and a non-negative amount of adult-equivalent labour

$$(\gamma - e)\,n \geq 0. \tag{9.4}$$

A child's education consequently has an opportunity cost, $w_1 e$, proportional to e. It also has a fixed out-of-pocket cost, denoted by p, which includes the tuition fees, the cost of the essential didactic material, and all those other items of expenditure that have to be incurred independently of how assiduously the child attends school, and how much time the child spends resting and carrying out school assignments when out of school. If this fixed cost is sufficiently high, children may not be enrolled at school.

At date 2, a child's income will be given by

$$y = w_2 + rs, \tag{9.5}$$

where r is the interest factor, and s the amount that the parents saved for each of their children at date 1. Given that children cannot commit, at date 1, to honour a debt incurred on their behalf, and having further assumed that, at date 2, parents will not be around to pay the loan back themselves, s cannot be negative,

$$ns \geq 0. \tag{9.6}$$

Using (9.5), we shall represent parental preferences by the Expected Utility Function

$$EU = u_1(c) + n\left\{\pi(e)\,u_2\left(w^S + rs\right) + [1 - \pi(e)]\,u_2\left(w^U + rs\right)\right\}, \tag{9.7}$$

where c denotes date-1 family consumption. The $u_t(.)$ function is increasing and concave, with $u_t'(c)$ tending to infinity as c approaches the subsistence level.[7] Under conditions of uncertainty, concavity implies risk aversion. For $e = 0$, there is no uncertainty, and (9.7) reduces to

$$U = u_1(c) + nu_2\left(w^U + rs\right). \tag{9.8}$$

If p, r, w_1, w^S, and w^U are such that children are enrolled at school, at date 1, parents choose c, e, and s so as to maximize (9.7), subject to the non-negativity constraints (9.4) and (9.6),[8] and to the budget constraint

$$c + n(p + s) = w_1[2 + n(\gamma - e)]. \tag{9.9}$$

Using (9.9) to eliminate c from (9.7), and appending (9.4) and (9.6), the maximand becomes

$$\begin{aligned} E\Lambda = {} & u_1(w_1[2 + n(\gamma - e)] - n(p + s)) + \\ & n\left\{\pi(e)u_2\left(w^S + rs\right) + [1 - \pi(e)]u_2\left(w^U + rs\right)\right\} + \\ & \lambda(\gamma - e)n + \mu ns, \end{aligned}$$

where λ is the Lagrange-multiplier of (9.4), and μ that of (9.6).

The First-Order Conditions on e and s, respectively given by

$$-nw_1u_1' + n\pi'\left[u_2\left(w^S + rs\right) - u_2\left(w^U + rs\right)\right] - \lambda n = 0 \tag{9.10}$$

and

$$-nu_1' + nr\left\{\pi(e)u_2'\left(w^S + rs\right) + [1 - \pi(e)]u_2'\left(w^U + rs\right)\right\} + \mu n = 0, \tag{9.11}$$

may be re-written as

$$MRE = w_1 + \frac{\lambda}{u_1'},$$

where

$$MRE := \frac{\pi'(e)\left[u_2\left(w^S + rs\right) - u_2\left(w^U + rs\right)\right]}{u_1'(w_1[2 + (\gamma - e)n] - (p + s)n)} \tag{9.12}$$

[7] This dispenses us from imposing a nonnegativity constraint also on c. The function $u_1(.)$ may differ from the function $u_2(.)$ due to time-preference or imperfect altruism.

[8] There is no need for a non-negativity constraint on e because, having paid to enrol their children at school, parents will give them some education.

is the expected Marginal Return to Education, and

$$MRS = r + \frac{\mu}{\pi(e)\,u_2'\left(w^S + rs\right) + \left[1 - \pi(e)\right] u_2'\left(w^U + rs\right)},$$

where

$$MRS := \frac{u_1'\left(w_1\left[2 + (\gamma - e)\,n\right] - (p + s)\,n\right)}{\pi(e)\,u_2'\left(w^S + rs\right) + \left[1 - \pi(e)\right] u_2'\left(w^U + rs\right)} \tag{9.13}$$

is the Marginal Rate of Substitution of c for y. For the Kuhn-Tucker theorem, at the optimum, either (9.4) is not binding, and MRE equals w_1, or it is binding, and MRE is then greater than w_1. Similarly, either (9.6) is not binding, and MRS equals r, or it is binding, and MRS is greater than r.

The partial derivatives of MRE with respect to e and s are

$$\frac{\partial MRE}{\partial e} = \pi''(e)\,\frac{u_2\left(w^S + rs\right) - u_2\left(w^U + rs\right)}{u_1'\left(w_1\left[2 + n(\gamma - e)\right] - n(p + s)\right)}, \tag{9.14}$$

$$- n w_1 \pi'(e)\,A(c)\,\frac{u_2\left(w^S + rs\right) - u_2\left(w^U + rs\right)}{u_1'\left(w_1\left[2 + n(\gamma - e)\right] - n(p + s)\right)}, \tag{9.15}$$

and

$$\frac{\partial MRE}{\partial s} = \pi'(e)\,r\,\frac{u_2'\left(w^S + rs\right) - u_2'\left(w^U + rs\right)}{u_1'\left(w_1\left[2 + n(\gamma - e)\right] - n(p + s)\right)}$$

$$- n \pi'(e)\,A(c)\,\frac{u_2\left(w^S + rs\right) - u_2\left(w^U + rs\right)}{u_1'\left(w_1\left[2 + n(\gamma - e)\right] - n(p + s)\right)}, \tag{9.16}$$

where

$$A(c) := -\frac{u_1''\left(w_1\left[2 + n(\gamma - e)\right] - n(p + s)\right)}{u_1'\left(w_1\left[2 + n(\gamma - e)\right] - n(p + s)\right)}$$

is the Arrow–Pratt measure of Absolute Risk Aversion. Both these derivatives are negative for concavity of $\pi(.)$ and $u_t(.)$. For any given value of s, therefore, the higher is e the lower is MRE. For any given value of e, the higher is s the lower is MRE.

If p, r, w_1, w^S, and w^U are such that children are not enrolled at school, e is set equal to zero. At date 1, parents then choose c and s so as to maximize

(9.8), subject to (9.6) and (9.9) with $p = e = 0$. Using (9.9) to eliminate c from (9.8), and appending (9.6), the maximand becomes

$$\Lambda = u_1\left(w_1\left(2 + n\gamma\right) - ns\right) + nu_2\left(w^U + rs\right) + \mu ns.$$

In this case, there is obviously no First-Order Condition on the parents' choice of e, but the one on s is the same as in the previous case, where e is positive.

In Figure 9.2, MRE and w_1 are measured on the vertical axis, L and en on the horizontal one (the former from left to right, the latter from right to left). The demand for L is represented by the **DD** line, more than unit elastic as in Figure 9.1, tracing (9.2). The **MR** curve traces the MRE schedule under the assumption that the Baland–Robinson, Pouliot, and Dessy–Pallage problems outlined above are all present. There are two possible equilibria. One is at point C, where the wage rate is w_1^C, and children work full time ($L = 2 + \gamma n$). If this is the equilibrium, at date 2, everybody will be unskilled ($w_2 = w^U$). The other possible equilibrium is at point B, where the wage rate is w_1^B, and children divide their time between work and study ($2 < L^B < 2 + \gamma n$).

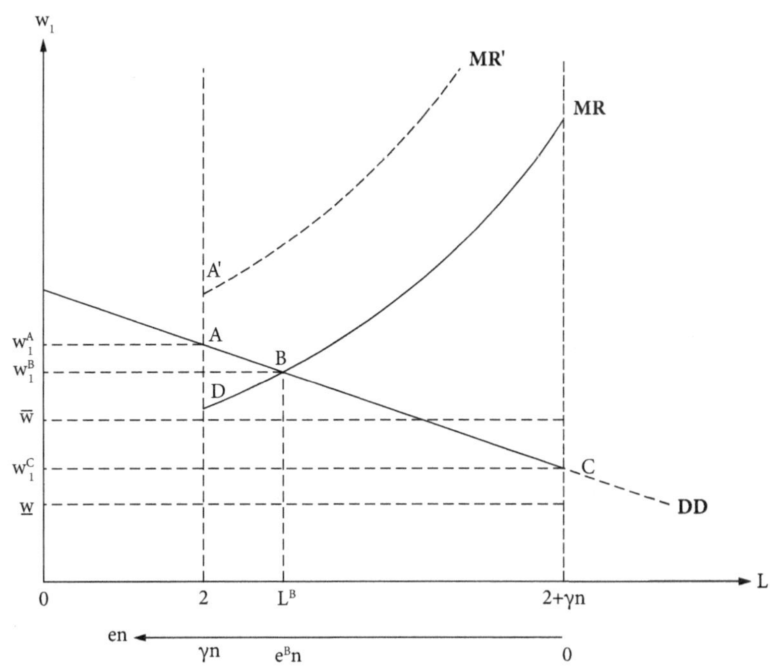

Figure 9.2 Education and child labour
Source: Cigno (2024)

If the equilibrium is initially at C, it can be nudged towards point B, where children work less and study more, by imposing a ceiling on child labour equal to $L^B - 2$. The same result may be achieved also by making education compulsory up to e^B. Once B is established, there will be no further need for a ceiling on child labour, or a floor below education. A partial ban would thus be self-enforcing. A total ban would not, however, because A is not an equilibrium. Intuitively, that is because family income decreases as child labour is reduced. Given that (9.6) is binding for the reasons explained earlier, current family consumption then decreases as child labour does. That would not matter if, above the subsistence level of consumption, parents were only concerned about child labour as in the Basu–Van model. It matters here, however, because parents care about current consumption.

Dessy and Pallage argue that the coordination problem they highlight would disappear if a total ban on child labour were announced with sufficient advance, because employers would then invest in skill-intensive technology at the level required to make the ban self-enforcing. For that to be true in the model we are examining, the **MR** curve would have to move up sufficiently to cut the **DD** line at or above point A. Is that what would happen? If the announcement leads parents to expect an increase in w^S, the numerator of *MRE* will rise. Given that parents are risk-averse, however, and assuming diminishing Absolute Risk Aversion, this effect becomes smaller as child labour and consequently current income are reduced. The denominator of *MRE* also will rise, because the marginal utility of current consumption increases as current income decreases. Indeed, $u_1'(c)$ tends to infinity as c falls towards its subsistence level. Even if the numerator increases, the denominator will thus tend to infinity, and *MRE* tend to zero, as w_1 rises towards w_1^A. The incentive for parents to invest in their children's education generated by the ban is choked off by the rise in the opportunity-cost, and in the parents' aversion to take risks. In conclusion, the **MR** curve may well shift upwards as child labour is banned, but not enough for it to cut the **DD** line at or above point A. For a total ban on child labour to be self-enforcing, it has to be complemented by other policy measures. Let $w_2 = \omega(e^*)$, where e^* is the equilibrium value of e (which families and firms take as a parameter), and $\omega(.)$ is an increasing function taking value 1 for $e = 0$, and value greater than 1 for $e > 0$. Suppose that, at the internationally determined risk-free interest factor, that we normalize to 1, the efficient level of e^* is γ, meaning that the expected return to full-time education is at least equal to the full cost,

$$\pi(\gamma)[\omega(\gamma) - 1] \geq \sigma, \tag{9.18}$$

where

$$\sigma := p + \gamma F'(2). \tag{9.19}$$

The argument that follows goes through even if, as may well be the case in a poor developing country, the efficient level of e is lower than γ.

Let the government announce in advance that, at date 1, it will borrow from the international credit market a sum of money equal to σ times the number of school-age children in the country, subsidize parents at the rate σ per school-age child, and ban child labour so that, for the Dessy–Pallage argument, at date 2,

$$w_2 = \omega(\gamma).$$

Let the government also announce that, at date 2, it will levy a tax

$$\tau = \omega(\gamma) - 1 \tag{9.20}$$

on every skilled worker. The latter will remove the incentive for parents to invest in education, because it will equalize the after-tax skilled and unskilled wage rates. That does not matter, however, because the ban leaves parents with no choice over the choice of e. Parents are compensated for this imposition, because they receive a subsidy σn that covers the full cost of letting their children study full time. Children actually benefit, because each of them will receive, at date 2, a bequest equal to σr, instead of nothing as they would without the policy.[9] In light of (9.18), (9.19), and (9.20), the tax revenue is sufficient for the government to pay its international creditors back with interest.

The government can thus do what parents cannot, borrow on the children's behalf. The reason is that the government has the power to claw back any subsidy it gives to the parents by taxing their children. This is one of those circumstances, mentioned in the last chapter, where the enforcement of a socially beneficial norm is better left to a 'specialized agency' (the government, with its judicial and police apparatus) than to spontaneous community initiative. With the policy, the Marginal Return to Education is

[9] The parents benefit also, because they altruistically derive utility from their children's expected future income.

$$MRE := \frac{u_2(1+rs)}{u_1'(2w_1 + (\sigma - s)n)}, \tag{9.21}$$

and thus certain. In Figure 9.2, (9.21) is represented by the dashed **MR'** curve, higher than **MR**. The equilibrium is at point A', higher than A. At point A', MRE is greater than w_1, because (9.4) is binding, but MRS is equal to r, because (9.6) is not binding. The policy package solves at once the Baland–Robinson problem, because it relaxes the credit constraint, the Pouliot problem, because it fully insures parents against the risk of an educationally unfavourable outcome, and the Dessy–Pallage problem, because it makes families and firms' investment decisions mutually compatible. The outcome is a First-Best Social Optimum.

9.3 Asymmetric Information

The optimistic conclusion reached in the last subsection overlooks the fact, noted in Section 1.2.2 of Chapter 1, that a large part of the work children do takes place within the family. We shall call this 'domestic work' for short, even though it may take place not only within the domestic walls, carrying out household chores, but also in the family farm, or the family business. That makes a difference from the policy point of view, because this kind of work is not as easily observable by the government as, and cannot thus be banned like, market work. Similar considerations apply to education. The government observes school enrolment and can thus make it compulsory. School attendance also is observable, but it is difficult to make compulsory, because children can falsely claim to be ill when they are actually working for their parents.[10] And, even if children attend school, their school performance is adversely affected if they do not allow sufficient time for rest, and for carrying out school assignments outside school hours. That is why we defined e to include not only school attendance, but also rest and homework. Given that domestic work is not observable by the government, we shall then assume that education also is private information.

Let a child's domestic work be denoted by d, so that a child's labour market work is equal to $\gamma - d - e$. Like e, also d is measured in adult-equivalent time units. Let $G(nd)$ be the income produced by the children's domestic work, where $G(.)$ is another production function, increasing and strictly concave

[10] As reported in Fasih (2008), the probability that a child will be absent from school, officially because unwell, is highest at the times when the child's work contribution is most needed in the family farm or family business.

like $F(.)$. If children are enrolled at school, the parents now choose d, e, and s so as to maximize (9.7), subject to the nonnegativity constraints

$$nd \geq 0, \tag{9.22}$$

$$(\gamma - d - e)\, n \geq 0, \tag{9.23}$$

and (9.6), and to the budget constraint which now reads

$$c + n\,(p + s) = w_1\,[2 + n\,(\gamma - d - e)] + G\,(nd)\,. \tag{9.24}$$

Using (9.24) to eliminate c from (9.7), and appending (9.6), (9.22), and (9.23), the maximand becomes

$$\begin{aligned} E\Lambda = {} & u_1\,(w_1\,[2 + n\,(\gamma - d - e)] + G\,(nd) - n\,(p + s)) \\ & + n\left\{\pi\,(e)\, u_2\left(w^S + rs\right) + [1 - \pi\,(e)]\, u_2\left(w^U + rs\right)\right\} \\ & + \lambda\,(\gamma - d - e)\, n + \mu ns + \varphi nd, \end{aligned}$$

where δ, λ and μ are the Lagrange-multipliers of, respectively, (9.22), (9.23), and (9.6). If children are not enrolled at school, the parents maximize (9.8) subject to (9.23) and (9.24) with $e = p = 0$. Except for the fact that e is held at zero, the solution has the same properties as in the case where children are enrolled.

The First-Order Conditions on the parents' choice of d, e, and s are, respectively,

$$\left[-w_1 + G'\,(nd)\right] nu_1' + (\varphi - \lambda)\, n = 0, \tag{9.25}$$

$$-w_1 nu_1' + n\left\{\pi'\left[u_2\left(w^S + rs\right) - u_2\left(w^U + rs\right)\right] - \lambda\right\} = 0, \tag{9.26}$$

and

$$-nu_1' + nr\left\{\pi\,(e)\, u_2'\left(w^S + rs\right) + [1 - \pi\,(e)]\, u_2'\left(w^U + rs\right)\right\} + \mu n = 0. \tag{9.27}$$

Condition (9.25) implies

$$G'\,(nd) = w_1 + \frac{\lambda - \varphi}{u_1'}.$$

Given that either or both (9.22) and (9.23) may be binding, this tells us that the Marginal Product of domestic work may be greater than, equal to, or smaller than, the current wage rate. Conditions (9.26) and (9.27) may be re-written as, respectively,

$$MRE = w_1 + \lambda,$$

where

$$MRE := \frac{\pi'(e)\left[u\left(w^S + rs\right) - u\left(w^U + rs\right)\right]}{u_1'\left(w_1\left[2 + n\left(\gamma - d - e\right)\right] + G(dn) - n\left(p + s\right)\right)}, \tag{9.28}$$

and

$$MRS = r + \frac{\mu}{\pi(e)\, u_2'\left(w^S + rs\right) + \left[1 - \pi(e)\right] u_2'\left(w^U + rs\right)},$$

where

$$MRS := \frac{u_1'\left(w_1\left[2 + n\left(\gamma - d - e\right)\right] + G(nf) - n\left(p + s\right)\right)}{\pi(e)\, u_2'\left(w^S + rs\right) + \left[1 - \pi(e)\right] u_2'\left(w^U + rs\right)}. \tag{9.29}$$

The former tells us that, either (9.23) is not binding, and $MRE = w_1$, or it is binding, and $MRE > w_1$. The latter similarly tells us that, either (9.6) is not binding, and $MRS = r$, or is binding, and $MRS > r$.

In Figure 9.3, the horizontal axis measures market and domestic work from left to right, and education from right to left. The vertical axis measures the marginal return to the three different uses of the children's time. The MRE schedule is again represented by the **MR** curve, and $F'(L)$ by the **DD** line. The $G'(nd)$ schedule is represented by the **MP** line. In the case illustrated, the possible equilibria are B' and C. At B', children divide their time between education and domestic work. Given that only adults work in the labour market, the equilibrium wage rate is w_1^A. At C, education is equal to zero. Children work full time in the labour market, and the equilibrium wage rate is w_1^C, lower than w_1^A.

Suppose that the equilibrium is initially at C. If the government bans child labour, C ceases to be an equilibrium. The equilibrium then shifts to B'. Paradoxically, asymmetric information seems to facilitate instead of hindering the policy, because it makes a total ban on child labour self-enforcing. But, the paradox is only apparent, because the ban does not send child work away, it only sends it underground. Nonetheless, it succeeds in reducing the total amount of time that a child spends working, because it makes the opportunity-cost of e equal to $G'\left(nd^{B'}\right)$, which in equilibrium is lower

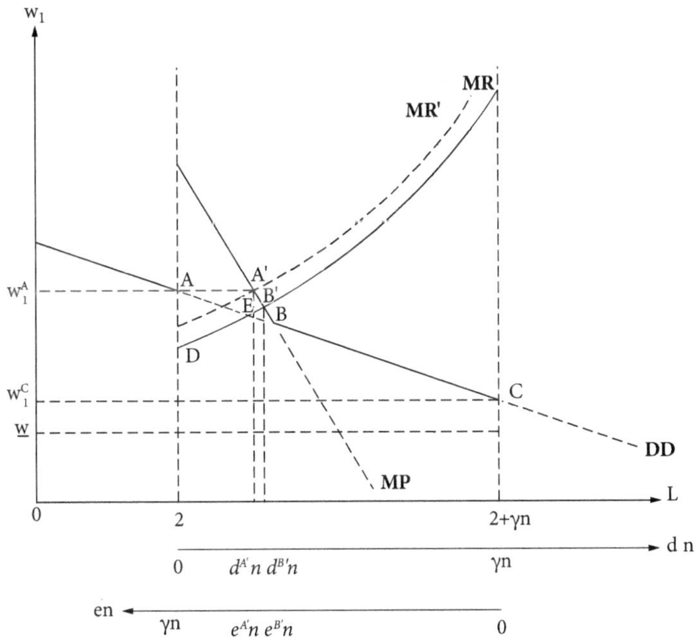

Figure 9.3 Education and child labour with asymmetric information
Source: Cigno (2024)

than w_1^A. Therefore, parents have an incentive to let their children study more than they otherwise would.

Is it still true that a ban on child labour can be usefully complemented by a credit-backed combination of subsidies for parents and taxes on skilled workers as in the case where a child's use of time is fully observable by the government? If government does not observe d and e, it cannot forbid the former or make the latter compulsory. It can only stop children working in the labour market so that

$$\gamma - d - e = 0. \tag{9.30}$$

Suppose that, as in the previous case, the government announces that, at date 1, it will forbid child labour, borrow from the international credit market a sum equal to σ times the number of school-age children in the economy, and subsidize parents at the rate σ per school-age child. At date 2, it will then levy a tax τ on each skilled worker large enough to allow it to pay its international creditors back with interests (we will see that σ and τ are smaller than in the previous case).

Having lost a decision variable because of (9.30), parents now choose (d, s) so as to maximize the Lagrangian obtained substituting (9.24) and (9.30) into (9.7), and appending (9.6) and (9.22),

$$
\begin{aligned}
E\Lambda = {} & u_1 \left(2w_1 + G(nd) - n(p+s) + \sigma\right) \\
& + n\left\{\pi(\gamma - d)\, u_2\left(w^S - \tau + rs\right) + \left[1 - \pi(\gamma - d)\right] u_2\left(w^U + rs\right)\right\} \\
& + \mu ns + \varphi nd.
\end{aligned}
$$

The First-Order Conditions on their choice of d and s are now, respectively,

$$
\left[-w_1 + G'(nd)\right] nu_1' + \varphi n = 0 \tag{9.31}
$$

and

$$
\begin{aligned}
-nu_1' + nr\{\pi(\gamma - d)\, u_2'\left(w^S - \tau^{SB} + rs\right) \\
+ \left[1 - \pi(\gamma - d)\right] u_2'\left(w^U + rs\right)\} + \mu n = 0.
\end{aligned} \tag{9.32}
$$

Condition (9.31) may be re-written as

$$
G'(nd) = w_1 - \frac{\varphi}{u_1'}. \tag{9.33}
$$

With the policy, therefore, the Marginal Product of domestic work cannot be larger than the current wage rate as it would without the policy. It will be equal to the current wage rate if (9.22) is not binding, smaller if (9.22) is binding. Condition (9.32) may be re-written as

$$
MRS = r + \frac{\mu}{\pi(\gamma - d)\, u_2'\left(w^S - \tau + rs\right) + \left[1 - \pi(\gamma - d)\right] u_2'\left(w^U + rs\right)},
$$

where MRS is now given by

$$
MRS := \frac{u_1'\left(2w_1 + G(nd) - n(p+s) + \sigma\right)}{\pi(\gamma - d)\, u_2'\left(w^S - \tau + rs\right) + \left[1 - \pi(\gamma - d)\right] u_2'\left(w^U + rs\right)}.
$$

Depending on whether (9.6) is or is not binding, therefore, the Marginal Rate of Substitution of c for y may still be greater than, or equal to r.

If the government's objective is to increase education and reduce child work, but the government does not observe the former and observes only the market component of the latter, it must then use the policy instruments at its disposal to induce parents to choose a smaller value of d. Given that the parents' choice of this variable satisfies (9.33), and that $G'(.)$ is a decreasing function, the government knows that the lowest possible value of d it can achieve is that which equates $G'(nd)$ to w_1. Therefore, the government will tax and subsidize to the point where (9.22) ceases to be binding. At that point, φ is zero, implying that $G'(nd)$ is equal to w_1. In other words, the government cannot induce parents to reduce their children's domestic work to zero. It can only induce them to reduce d to the point where its marginal product is equal to the current wage rate.

Put a little more technically, given that d and e are private information, the government's choice of policy is subject to the incentive-compatibility constraint represented by (9.33). Geometrically, this means that, with the policy, the equilibrium is a point on the **MP** line. The best the government can do is then to choose σ and τ so that the curve representing the *MRE* schedule becomes **MR'**, higher than **MR**. This curve cuts the **MP** line at point A', where $G'(nd)$ is equal to w_1^A. At this point, children work less than at point B'. The policy yields a Second-Best Social Optimum.

The Second-Best values of σ, τ, d and s are simultaneously determined by

$$G'(nd) = F'(2),$$
$$\sigma = \pi(\gamma - d)\tau,$$
$$MRE^{SB} = w_1$$

and

$$MRS^{SB} = r, \tag{9.34}$$

where

$$MRE^{SB} := \frac{\pi'(\gamma - d)\left[u_2(\omega(\gamma - d) - \tau + rs) - u_2(1 + rs)\right]}{u_1'(2F'(2) + G(dn) - n(p + s) + \sigma)}$$

is the expected Marginal Return to Education, and

$$MRS^{SB} := \frac{u_1'(2F'(2) + G(dn) - n(p + s) + \sigma)}{\pi(\gamma - d)u_2'(\omega(\gamma - d) + rs) + [1 - \pi(\gamma - d)]u_2'(1 + rs)} \tag{9.35}$$

the Marginal Rate of Substitution of present consumption for future income, given the policy. Given that (9.22) is not binding, the Second-Best level of e

is lower than γ. Consequently, σ and τ are not large enough for the policy to fully insure parents against the risk of an unsuccessful educational outcome.

The distance between First and Second Best increases if we drop the assumption that the children's current consumption is proportional to the parents'. Realistically assuming that the way parents allocate consumption between themselves and their children is private information, the government's Second-Best choice of σ and τ will then be subject to a further incentive-compatibility constraint, constituted by the First-Order Condition on the parents' choice of their own consumption level. In order to give parents an incentive to consume less, and allow their children more time for rest and study, Cigno (2012a) proposes to include in the subsidy a 'merit' component positively dependent on education results. In practice, future adults would then be paying the difference (positive, zero or negative) between a tax and a scholarship. In any case, the size and the sign of the overall effect will depend on how the policy is financed. If the net cost of the policy is covered by an increase in general taxation, rather than by an international loan (or foreign donations), the policy gives with one hand, and takes with the other. The overall effect is then likely to be small.[11]

In practice, primary school enrolment is compulsory, and work at a very young age forbidden, in most countries, but enforcement is often partial or ineffective. Subsidies usually do not cover the full cost of education. Is that better than nothing? In light of what we have established, the answer may be no, because compulsory schooling obliges parents to bear an extra cost, and faces them with an additional risk against which they have no way of insuring. Furthermore, the policy distorts the allocation of the children's total work time between domestic and market activities. In a Second-Best policy package, the efficiency cost of this distortion is traded-off against the benefit of a reduction in the opportunity-cost of education. As we will see in the next chapter, however, that is generally not the case in practice. In some cases, the subsidy is conditional on the child actually attending school (for example if it consists in a free school meal). This increases the incentive to attend school, but does not reduce the incentive to work outside school hours. Consequently, as we will see in the next chapter, school attendance may rise, but rest and homework time may not fall by the same amount. Besides, as we will see, many real-life schemes are often small, and never get past the pilot stage. If, without the policy, parents are at a corner (i.e., if their children do not go to school at all), the policy may

[11] If the policy is financed by reallocating public expenditure from other items, it all depends on whether and how those items affect families with children.

thus be insufficiently generous, or not last long enough, to get them off the corner.

Giving parents money and subsidizing education are not the only ways of encouraging the latter. Another is for the government to reduce the opportunity-cost of education by making it unnecessary for children to engage in activities like fetching water or gathering fuel for the home. As we saw in Chapter 4, there is empirical evidence that bringing piped water or mains electricity to the homes of families with children reduces child work. Adding this form of intervention to the government armoury is all the more helpful if the kind of children's work that the intervention makes unnecessary is not observable by the government.

9.4 Fertility

All of this was on the assumption that policy measures aimed at encouraging education, or discouraging child work, do not affect the number of school-age children a couple will have. That is not true in general, however.[12] As we know from Chapter 1, other things being equal, the larger is the number of school-age children n a couple have, the less education e will each of these children get, and the more will each of them work. Except in the extreme case where the expected marginal return to education is lower than the interest factor, therefore, the greater is n, the lower is the utility $U^* (c_2, m + h\omega)$, where c_2 is school-age consumption, m transfers from parents, h adult human capital, and ω the return to this capital, that each of those children gets over what is left of her or his life. We know from Chapter 2, however, that the higher is the net marginal utility $v' (n)$ that school-age children are expected to have for their parents, the larger is those children's expected number. If a policy aimed at raising education, or lowering child labour, raises the net cost of a school-age child, denoted by z, that will reduce $v' (n)$ for any given n, and thus the average n.[13] If that is the case, the policy's indirect effect via n will compound the direct effect. Otherwise, the indirect effect will tend to offset the direct effect. In the absence of direct or indirect child-related subsidies, for example, a ban on child labour, or making education compulsory, would definitely raise z. By contrast, child-related subsidies tend to reduce z,

[12] As pointed out in Chapter 2, fertility is part of the economic calculus at least since Becker (1960), and Becker and Tomes (1979). An early analysis of the policy implications is in Cigno (1986).

[13] The average, rather than the number in each family, because the realized value of the latter depends partly on chance.

all the more if child labour is not effectively banned, or education not effectively compulsory. Therefore, endogenizing n further complicates the design of the optimal policy, especially if parental actions, such as birth control and expenditure on pre-school children, are private information. We are then all the more in Second-Best country.

Second-Best policy is modelled by Cigno et al. (2003) as a Principal-Agent problem,[14] with the government in the role of Principal, and parents in that of Agents, in an endogenous fertility setting (more general than the one envisaged in the present section), where parents are differentiated by income, and the children's consumption (not observable by the government) is not a fixed share of total family consumption. The Second-Best policy is shown to include indirect taxes,[15] and two transfers, one conditional on n, and the other on h. Both these transfers may be positive for some, and negative for others. Given heterogeneity in parental incomes, they thus have a redistributive role. Given uncertainty about educational outcomes, they have an insurance role. Depending on whether h is measured by the child's educational results or future earning capacity, the transfer may be interpreted either as a scholarship for the child or, realistically assuming that a person's lifetime income can be assessed only when this person's parents reach retirement age, as a pension benefit for the parents. Both the scholarship and the pension benefit are effectively a transfer to the parents, because the government does not observe how the latter divide their income between themselves and their children. Both are thus an incentive for parents to invest in their children's education. As in the model examined in the last subsection, the policy redistributes and insures, but not as far as it would in a First-Best world, because it must satisfy the incentive-compatibility constraints represented by the first-order conditions on the parents' choice not only of e, but also of c_0, c_1, and m.

9.5 Social Security

In the first section of Chapter 8, we saw that individual behaviour may be governed by family constitutions, and that the hypothesis is not rejected by the data. We also discovered that compulsory participation in a public pension system ('social security') crowds out family constitutions. Barnett et al. (2018) argue that, in the presence of family constitutions, social security cannot be justified on efficiency grounds, because it replaces spontaneous arrangements that guarantee an efficient allocation of resources, including an

[14] See Laffont and Martimort (2002).

[15] On the role of indirect taxation in particular, see also Cigno and Pettini (2002).

efficient level of fertility, with a mandatory one that does not.[16] It can be justified on equity grounds, however, if different families have different incomes, because it allows the government to redistribute from the rich to the poor (and, we would add, in the presence of uncertainty, from the lucky to the unlucky). In light of the Second-Best policy analysis carried out in the last subsection, the introduction of a public pension system may be justifiable also on efficiency grounds, because it may be possible to trade-off the distortions caused by social security against those caused by asymmetric information. The theory developed in chapters 1 and 2 predicts, in fact, that exogenous (with respect to child labour decisions) fertility changes are positively related to child labour supply. The theory developed in the first section of Chapter 8 predicts that social security reduces the fertility rate and may raise the saving rate. Putting these two sets of theoretical predictions together, it then follows that social security may be usefully included in the policy package to avoid that the fertility incentive provided by other package components will prevail over the education incentive.

Social security has three dimensions: the number of persons included in the scheme, the extent to which each person included is covered, and the extent to which the scheme is actuarially fair. The first dimension (the 'extensive' measure of coverage) is measured by the ratio of the number of persons receiving public pension benefits to the number of persons of retirement age. The second is measured by the average pension benefit received by the persons included in the scheme. The ratio between total pension payments and number of persons of retirement age (the 'intensive' measure of coverage) reflects both these dimensions. The third dimension is measured by the difference between the present value of the expected pension benefit stream, and the capitalized value of the pension contributions paid by each generation at the date of retirement. If this difference is positive, the policy is an implicit subsidy to the current generation at the expense of future ones. It thus raises the demand for all normal goods. If this difference is negative, it is an implicit tax, and its effect is the opposite of that of the implicit subsidy.

Using cross-country data, Hohm (1975) and several others find a negative correlation between fertility and some measure of pension coverage. Nugent and Gillaspy (1983), and Entwisle and Winegarden (1984) do the same specifically for developing countries. Ehrlich and Zhong (1998) and Zhang and Zhang (2004) treat fertility as jointly determined with per capita income growth and household saving (in the case of Zhang and Zhang, also

[16] See also Cigno and Werding (2007).

private educational expenditure). The last two studies contradict each other over a number of points, but concord with each other, and with the earlier studies, in finding that the extensive measure of pension coverage has a negative effect on fertility. As none of these cross-country studies controls for actuarial fairness (and for child benefits, which encourage fertility), however, the estimates may be biased.

One of the problems with cross-country studies is that information on child benefits and actuarial fairness is available only for a limited number of countries. A better alternative is time-series studies for countries that do provide this information. The drawback is that none of these countries can be classified as low income. We now report on a family of such time-series studies that use co-integration techniques to get at the long-term relationships between the relevant variables. In all these studies, fertility is measured by the total fertility rate. Pension coverage is measured either at the extensive or at the intensive margin. The degree of actuarial fairness is proxied by the pension administration deficit or surplus, the difference between annual pension benefits and annual pension contributions. In steady state, this difference coincides with the one between the present value of pension benefits received, and the capitalized value of pension contributions paid, by each generation at the date of retirement. Over a sufficiently long run of years, it may thus be expected that the pension deficit (surplus) in the yearly current account of the pension administration will tend to behave like the surplus (deficit) in the life-time account of the representative individual.

Cigno and Rosati (1992) use Italian time series to estimate reduced-form equations for saving and fertility. The paper shows that the pension deficit has no significant impact on fertility, but pension coverage has a strong negative one. Controlling for capital markets (which also compete with family transfer systems for the provision of old-age security) accessibility, the paper finds that as much as three-quarters of the total fertility reduction which occurred between 1930 and 1984 can be attributed to the increase in the proportion of the population covered by mandatory pension arrangements. This confirms the role not only of social security, but also of capital markets, as an alternative to intra-family arrangements. Foster and Rosenzweig (2000) find the same for a developing country. Controlling for per capita household income, or male and female wage rates, and for the interest rate (proxied by the yield on long-dated government bonds), Cigno and Rosati (1996, 1997) find similar effects to Cigno and Rosati (1992) in the post-war time series of West Germany, Italy, Japan, the UK, and the USA. The male wage rate (or household income) is found to affect fertility positively, and the female wage rate to affect it negatively. This is as family constitution theory predicts. The effect of the interest rate is negative in some countries as family constitution theory predicts, but positive in others. Where data are available, the fertility effect of the child benefit rate (equivalent to that of a reduction in the fixed cost of a child) is found to be positive as the theory predicts.

In all these studies, the saving and fertility equations are estimated separately. Cigno et al. (2003) redo the analysis in Cigno and Rosati (1992) for West Germany only using VAR (Vector Autoregressive) methods, which allow for all possible interactions among the variables concerned, without any a priori assumption about the direction of causation. The econometric analysis establishes that causality runs from social security policy to fertility, and confirm that this effect is negative. These findings relate to developed economies, but are consistent with those, already mentioned, concerning developing economies. Similar results are obtained using either macro or micro data by several other authors, including Gabos et al. (2009), Galasso et al. (2009), Billari and Galasso (2014), Boldrin, De Nardi and Jones (2015), Fenge and Scheubel (2017), and Danzer and Zyska (2023). The last one is especially relevant for our discourse, because it refers to a middle-income country, Mexico, rather than to developed countries like the rest.

Like the direct tests of the family constitution model reported at the end of the first section of Chapter 8, these empirical findings are evidence that family constitutions exist. They also validate the policy implication that introducing or extending a public pension system in a developing country would reduce fertility, and thus help trigger a demographic transition,[17] without incurring the negative consequences of compulsory measures like forced sterilization, or fertility penalties, already mentioned in Chapter 2. As Zhang and Zhang (2004) conclude from their cross-country analysis, 'social security may indeed be conducive to growth through tipping the trade-off between the number and quality of children toward the latter'.

[17] In developed countries past the demographic transition, the problem is not excessive, but rather insufficient fertility. In these countries, the fertility effect of social security has to be tempered by policy measures aimed at restoring the incentive to have children; see Cigno and Werding (2007).

10 Impact Evaluation of Child Labour Reduction Policies

This chapter presents evidence on the effectiveness of policies aimed at reducing child labour, and on the unintended effects of policies designed with different aims in mind. The former tend to have the intended results, but these are often disappointingly small. In some cases, they are actually counterproductive. As the quotation of Carlos Puebla warns us, well-intentioned actions can backfire. That is small wonder in view of the fact that, as anticipated in the last chapter, actual policies tend to fall short of the recommendations that come from economic theory. In particular, they overlook the complex interactions that exist between fertility, education, and other forms of investment decisions. We shall restrict our attention to empirical studies that can reasonably claim to have identified a causal link between ends and means.

10.1 Legislation and Regulation

Setting legal standards with respect to child labour is often the first step towards a commitment to eliminate child labour. The question is whether such restrictions actually reduce child labour and raise welfare. There is some evidence of the former, but little of the latter. We begin our discussion from the highest source of law, international conventions. The ratification of an international convention commits a government to take all the measures that are necessary to realize the aim of that convention. In the case of child labour, two international conventions are particularly important: ILO convention 138 on minimum working age, and ILO convention 182 on the worst forms of child labour. Of course, it is very challenging to identify a counterfactual to the signing of a convention, and this has substantially limited the scope for sound empirical analysis.

Boockmann (2010) addresses the question using cross-country data and individual datasets for a subset of countries, focusing on the ratification of

The Economics of Child Labour. Second Edition. Alessandro Cigno and Furio C. Rosati, Oxford University Press.

DOI: 10.1093/oso/9780198903000.003.0011

minimum age conventions. As the author himself admits, the identification strategy adopted in the paper is not fully convincing. In the analysis of individual data, school attendance is used as a proxy for child labour. Given that most of the children in the sample work and attend school, this approach could be flawed by substantial measurement errors. The results of the exercise indicate that the ratification of a convention on minimum work age does not have an impact on child labour. Edmonds and Shrestha (2012) also make use of cross-country data. They use individual data for 59 countries drawn from the broadly comparable MICS-UNICEF surveys. They do not look at the possible impact of convention ratification, but at that of national minimum age legislation. In order to have enough variability in the data, they look, in particular, at the minimum age for light work. Minimum age restrictions typically apply only to work for pay and not to work in the family farm or business. If labour markets were perfect and adult and child labour had a similar productivity (up to a constant), then an increase in the minimum age for (light) work would not have any income effect. It would only reallocate child work from work for pay to work within the household economic activity, with a specular reallocation of adult labour. If labour markets are not perfect, or adult and child labour are intrinsically different (e.g., only children or only adults can perform certain tasks), minimum age legislation can generate an income effect affecting the overall supply of child labour. The authors find that an increase in the minimum age for (light) work does not reduce work for pay, nor does it increase work within the household, and conclude that minimum age legislation is not actually enforced. We know from Chapter 1, however, that the observed ineffectiveness of minimum age legislation may reflect labour or credit market imperfection, rather than imperfect enforcement.

The identification of child labour legislation effects using cross-country data as in the two studies we have just looked at suffers from the difficulty of building a credible counterfactual. We turn thus to the discussion country-based studies, where a counterfactual is easier to build. The work of Bharadwaj et al. (2020) on India provides a useful starting point for our discussion, as it also allows us to focus on what happens when a ban is not self-enforcing (i.e., as explained in the last chapter, the policy does not move the economy from an equilibrium with, to an equilibrium without or with less child labour). They focus on the 1986 Child Labour Act, which banned employment of children under the age of 14 in some occupations and industries. The ban, however, did not extend to agriculture, or to family run businesses. The data come from several rounds of the National Sample Survey employment schedule. It is important to note that such a survey identifies an individual's occupation of the basis of the person's 'main activity', implying that children working, attending school, or performing household chores belong to mutually exclusive categories. Given the relative large number of children who both work and attend school, this makes the estimates difficult to interpret.

The authors follow two approaches to identify the effects of the legislation. The first is a simple Difference-In-Difference (DID) procedure comparing children below 14 years of age affected by the legislation, with those who are not affected. The second compares children with siblings aged 10 to 13 potentially affected by the change in legislation, with children who have siblings younger than 10 or older than 13. The results show that the introduction of more restrictive child labour legislation did increase children's labour participation in both banned and not banned occupations, with the most relevant increase in the latter. Both paid and unpaid work activity increased, but the largest effect was on paid activities. The estimates that use the sibling sample show also a significant decrease in children declaring that attending school is their main occupation. These results can be rationalized in the context of a partial ban fully enforced only where households below or close to the subsistence level are concerned. If the partial or total ban is not fully enforced, employers may continue to hire children despite the risk of a fine or other punishment. The latter can be thought of as a tax on the employment of children in selected occupations. If the supply of child labour is in its inelastic range (i.e., if the solution is at a corner where the use of the children's time is concerned; see Chapter 1), the 'tax' is fully borne by the family. Given that adults already supply as much work as they can, as the child wage rate is reduced by the ban, children will then need to work more in order to meet the family's subsistence requirements.

Of course, wage information is available only for individuals who are formally employed or doing casual work, not for individuals who work within the family farm or family business. The use of wage data thus suffers from a selection problem that is particularly important in low- and middle-income countries. With this limitation in mind, it is interesting to note that the estimates show a substantial reduction in observed children's wage rates following the introduction of the legislation. This lends credibility to the just discussed interpretation of the empirical results. Bharadwaji et al. (2020) give a preliminary look also at the impact of legislation on household welfare, using different indicators relative to expenditure, quality calories intake, and assets. Coherently with their explanatory framework, they find a small but significant reduction in the intake of quality calories, and in asset holdings.

Somewhat different results are obtained in studies that look at the change in the Constitution of Brazil introduced in 1998, which raised the minimum employment age from 14 to 16 years. Both Bargain and Boutin (2021) and Piza and Souza (2017) look at the Brazilian experience but with different conclusions. Piza and Souza (2017) employ a DID approach comparing children who turned 14 after the change in legislation with those who turned 14 before that. They find that the change in legislation reduced the labour force participation of boys, but not of girls. They find that this effect is driven by the impact on children working in the informal sector and not on those working in the formal sector. This is somehow surprising, as one would expect the legislation to produce larger effects on firms that operate in the formal sector, where monitoring is more likely. The definition of informality is always complex. The authors define as formally employed individuals who have a working permit issued by the Ministry of Labour. They argue that firms hiring children informally might be worried about fines, but the chance of verification by the authorities might be reduced by the change in legislation, which made it impossible for children below the age of 16 to obtain a work permit. While this can explain the reduction in the number of children hired informally, it does not explain why we do not observe any reduction in the number of children hired formally.

Bargain and Boutin (2021) study the effect of the same change in legislation using a Regression Discontinuity, and a Difference in Discontinuity approach, the latter being their preferred approach. They find that, overall, the change in legislation had no impact on child labour. However, the effect seems to depend on the probability of receiving an inspection, and on the characteristics of the work performed by the children. Where children who work in 'visible' activities (mainly work for pay) are concerned, in states where the inspection rate is above the national average, it is possible to identify a significant reduction in the number of working children. Verifiability of the activity carried out by the children, and propensity on the part of the authorities to actually carry out inspections, appear to be the crucial elements for the effectiveness of legislation. Neither of the two papers on Brazil looks at the impact of legislation on any measure of the welfare of the household.

The desire on the part of firms to avoid inspections, and their preference for informal labour relations, appear to have played an important role also in the case of Bolivia, where we observe that a reduction in the age at which children can be employed has in fact reduced child labour. The case of Bolivia is interesting as this is the only country that in the recent past has reduced the minimum age of employment. In 2014, the Government of Bolivia approved legislation that reduced the minimum working age, from 14 to 10. Specifically, the law allowed children older than 12 to work for others provided that they acquire a work permit, while simultaneously extending benefits and protections to child workers. For example, the law entitled working children to the same minimum wages that applied to adult labour, and to two hours of pay per day to devote to school or study. The law also allowed children between the ages of 10 and 12 to work on their own account. To ensure enforcement, the government tasked local child advocacy offices, *Defensorias de la Ninez y Adolescencia* (DNAs), with issuing work permits, and local offices of the Ministry of Labour with adding child labour inspections to their regular labour and workplace inspections. Following national and international pressure the legislation was retracted in 2018.

Lakdawala et al. (2023) evaluate the Bolivian expereience using a difference-in-discontinuity approach that takes advantage of differences in the age groups affected by the legislation. The results show that, as a consequence of the law, there was a decrease in child labour both at the intensive and at the extensive margin. The decrease was mainly due to the reduction in work for pay outside the household in the sectors were child labour was allowed, subject to obtaining a work permit. To validate their results, they look at the consequence of the abolition of the law in 2018, that brought the minimum age for work back 14 years. The results indicate an increase in child labour following the increase in minimum age at both the intensive and the extensive margin, due mainly to an increase in work outside of the household. As already mentioned, the legislation not only allowed children below the age of 14 to work but also instituted and promoted a system of controls to ensure that the children's rights at work were respected. Moreover, to work legally, children had to obtain a work permit. The salience of the regulation of child labour and the ensuing probability of inspections might have made informal firms (where most of the children work) reluctant to hiring children to avoid inspections that might results in heavy fines. The authors corroborate such a hypothesis with estimates showing that the reduction in child labour was mainly observed in areas close to the office of the Ministry of Labour and so more likely to be the object of an inspection.

The evidence on the effects of legislation and similar measures is not conclusive, as we have seen. The adoption of international instruments, like the ILO conventions on minimum working age do not appear to have had any direct effect on child labour. The validity of this result, however, is limited by the identification problem that makes it difficult to build a solid counterfactual. Moreover, underwriting the international convention could reflect a general commitment to deal with child labour, but actual action followed with substantial delay. Hence, the effect may not be captured by estimates that use the year of ratification as the date of treatment. Adoption of national minimum age legislation also does not appear to have affected child labour. The cross-country study discussed indicates that no substantial impact could be identified. The picture changes when we look at individual country experiences. The results are not concordant, but two elements emerge as critical in determining the effect of child labour legislation: the possible effect on household income and the role of enforcement.

Given the non-perfect enforceability of the legislation, that in any case only applies to work outside the household, all the studies considered view the introduction or tightening of minimum age, and other child labour legislation, as a tax on hiring children. The incidence of the tax depends on the probability of receiving an inspection. In the case of India, the (not tested) reduction in the wages paid to children is seen as the reason that pushed households close to subsistence to increase children's labour supply. In the case of Brazil, the authors link the small observed reduction in child labour to the desire on the part of firms to avoid controls. As we have seen, the reduction in child labour appears to be significant only in areas where the probability of an inspection is higher. Similarly, in the case of Bolivia, it is the desire to avoid inspections and controls that appears to generate the reduction in child labour following a reduction in the minimum age of employment, and the formalization of child employment. While it is difficult to draw general conclusions from the studies discussed given their limited external validity, the results clearly identify the channels which determine the effects of child labour legislation and can thus be used as guidelines to assess the efficacy of policy measures in this subject area.

10.2 Cash Transfers

Cash transfers are widely used to address household vulnerability and promote specific activities like human capital investment. In some schemes, the transfer is in kind. In the vast majority of cases, however, the transfer is in cash. Only a small number of these schemes are explicitly targeted at reducing child labour. They come in two forms. Unconditional cash transfers (UCT) provide support to households normally on a means tested base. Conditional cash transfers (CCT) schemes require, besides meeting certain eligibility criteria, compliance with certain behavioural conditions, generally in terms of school attendance or health care.

10.2.1 Unconditional Cash Transfers

Not being associated with any behavioural requirement, UCT is the policy instrument that most closely resembles a lump-sum transfer. It should thus produce a pure income effect. Increasing the resources available to households supplying an inefficiently high level of child labour should have a negative effect on children's employment. However, the results obtained from several impact evaluations are far from unambiguous. Two relatively recent studies (de Hoop and Rosati 2014 and Dammert, de Hoop, Mvukiyehe, and Rosati 2018) review in some detail the various impact evaluations that have been carried out. They show that both negative, null, and positive impacts on child labour have been observed. Here is a non-exhaustive list of examples. The *Bono de Desarrollo Umano* implemented by the Ecuador Government reduced child labour, while the Malawi Social Cash transfer scheme reallocated child labour from work for pay to work within the household. More recently, Meza-Cordero (2023) analysed the pilot *Niños, Niñas y Adolescents Trabajadores* programme implemented by the Government of Costa Rica. He finds that the programme did not change the children's work participation rate, but marginally reduced the number of hours worked. Chong and Yáñez-Pagans (2019) find that a cash transfer implemented in Bolivia increased child labour.

It is obviously difficult to compare the results of different impact evaluations and to understand what might have generated the difference in the results. Such differences can be due to several factors and are in general linked to the limited external validity of the impact evaluation themselves. For example, the amount of the transfer as well as the delivery modality differ across programmes. The criteria utilized for the selection of beneficiaries also differ, as do other implementation characteristics. Also the outcome of interest, child labour in our case, can be defined differently, especially as child labour is very often not the main focus of the impact evaluations. Moreover, given the limited number of impact evaluations dealing with child labour for each type of programme, it is not possible to carry out a robust meta-analysis. There are, however, two aspects that might contribute to explain the observed differences in the impact of unconditional cash transfers. The first refers to the possible non-linearity of the income effects, the second to the fact that the transfer might be used in a way that will alter the returns to child labour. We will address these two issues in turn.

As already mentioned, in principle, UCT should generate a pure income effect leading parents to increase the investment in their children's human capital, and to reduce child labour supply. However, cross-sectional and cross-country studies do not identify a substantial child labour income elasticity. Edmonds (2005) suggests that this can be due to endogeneity problems, and also to the inherent nonlinearity in the relationship between child labour and income. This is consistent with the theory set out in Chapter 1, but the empirical evidence is not very large. Edmonds (2005) shows that the effect of the increase in income in Vietnam, between 1993 and 1998, was present mainly for the households that moved from below to above the poverty line. Pellerano, Porreca, and Rosati (2020) find that the income elasticity of child labour is null for extremely poor households, becomes negative and decreasing in income for relatively less poor households, and is again zero in the more affluent households where children do not work at all.

Only Pellerano, Porreca, and Rosati (2020) provide evidence on the nonlinear relationship between child labour and income in the context of an UCT impact evaluation. In particular, they study the effect of the Child Grant Program (CGP) introduced in 2009 by the Ministry of Social Development of the Government of Lesotho, an UCT aimed to support poor and vulnerable households with children. The main goal of CGP 'is to improve the living standards of Orphans and Other Vulnerable Children (OVC) so as to reduce malnutrition, improve health status and increase school enrolment among OVCs'.[1] The programme did not include any conditionality, but a form of 'nudging' about the use of funds, as the beneficiaries received at each payment round the message that the transfer should be spent in the interest and for the needs of children. The analysis exploits the random allocation of Phase 1–Round 2 of the programme. Because of lack of financial resources, it was decided to randomly choose beneficiary households among the eligible ones. Since there were a total of 96 Electoral Divisions (EDs), 48 EDs were randomly assigned to the treatment group, and 48 to the control group in public lottery events. Eligibility criteria were based on a combination of Proxy Means Testing (PMT) and community validation. Eligible households were selected in both treatment and control EDs, but the transfer was provided only to households living in treatment EDs, thus leading to a valid control group.

Given the satisfactory randomization process, as also confirmed by the balance test, Pellerano, Porreca, and Rosati (2020) estimate a simple OLS model for a set of children outcomes. The results for all the beneficiaries indicate that the programme increased school enrolment, without any effect on child labour. Participation in economic activities did not change and there was a marginally significant decrease in days and hours worked in

[1] Manual of operation in use for round 1A of the CGP pilot. November 2008.

agricultural activities. Treated children were more likely to be enrolled in school and spent six minutes more doing homework on a typical school day, an increase of 4% in enrolment rate and of 13% in time spent studying with respect to pre-treatment values. Involvement in economic activities did not decrease. The transfer not only increased school attendance, but also increased expenditures for school uniforms and shoes by a large amount.

The results look rather different if one considers household heterogeneity by level of income. The transfer appears to affect children's time allocation only for the relatively less poor households. The latter experience a 17% reduction in the participation of children to economic activities. The amount of time devoted to work declines by almost one day in the top quartile. These effects are not present in the first three quartiles of the expenditure distribution. Also, the increase in school enrolment, time spent studying, and school expenditures on fees is larger for children belonging to the highest quartile (14% points on school enrolment, 9 minutes on studying, and about M 150 on expenditure on school fees), but statistically insignificant for children belonging to the first three quartiles. However, the lower the pre-treatment income of the household, the higher the increase in school expenditure on uniforms and shoes. In light of the theoretical model set out in Chapter 1, this tells us that, if transfers are not large enough to move the household from a corner to an interior solution, unconditional cash transfers might prove ineffective in altering child labour and school participation. This can be seen very clearly by looking at Figures 1.5 or 1.6 of Chapter 1. If the production point **P** is at the corner where children work full-time because the interest factor r (and thus the marginal return to conventional forms of investment, or to lending) is high, a lump-sum subsidy shifting the frontier to the right would raise welfare but would have no effect on child labour. For the latter to fall, the marginal return to education would have to rise by a sufficiently large amount. Recent evidence (Balboni, Bandiera, Burgess, et al. 2022) reveals the presence of poverty traps and emphasizes the need for 'big push' interventions to help people escape from those traps. This implies, among other things, that policies aimed at child labour could only be effective if they have a minimum scale.

Another factor that can contribute to explaining the wide range of results observed in terms of impact of cash transfers is that the latter might not be used only for consumption and education, but also to invest in productive assets. As we know from Chapter 1, if the expected return to education is lower than the expected return to alternative forms or investment, it is in fact inefficient to invest in human capital. If that is the case, the transfer will be used to buy productive assets, that may affect the marginal productivity of child labour employed in the family farm or family business. If those assets are a complement rather than a substitute for child labour, these investments raise the marginal productivity of child labour, and the substitution-effect of the transfer will then counteract the income-effect of the transfer. For example, Malawi's Social Cash Transfer Scheme offered a transfer that ranged from 4 US$ per month for a household with one eligible member to 13 US$ per month for households with four or more eligible members, with no conditions attached. In addition, the programme offered a schooling attendance bonus ranging from 1.30 US$ per month for primary school age children to 2.60 US$ per month for secondary school age children. The target population was the poorest 10% of the households. Covarrubias, Davis, and Winters (2012) show that eligible households increased their investment in productive agricultural assets (ownership of agricultural tools and livestock) and reduced adult participation in labour activities outside the household. At the same time children increased their involvement in household chores and increased the hours worked on the family farm or family business, especially during harvest. Chong and Yanez-Pagans (2019), already mentioned, find that an UCT in Bolivia led to an increase in child labour. They argue, but do not formally test, that this effect is due to increased investment in productive assets by the beneficiary households. It appears, therefore, that if cash transfers are used in a way that increases the children's productivity in domestic or economic activities, they can generate unintended effects in terms of child labour and school attendance. The impact that well intended programmes have on the relative returns of children activities is a theme that will permeate most of the discussion of the various programmes implemented.

10.2.2 Conditional Cash Transfers

Conditional cash transfers (CCT) link the benefit to a behavioural requirement of the beneficiary. The so called 'condition'. In most cases such a condition is relative to the school attendance of the children of the household. It can take different forms and be relative to enrolment, progress, etc. The conditionality can also be relative to health, including visit to clinics, vaccination, etc. and sometime the programmes. Mexico's 1997–2014 *Oportunidades* (*Programa de Desarrollo Humano*, formerly *Progresa*) combines education and health conditionalities. In what follows, we concentrate on programmes that include an education conditionality. The CCT offers the beneficiary a choice. If she complies, she sends her children to school, thus facing the direct costs involved and the opportunity cost of foregone child labour, in exchange for an income transfer. It is clear that, besides the other characteristics of the programme, the amount of the transfer plays a crucial role in determining its effectiveness. If the transfer fully compensates for the direct and opportunity cost, then the household will always comply: send the children to school and not to work (or at least substantially reduce their participation in economic activities). This is a sufficient, but not a necessary condition. Even if the transfer does not fully compensate for the direct and opportunity costs of sending the children to school, the household could still accept the offer depending on the characteristics of the utility function. Moreover, as schooling and work are not mutually exclusive it is possible, as we will see below, that a CCT which does not fully compensate for the direct and opportunity costs increases both school attendance and child labour.

The available evidence suggests that CCT programmes have, in the majority of cases, demonstrated a positive impact by increasing school attendance and reducing child labour, either on the intensive or extensive margin. In the comprehensive review by de Hoop and Rosati (2014) it is highlighted that, despite variations across programmes, conditional cash transfers generally lead to a reduction in child labour. The impact estimates vary, with eight out of 16 studies showing no statistically significant change. For example, Cambodia's Education Sector Support Project (CESSP) scholarship programme exhibited a noteworthy 10 percentage point reduction in child labour (see Ferreira et al., 2009). These results imply that the income-effect of an incentive for households to invest in productive assets, or to engage in activities that might involve children, is sufficiently large relative to the substitution-effect to keep children away from labour.

Remarkably, none of the programmes under consideration showed statistically significant increases in child labour—a relevant finding, given the ambiguous theoretical predictions regarding the impact of conditional cash transfers on child labour. However, as we shall see below, more recent studies have identified cases of a positive impact on child labour. It is also interesting to look at the correlation between the effects of cash transfer programmes on child labour and their impact on school participation. de Hoop and Rosati (2014) note that, among the eight studies showing a significant reduction in child labour, six also reveal a significant increase in school participation, whether in terms of enrolment or attendance, depending on the study's focus. Conversely, of the eight studies where no significant reduction in child labour is found, only three report a significant increase in school participation. A regression analysis identifies a substantial and statistically significant correlation between these impacts. Specifically, a one percentage point increase in school participation corresponds to a 0.31 percentage point reduction in child labour. This confirms that child labour is integral to households' decisions regarding human capital investment. Yet, the coefficient on school participation impacts differs significantly from 1, implying that changes in school participation are not entirely mirrored in changes in child labour. In fact, some programmes exhibit striking differences in programme impacts on school participation and engagement in work. As mentioned earlier, there are instances where conditional cash transfers significantly affected education without a corresponding impact on child labour (e.g., Path in Jamaica). Conversely, there are cases where conditional cash transfers had a significant negative effect on child labour, but no impact on school participation (e.g., female school stipends in Pakistan). This underscores the complexity of household adjustments in response to cash transfers, involving changes in working hours, leisure time, and the type of activities performed. In general, the impact of a cash transfer on child labour does not necessarily mirror its impact on education.

We now examine in more detail a case in which a CCT providing a transfer covering only part of the expenditures required for school attendance generates an increase in both school attendance and child labour. The Pantawid programme in the Philippines, discussed and analysed in de Hoop et al. (2019), aims to assist impoverished households in meeting their consumption needs while encouraging investments in the education and health of their children. The programme started in 2008, with the enumeration of potential beneficiary households. This involved a comprehensive listing exercise that gathered various sociodemographic and household asset indicators to formulate a Proxy Means Test (PMT) score. To be eligible for the CCT, households needed to have a baseline PMT score below the poverty threshold of around 2.15 US$ per capita per day (in 2011 dollars) and to include either a pregnant woman, or at least one child under the age of 14. The first set of beneficiary households were enrolled in the programme and started receiving benefits in the same year. Subsequently, the programme has undergone an expansion. In 2017, it covered approximately 4.5 million households. Pantawid provides both education and health grants to beneficiaries. The monthly education grant, amounting to 300 Philippine Pesos (approximately 7 US$), is designated for children aged 6–14 who consistently attend primary or secondary school (at least 85% of school days each month). Additionally, lump-sum monthly health grants of 500 Philippine Pesos (about 11.50 US$) are provided to beneficiary households under specific conditions.

In the study sample, the average household includes 2.6 children, resulting in a potential maximum monthly transfer of 30 US$, 20% of the average beneficiary's monthly household income (refer to World Bank 2013 for further details). The village-randomized evaluation was designed by the World Bank and the Philippine Department of Social Welfare and Development. In October 2008, a total of 130 villages were randomly assigned to treatment and control arms, with 65 villages in each, stratified across eight municipalities. Data for the PMT were collected in all 130 villages from October 2008 to January 2009. Subsequently, in April 2009, eligible households in the treatment villages commenced receiving transfers. The goal of Pantawid was to improve children's school participation. The estimates presented by the authors indicate that overall attendance increased by four percentage points relative to a control mean of 89%.

Notwithstanding the fact that Pantawid might have had an impact on child work as discussed above, the programme was not designed to address child work in its conditionalities or messaging. The probability of 10–14 years old children engaging in work in the 12 months before the interview increased by four percentage points. While not precisely estimated, the point estimate indicates a 20% increase with respect to the control mean. The increase in work is due almost exclusively to an increase in work for pay outside the household—a five percentage point increase quite significant as the control mean was 12%. The study also looks at how Pantawid affected the four mutually exclusive combinations of school only, work only, school and work, and neither school nor work and whether children worked while school was in session. The authors show that Pantawid caused a four percentage point decrease in the probability of children being neither in school nor work and a six percentage point increase in the probability of children both working and attending school. The probability of children working while school was in session increased by five percentage points. These results suggest that the programmes caused a transition from being neither at school nor at work to being in both, and especially in work for pay.

As Pantawid provided a transfer that did not fully cover the cost of education (during the evaluation period, it did not even cover the direct cost), it appears, therefore, that schooling and work for pay were complements. The theoretical maximum annual education transfer per child was approximately 70 US$, but on average the households received only about 55 US$. Estimated primary schooling cost in treated areas was 86 US$. Therefore, compliers had to face an additional cost of 31 US$ per enrolled child not covered by the programme. The authors' calculations show that the earnings of children that begun to work were very close to the excess of school attendance costs with respect to the transfer. Therefore, the children that started attending school in response to the programme represented a net cost to the household.

According to the theory developed in Chapter 2, this should have reduced fertility, but no attempt has been made, as far as we know, to verify this empirically.

10.3 Public Works

Public work programmes are widespread in developing countries. They provide temporary employment opportunities for unskilled workers, and support new or improved infrastructure by the like of road construction and maintenance, or water conservation (see Subbarao, Del Ninno, Andrews, and Rodríguez-Alas 2013). Public work programmes are usually self-targeting, as they offer wage rates and type of work that only poor people are willing to accept. In general, they do not aim to address child labour. On the one hand, these programmes reduce the need for child labour because they offer income support to vulnerable households. On the other hand, however, participation in public work programmes may reduce the availability of adult labour for the family's other, market and non-market, activities, and thus generate an increase in the demand for children to participate in those activities. Given the diffusion of such programmes and, in certain cases, of their size, it is important to assess what kind of impact they have on child labour. The available impact evaluations seem to indicate that public works programmes do not generate any relevant reduction in child labour, and in some instances increase it.

Despite their widespread use, evidence on the impacts of public work programmes on child labour (and other outcomes) is limited, also because of the difficulty of identifying a counterfactual for these, often temporary and large-scale, programmes. Gilligan et al. (2009) study the impact of Ethiopia's Public Safety Net Program on child school attendance and labour. This programme provided 30 days of work in labour-intensive projects to individuals from selected beneficiary households residing in chronically food insecure areas. The programme was complemented by other activities such as access to credit, agricultural extension, irrigation, and harvesting schemes. Given the non-random allocation of beneficiaries, the authors use propensity score matching. They find that children aged 6–10 years reduced their involvement in child labour thanks to a reduction in both household chores (see Chapter 4) and agricultural activities, but that older children were not affected. However, in the cases where the public works programmes were combined with transfers designed to increase agricultural productivity, young girls (aged 6–10) showed an increase in weekly hours worked, in particular in domestic chores.

Participation in public works might thus reduce the time available to women for their domestic activities, with the consequence that girls might be called on to fill the gap. According to Quisumbing and Yohannes (2004 this is what happened in the case of Ethiopia's public works programme. Shah and Steinberg (2021) systematically investigate the effects of the implementation of India's National Rural Employment Guarantee Scheme (NREGS), the world largest public works programme. Their analysis aims to identify the repercussions of increased demand for adult labour on individuals aged 5–16. The NREGS guarantees of up to 100 days of annual employment in rural infrastructure projects, remunerated at the minimum wage and requires one-third of its beneficiaries to be women. The study identifies significant effects on adolescents only (13–16 years), but not on younger children. The former group is old enough to substitute for adult labour, but too young to be part of the programme. Specifically, the research shows that adolescent girls increased the likelihood of substituting for their mothers in domestic labour, while boys are more likely to engage in remunerated labour outside the household. As in the case of Ethiopia, these findings are consistent with girls taking up domestic activities and boys spending more time in economic activities, because the involvement of adults in the workfare programmes reduced adults' involvement in both activities. Similarly, the Youth Employment Support Project in Sierra Leone, which includes a labour-intensive component known as the Cash for Work Program, has the objective to provide additional income and temporary employment opportunities to vulnerable youth. The programme rules included a quota of at least 30% participation by women. Rosas and Sabarwal (2016) exploit a randomized rolled-out design to examine its short-term impacts (3–4 months). The findings reveal an increase in school absenteeism with no increases in paid activities among children aged 6–14 years. Given the increase in labour participation among eligible household members, the higher school absenteeism could be due to higher needs for household chores, but this is not discussed in detail in the paper.

As predicted by the theoretical policy analysis in Section 9.1 of the last chapter, these empirical findings indicate that children may assume the responsibilities of parents, particularly in household chores, while the latter participate in public works programmes. The temporary nature of the employment programmes might explain why children redirect their time towards household tasks or activities traditionally undertaken by adults. The short-term nature of public work programmes could lead beneficiaries to resort to child labour temporarily, especially when adults are engaged in these programmes for brief periods (weeks or a few months). Subsequently, once the programme concludes, parents and children may revert to their usual activities, but no evidence is available on the impact after the involvement in the project is terminated. Implementing supplementary programmes that address the need for household labour while the adult beneficiary is employed, along with initiatives facilitating the transition into long-term employment, has the potential to mitigate reliance on child labour.

10.4 Microcredit

We know from Chapter 1 that, if markets are not complete, and households do not have access to credit markets, child labour may be inefficiently high. It might thus be thought that favouring access to credit for poor households would contribute to the reduction of child labour. As explained in Chapter 1, however, that is true only if the marginal return to education is higher than the marginal return to other forms of investment. If it is lower, relaxing the borrowing constraint will raise investment in financial or physical assets, rather than education. If the physical assets are used in the family farm or business and are complements rather than substitutes for labour in the production of family income, microcredit will then raise the marginal productivity of family members' labour (in particular of children if adult family members are already working full time). As this will raise the opportunity-cost of education, the marginal return to the same will then fall, and child labour rise. As we shall see, the very limited existing evidence seems to indicate that microcredit programmes do not lead to a reduction in child labour, and that in some cases increase it.

Hazarika and Sarangi (2008) use the Malawi Financial Market and Food Security Survey carried out in 1995 by the International Food Policy Research Institute (IFPRI) and the World Bank to assess the impact of microcredit on children's schooling and work. As a measure of access to credit they use the self-assessed credit limits reported by each household. They recognize that such a measure is likely to be endogenous, but do not address it any way. Therefore, the results must be taken as suggestive of a possible correlation, rather than of causality. They find effects only during the peak harvest season, when the demand for labour in farming is very high. Access to microcredit tends to increase child labour in proportion to the area of land owned and the non-farm retail sales enterprises the household manages. In particular, the children of these households increase their involvement in domestic work, but not in economic activities. It appears that, in the presence of imperfect labour market, access to credit increases the demand for labour within the household, as children are used as substitutes for adults in domestic work.

Islam and Choe (2013) focus on the impact of microcredit in Bangladesh using an ad hoc survey carried out by the Rural Employment Support Foundation in collaboration with the World Bank. They look at the impact of microcredit on children's work and on different measure of education participation and achievement. Access to credit is defined as the amount actually borrowed from microcredit institutions. To take care of the obvious endogeneity of this variable, the authors exploit the circumstance that the selection criteria for access to the microcredit programmes (namely that the household owns less than an acre of land) was not strictly enforced, and hence that participation in the programme was to a certain extent random. The results show that microcredit increases child labour especially for girl by more than 10%. This is mirrored by a reduction in school enrolment and, to a certain extent, in school achievements for both boys and girls. Again for Bangladesh, Hossain (2023) makes use of data from a randomized controlled experiment to examine the effect of an agricultural credit expansion programme on child labour and education. The results indicate that the programme generated and increase in child labour, and that such an increase is due to the opportunity that children have to work in the household's self-employment activities. The effect is stronger for household whose adult labour supply, as proxied by the number of adults, is smaller. Again, the role of imperfect labour markets appears clearly. This increase in child labour does not appear to be associated with a worsening of school outcomes, albeit the time budget survey reveals that children from treated areas spend significantly less time studying.

Therefore, fostering household investments in productive activities through microcredit could (although it seldom does) increase household income, but does not appear to reduce child labour. On the contrary, it is likely to have unintended effects. Of course, the evidence is scant and more research is necessary, but the experience documented so far points in that direction. Other programmes have been introduced with the same logic, but different instruments. These programmes aim to support the livelihood of the household by favouring the development of productive activities. To the extent that they increase household income, they should reduce child labour. As their success relies on household involvement in productive activities, however, these programmes can change the return to child labour in domestic or economic activities. The substitution-effect thus tends to offset the potential income-effect. We will discuss some studies that seem to indicate that such programmes do not appear effective in addressing child labour.

De Hoop et al. (2016) utilize a regression discontinuity approach to assess the impact of the ILO Eliminating Child Labour in El Salvador through Empowerment and Social Inclusion project. The project consisted of a set of intervention aimed to support the creation of micro enterprises by the mothers of working children, as well as of the so-called 'flexible education intervention' aimed at bringing out-of-school children back to school in the appropriate grade. The programme succeeded in increasing the participation of women in economic activities, especially in own businesses. This did not affect the labour supply of the other household members. Child labour did not decrease, but enrolment did increase, at least in the short run. Therefore, treated children continued to work, but made room for school attendance by reducing their working hours.

Edmonds and Theoharides (2020) analyse the impact of the KASAMA programme in the Philippines, financed partly by the US Department of Labour. The programme provides to household with a least one child labourer a one-time, in-kind productive asset transfer (the specific asset is chosen by the beneficiary) worth 518 USD$, and three days' worth of business training and child labour. Participation in the programme did not affect the labour supply of adolescents who worked before the beginning of the programme. The authors find an increase in economic activity for those children who were not working before the beginning of the programme. It thus appears that the availability of productive assets raises the demand for labour within the household, and that households who are limited in the possibility of utilizing adult labour recur to child labour to support their expanded household business. To support this view, the authors observe that the increase in child labour was especially large in families running a non-farm business. These families have a smaller number of adult members compared with those involved in agriculture. Therefore, they have a smaller number of adults that can be employed in productive activities. As a consequence, this group of families had to make use of children's time to meet the increase in labour requirement generated by the increase in the scale of their economic activities. The programme led to an increase in child labour, including labour of the hazardous kind. Moreover, the increased level of economic activity did not lead to an improvement in other dimensions of children's welfare that, it could be argued, would compensate for their involvement in work. The same study finds similar results in another group of families who had a relatively large number of children neither working nor attending school. Also in this case, the households utilized labour resources that were available within the household itself. Children neither working nor going to school begun to work, some of them also in hazardous occupations.

The results from the study of the impact of microcredit and 'livelihood' programmes seem to agree that these forms of intervention do not represent a promising way to address child labour. In the best-case scenario, they leave child labour unaffected. In the worst, but not uncommon, case, they even increase it. Households seem ready to participate in programmes that promise them the opportunity of improving their income through the expansion or creation of micro farm and non-farm enterprises. However, the demand for labour generated by the development of such activities, in the absence of perfect labour and credit markets, is met by making recourse to labour resources, including children, available within the family. The substitution effect generated by the increase in child labour productivity appears to dominate any possible income effect due to the successful development of the new or expanded micro enterprise activities. It should be mentioned, however, that we have no studies of the long-term effect of the class of programmes discussed here. It is possible to speculate that, to the extent that the new business is successful, as time passes, the income effect might become larger and eventually support the decision of sending children to school rather than to work. The long term, however, should not be too long, or children will then be adults and have thus missed the chance of accumulating human capital through education.

10.5 Pensions

The theory developed in Chapters 1 and 2 predicts that exogenous (with respect to child labour decisions) fertility changes are positively related to child labour supply. The theory developed in Chapter 8 predicts that pension policy, child benefits, male and female wage rates, and the rate of interest can affect fertility behaviour. We focus on the evidence available on the impact of pension policy. We begin by considering that pension policy has three dimensions: the number of persons covered, the level of coverage, and the extent to which it is actuarially fair. The first is the ratio of the number of persons receiving public pension benefits to the number of persons of retirement age (the 'extensive' measure of coverage). The second is the amount of pension benefits received on average by persons covered by a public pension scheme. The ratio between total pension payments and number of persons of retirement age (the so-called 'intensive' measure of coverage) reflects both these dimensions of pension policy. The third dimension is measured by the difference between the discounted value of pension benefits received, and the capitalized value of pension contributions paid, by a generation at the date of retirement. If this difference is positive, the policy is a subsidy to the current generation at the expense of future ones, and it thus raises the demand for all normal goods. If this difference is negative, it is a tax, and its effect is then the opposite.

Using cross-country data, Hohm (1975) and several others find a negative correlation between fertility and some measure of pension coverage. Nugent and Gillaspy (1983) and Entwisle and Winegarden (1984) do the same specifically for developing countries. Ehrlich and Zhong (1998) and Zhang and Zhang (2004) treat fertility as jointly determined with per-capita income growth and household saving (in the case of Zhang and Zhang, also private educational expenditure). These last two studies contradict each other over a number of points, but concord with each other and with the earlier studies in finding that pension coverage has a negative effect on fertility. As none of these cross-country studies controls for actuarial fairness and child benefits, however, the estimates may be biased.

One of the problems with cross-country studies is that information on child benefits and actuarial fairness is available only for a limited number of countries. A better alternative is time-series studies for countries that do provide this information. The drawback is that none of these countries can be classified as low income. We now report on a family of such time-series studies that use co-integration techniques to get at the long-term relationships between the relevant variables. In all these studies, fertility is measured by the total fertility rate. Pension coverage is measured either as the ratio of the number of persons receiving pension payments to the number of persons over the age of 65 (the 'extensive' measure), or as the ratio between total pension payments and number of persons aged 65 or over (the 'intensive' measure). The degree of actuarial fairness is proxied by the pension fund deficit, the yearly difference between pension benefits and pension contributions. In steady state, this difference coincides with that between the discounted value of pension benefits received, and the capitalized value of pension contributions paid, by each generation at the date of retirement. Over a sufficiently long run of years, it may thus be expected that the pension deficit (surplus) in the annual account of the pension administration will tend to behave like the surplus (deficit) in the lifetime account of the representative individual. The interest rate is proxied by the yield on long-dated government bonds.

Cigno and Rosati (1992) use Italian time series to estimate reduced-form equations for saving and fertility. The paper shows that the pension deficit has no significant impact on fertility, but pension coverage has a strong negative one. Controlling for the expansion of capital markets, which also compete with family transfer systems for the provision of old-age security, the paper does indeed find that as much as three-quarters of the total fertility reduction which occurred between 1930 and 1984 can be attributed to the increase in the proportion of the population covered by mandatory pension arrangements. This confirms the role of these markets as an alternative to intra-family arrangements. Foster and Rosenzweig (2000) find the same in a developing country.

Cigno and Rosati (1996, 1997) find similar effects as Cigno and Rosati (1992) in the post-war time series of West Germany, Italy, Japan, the UK, and the United States. In all these studies, the male wage rate (or household income) is found to affect fertility positively, and the female wage rate to affect it negatively. The effect of the interest rate is positive in some countries, and negative in others. Where data are available, the fertility effect of the child benefit rate (equivalent to that of a reduction in the fixed cost of a child) is estimated to be positive. These findings relate to developed economies, but are consistent with earlier findings on developing economies, and with the predictions of the theory. However, in all these time-series studies, the saving and fertility equations are estimated separately. Cigno et al. (2003) redo the analysis for West Germany only using VAR methods that allow for all possible interactions, and directions of causation, among the variables concerned. The econometric analysis establishes that the relationship between policy and fertility is causal, and that causality runs from policy to fertility. The new estimates confirm the negative effect of pension coverage on fertility. Similar results are obtained using either macro or micro data by several other authors, including Gábos, Gál, and Kézdi (2009), Galasso, Gatti, and Profeta (2009), Billari and Galasso (2014), Boldrin and Rustichini (2015), Fenge and Scheubel (2017), and Danzer and Zyska (2023). The last one is especially relevant for our discourse, because it refers to a middle-income country, Mexico, rather than to developed countries like the previous ones. Like the direct tests of the family constitution model reported at the end of the first section of Chapter 8, these empirical findings are evidence that family constitutions exist and that they condition behaviour. More to the point, they validate the policy implication, discussed in the first section of Chapter 9, that introducing or extending a public pension system in a developing country reduces fertility, and will thus help trigger a demographic transition, without the negative consequences of compulsory measures like forced sterilization, or fertility penalties, already mentioned in Chapters 2 and 9.

11
International Trade and International Policies

So far, we have reasoned as if the economy were completely isolated from the rest of the world. Relaxing that assumption has major implications. We know that international trade and emigration affect relative prices, including relative wage rates. So do bans on certain imports. International capital mobility, and the removal of obstacles to direct foreign investment, also affect prices, wages, and interest rates. In the present chapter, we examine the child labour, education, and fertility effects of trade and foreign investment liberalization on developing countries, and discuss the advantages or disadvantages of using this as a policy tool. We also briefly examine the effects of an international ban, or other forms of boycott, on imports of goods produced with child labour.

11.1 Trade and Offshoring

Standard Heckscher–Ohlin trade theory tells us that, if a country opens itself to trade, it will specialize to some an extent in the production of the good that makes intensive use of its comparatively more abundant non-traded factor. As the relative price of the good in question will fall from its autarchy level, the relative price of the non-tradable factor will rise for the Stolper–Samuelson theorem.[1] The benefits of trade will thus accrue to the comparatively more abundant non-tradable factor. Comparative statics further tell us that an increase in a trading country's endowment of a non-tradable factor may either raise or lower the price of that factor, depending on whether the factor is used intensively in the exporting sector or in the import competing one.

In traditional classroom accounts of trade theory, the non-tradable factors are capital and labour. Participation in international trade is thus predicted to bring about an increase in the wage rate relative to the rental price of capital if the country in question has a comparatively large endowment of labour,

[1] See Stolper and Samuelson (1941).

The Economics of Child Labour. Second Edition. Alessandro Cigno and Furio C. Rosati, Oxford University Press.
 DOI: 10.1093/oso/9780198903000.003.0012

a reduction if the country has a comparatively large endowment of capital. Wood (1994) points out, however, that financial capital is highly mobile, and that physical capital (hence, the technology embodied in it) follows financial capital with only a short lag. If any factor other than land and natural resources is sluggish in moving from one country to another, it is labour. That is all the more true today that most destination countries refuse to take in immigrants legally, and raise high barriers against illegal immigration. Since the skill composition of a country's stock of workers (as distinct from the flow of new workers) takes a long time to change, trade will then affect the relative wage rates of workers with different skill levels. Thus reformulated, trade theory leads us to expect that, if a country opens itself to trade, the skilled wage rate will rise relative to the unskilled wage rate if the country has a comparative abundance of skilled workers, fall if the country has a comparative abundance of unskilled ones. In the first case, the skill premium will rise, in the second it will fall. If the number of skilled workers increases in a trading country with a comparative abundance of unskilled workers, the skill premium will then increase too.

This is not what happens in reality however. Leamer (1996, 1998) does not find a Stolper–Samuelson effect in the US economy. Feenstra and Hanson (1996), Robbins (1996), Wood (1997), and Freeman and Oostendorp (2001) find that participation in international trade raises the skill premium not only in skill-abundant countries, but also in some skill-scarce ones. Goldberg and Pavcnik (2007) find that, in developing countries where unskilled labour may be presumed to be the abundant factor, trade participation did not raise the wage rates of the less skilled or educated workers relative to those of the more skilled or educated ones. Chaudhuri and Dwibedi (2007) and Cigno et al. (2018) also find that trade participation has different effects in different developing countries. Why is that? Traditional trade theory assumes that all trading countries have fixed endowments of non-tradable factors, have access to the same technology, and trade in final goods only, but none of this is entirely true, or true any more.

First, some non-tradable factors such as land may be regarded as fixed, but labour is not. At any given date, a country has given numbers of skilled and unskilled adult workers, but the number of adult-equivalent unskilled workers is endogenous, because children may work. The number of children, weighted with the share of the time for which they work, and converted into adult-equivalent units, must be added to the number of adult workers. If children receive an education, some of them will be skilled workers when they become adults. As we saw in Chapter 2, the number of children also is endogenous. And, the more they are expected to work, the more of them will be born.

Second, not all technology is freely available to all countries. Some goods are produced with freely available traditional technology, but some other are produced with new technology, which is the result of costly research and development (R&D). For a period, new discoveries are protected by patents. When patents expire, they are covered by industrial secrecy. Given that R&D is generally carried out in the more developed part of the world, new technology is available in the less developed part only to subsidiaries, or licensees, of companies based in the more developed one.

Third, new production processes tend to be more 'roundabout' than traditional ones, meaning that final goods are not produced by directly transforming primary factors, but by assembling intermediate goods that are in turn produced by transforming primary factors. The lowering of transport costs and other barriers to trade that has occurred since the end of the Second World War has made it profitable for the companies that detain the new technology to carry out different segments of the same production process in different countries in order to take advantage of factor price differences. Most international trade is now in intermediate, rather than final goods.

11.1.1 A Sketch of the Theory

Let the world economy consist of three countries, North, South 1, and South 2.[2] Following Wood (1994), we assume that capital is perfectly mobile, and labour immobile (no migrations). There are two dates, labelled $t = 1, 2$. At date 1, country $i = 1, 2, N$ has a given number S_i of skilled, and U_i of unskilled adult workers, and an unspecified number of school-age children. The ratio of skilled to unskilled adult workers is highest in North, and lowest in South 2,

$$\frac{S_2}{U_2} < \frac{S_1}{U_1} < \frac{S_N}{U_N}. \tag{11.1}$$

At date 2, the ratio of skilled to unskilled adult workers in any country will depend on the education that the children received in that country at date 1.

There are three non-tradable final goods, X produced and consumed only in North, Y_1 produced and consumed only in South 1, and Y_2 produced and consumed only in South 2. That is an acceptable simplification if we think of X, Y_1, and Y_2 as composite goods reflecting the country's climate, tastes, and culture. Of these composite goods, Y_1 and Y_2 are produced with skilled and unskilled labour by constant-returns-to-scale production functions,

[2] The analysis that follows draws on Cigno et al. (2018), but a similar argument is developed in Dwibedi and Chaudhuri (2007).

$$Y_i = F^i(S_i, U_i), i = 1, 2. \quad (11.2)$$

By contrast, we follow Feenstra and Hanson (1996) in assuming that X is costlessly assembled from three intermediate goods, x_1, x_2, and x_3, each of which is produced using skilled and unskilled labour in accordance with constant-returns-to-scale production functions,

$$x_j = f^j(S_j, U_j), j = 0, 1, 2. \quad (11.3)$$

The constant-returns-to-scale assumption, common in trade theory, is justified by saying that production takes place in optimally sized plants.

In principle, any of x_1, x_2, and x_3 could be produced in any country. Given, however, that the demand for these intermediate goods comes only from firms producing the final good X, and that X is produced and consumed only in North, there is no point in producing any of the intermediate goods x_1, x_2, or x_3 anywhere else, unless it can be exported to North. We assume that tariffs and transport costs are prohibitively high at date 1, but are confidently expected to be negligible at date 2. In North all children are in full-time education at date 1, but not all of them will be skilled workers at date 2, because educational outcomes are uncertain. In the other two countries, expectations and endowments are such, that children divide their time between market work and education, but education is higher in South 1 where the skill endowment is $\frac{S_1}{U_1}$, than in South 2 where it is $\frac{S_2}{U_2} < \frac{S_1}{U_1}$. Therefore, (11.1) remains true at date 2.

As in the Chapter 9, we normalize the unskilled wage rate to 1, and denote the skilled wage rate (the skill premium) by $\omega > 1$. Given constant returns to scale, the cost-minimizing ratio of skilled to unskilled labour employed, and thus the minimum cost of producing a unit of x_j in country i, depends only on ω. Let $c(x_j)$ denote the unit cost of x_j. We assume that x_0 is more skill-intensive than x_1, and x_1 more skill-intensive than x_2, so that there is a value of ω, call it ω_1, such that $c(x_0) < c(x_1) < c(x_2)$ for $\omega < \omega_1$, and another value of ω, call it ω_2, such that $c(x_2) < c(x_1) < c(x_0)$ for $\omega > \omega_2$. This is illustrated in Figure 11.1, where the line labelled x_j represents the relationship between $c(x_j)$ and ω.[3] The most skill intensive intermediate good, x_0, is cheapest to produce if ω is lower than ω_1. The second most skill intensive intermediate good, x_1, is cheapest to produce if ω is higher than ω_1, but lower than ω_2.

[3] The diagram is adapted from Feenstra and Hanson (1996). There, however, the horizontal axis measures the ratio of skilled to unskilled labour, rather the skilled wage rate as it does here. The unit-cost ranking is thus inverted.

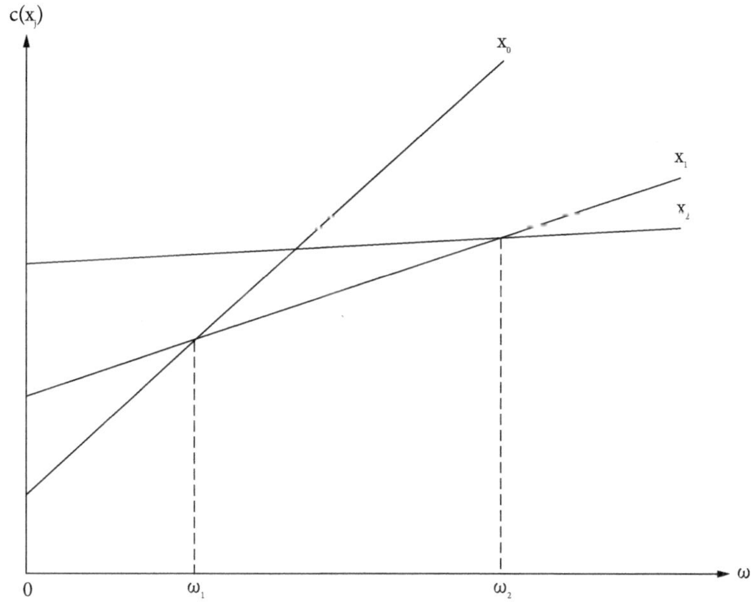

Figure 11.1 Skill intensity and the skill premium

The least skill intensive intermediate good, x_2, is cheapest to produce if ω is higher than ω_2.

Let relative skill endowments differ sufficiently across countries, at date 1, for ω to be lower in North than in South 1, and in South 1 than in South 2, not only at date 1, before trade and offshoring, but also at date 2, after trade and offshoring. For simplicity, we assume that, in autarchy, relative factor prices reflect relative factor endowments (same as saying that relative factor scarcities predominate over relative factor requirements in the determination of comparative advantages). At date 2, when goods can be exported from one country to another at negligible cost, the companies that own the production technology of x_0, x_1, and x_2 may then find it profitable to relocate some of their plants from North to South 1 or South 2. In equilibrium, the values of the skill premium in each of the three countries at each of the two dates are determined simultaneously with the localization of the plants that produce the three intermediate goods at date 2. Assuming rational expectations, the equilibrium values of the skill premium are correctly anticipated by companies deciding where to locate their intermediate-good producing plants at date 2, and by parents deciding how much education to give their children at date 1.[4]

[4] The equilibrium will not necessarily imply offshoring. Without offshoring, however, there will be no international trade. We thus assume that there is offshoring.

Suppose that, in equilibrium, the date-2 skill premium is lower than ω_1 in North, higher than ω_1 but lower than ω_2 in South 1, and higher than ω_2 in South 2. Therefore, at date 2, x_2 is produced in South 2, x_1 in South 1, and x_0 in North. This type of equilibrium is illustrated in Figure 11.2 for the case in which x_1 is more skill- intensive than Y_1, but x_2 is less skill-intensive than Y_2. The two rectangles are Edgeworth boxes, showing the date-2 allocation of skilled and unskilled labour in South 1 and South 2. The width of the rectangle measures the country's date-2 skilled labour endowment. The length measures the country's date-2 unskilled labour endowment. The convex-to-the-origin curves emanating from point O_{Y_i} are the isoquants of Y_i. Those emanating from O_{x_j} are the isoquants of x_j. The upward-sloping curve joining the SW to the NE corner is the locus of the efficient labour allocations. This curve is concave in the case of South 1, because Y_1 is assumed to be less skill-intensive than x_1, convex in that of South 2, because Y_2 is assumed to be more skill-intensive than x_2.

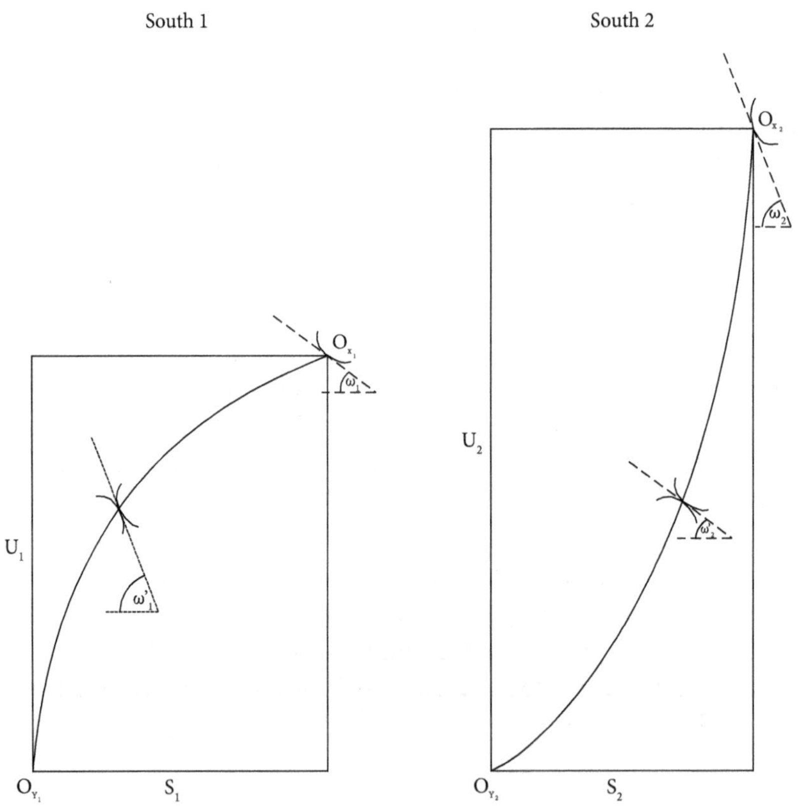

Figure 11.2 Labour allocation and international trade

Without trade and offshoring, the equilibrium point would be at the upper-right corner of the Edgeworth box, where only the local final good is produced. With trade and offshoring, the equilibrium will be somewhere further down the efficiency locus, where the country produces also a certain amount of an intermediate good. In South 1, the equilibrium value of ω would then be ω_1 if only Y_1 were produced, but it will be $\omega_1' > \omega_1$ if some x_1 is also produced. In South 2, the equilibrium value of ω would be ω_2 if only Y_2 were produced, $\omega_2' < \omega_2$ if x_2 also is. Therefore, trade and offshoring raise the skill premium in South 1, reduce it in South 2. As we know from Chapter 9, at date 1, children will then receive more education and work less in South 1, than in South 2. At date 2, South 1 will consequently look a little more like North, and South 2 a little less, than they did at date 1, and than they would without trade. The reason is that, at date 1, South 1 was sufficiently better endowed with skilled labour than South 2 to attract relatively more skill-intensive investments from North at date 2.[5]

Contrary to traditional trade theory, trade liberalization would thus induce South 1 to specialize less in low-skill production activities than it otherwise would have done. In agreement with traditional trade theory, however, it would induce South 2 to specialize even further in low-skill production activities. But, trade liberalization has also another effect. By allowing a country to specialize further in accordance with its comparative advantage, and independently of the direction in which the country specializes, trade liberalization enhances productivity.

Let us now go back to the parental decision model set out in Chapters 1 and 2 to see how trade affects parental decisions in different kinds of developing country. We have just established that, if initial conditions are 'right', in the sense that a sufficiently large part of the adult population is educated at the level required to operate skill-intensive technology, trade raises the skill premium, and thus the incentive for parents to invest in their children's education. Otherwise, trade has the opposite effects. If credit and insurance markets were perfect, we could then conclude that trade raises education and lowers child labour in comparatively skill-rich developing countries, while doing the opposite in comparatively skill-poor ones.[6] The fertility implications are also clear-cut. In comparatively skill-rich developing countries, where the net cost of a school-age child increases, fertility falls. In comparatively skill-poor ones, where the net cost of a school-age child falls, fertility rises.

[5] In Chapter 9, the high-skill equilibrium was associated with more skill-intensive investments on the part of local firms. Here, the skill-intensive investment comes from abroad.

[6] As a matter of fact, all children will study full time in the former, and work full time in the latter, because the efficient time allocation is always at a corner (see Chapter 1).

Given credit and insurance market imperfection, however, parental decisions are constrained by current income. If that is the case, poor parents cannot afford to send their children to school. By increasing per capita income, trade relaxes this constraint. In countries where trade raises the skill premium, therefore, education will rise and child labour will fall, more than it would without this effect. In countries where trade lowers the skill premium, by contrast, education will fall less and child labour will rise more than it otherwise would. These theoretical predictions conflict with public opinion in developed countries, that international trade is responsible for child labour in developing countries, because some of the goods children help to produce in poor countries are exported to rich ones. Public opinion is right, according to the theory, only of countries where the educational level is so low that they only attract production activities with low skill requirements. Elsewhere, the opposite is true.

Recalling from Chapter 2 that the more education parents intend to give their children the fewer babies they will beget, and the more they will spend on each of them to increase their survival probability, fertility and infant mortality can be expected to fall in developing countries where trade liberalization leads to an increase in education, and to fall in those where the opposite is true.

11.1.2 Evidence of Child Labour and Fertility Effects

Cigno et al. (2002) find cross-country evidence that trade openness (represented by a dichotomous variable according to which a country is classified as 'open' if it satisfies a number of criteria, ranging from low tariffs and quotas, to absence of state monopolies) reduces child labour. Edmonds and Pavcnik (2006) similarly find cross-country evidence that participation in international trade reduces child labour. They estimate that much of this effect is attributable to the induced increase in per capita income. Examining the effects of India's 1991 tariff reform, Edmonds et al. (2009, 2010) find that trade liberalization greatly reduced child labour and increased education. The effect was smaller in communities that, before liberalization, relied more heavily on protected industries. Topalova (2010) attributes this adverse effect to limited factor mobility. Using a Difference-in-Difference approach, she finds that rural districts, where the production activities worst affected by trade liberalization were concentrated, experienced slower poverty decline than the rest of the country. The impact was most pronounced in the least geographically mobile part of the population, that at the bottom of the income distribution, or living in Indian states where inflexible labour laws make factor reallocation across sectors more difficult. Given that this is not a peculiarity of India, it is to be expected that the same may apply also elsewhere.[7]

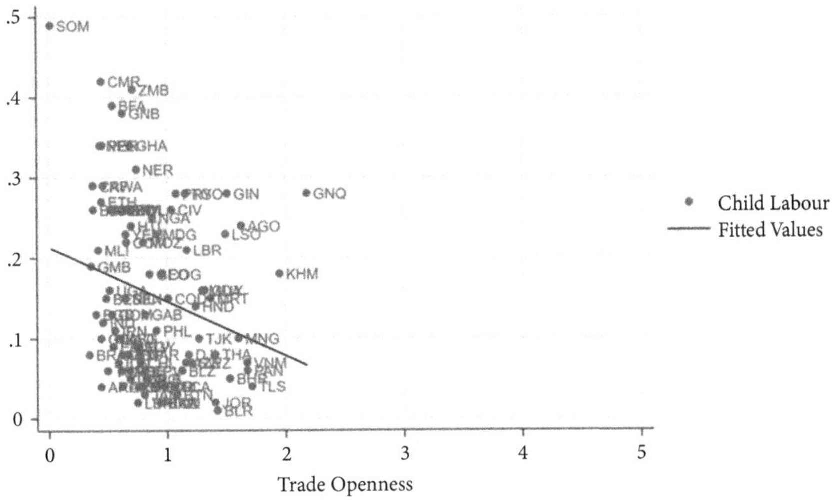

Figure 11.3 Child labour and trade openness in countries with above-median skill endowment

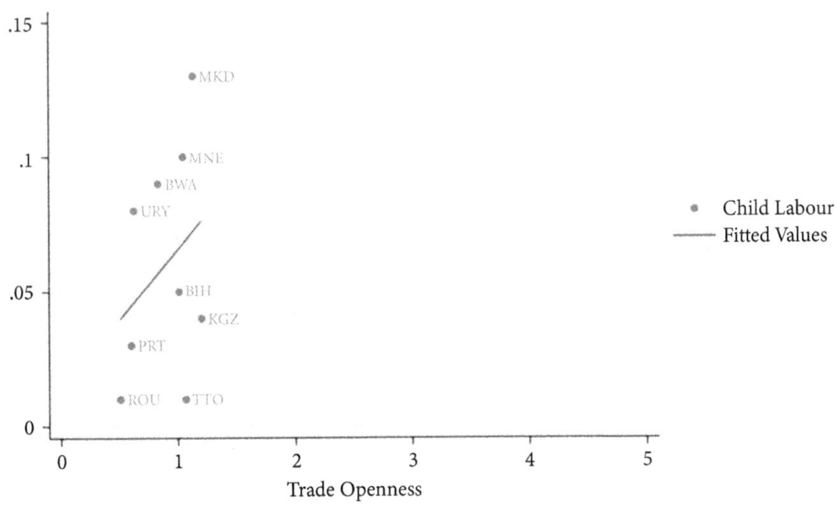

Figure 11.4 Child labour and trade openness in countries with below-median skill endowment

[7] See, among others, Grossmann and Michaelis (2007).

Figure 0.4 of the Introduction plots a measure of child labour incidence against a measure of trade openness for a sample of developing countries. The correlation is clearly negative, but small at low trade levels. As shown in Figures 11.3 and 11.4, if the sample is cut at the sample median of a skill endowment measure, the correlation remains negative in the sub-sample of countries where the skill endowment is above the sample median, but becomes positive (and statistically insignificant) in the sub-sample where the skill endowment is below the sample median.

Using a cross-country panel, Cigno et al. (2018) estimate two reduced-form equations, one for the skill premium,

$$\begin{aligned} Skillpremium_t = {} & \beta_{0S} + \beta_{1S}\, Skillendowment_{t-5} + \beta_{2S}\, Tradeopenness_{t-5} \\ & + \beta_{3S} FDI_t + \beta_{4S}\, Tradeopenness_{t-5} * Skillendowment_{t-5} \\ & + \beta_{5S} GDP_{t-1} + \varepsilon_S, \end{aligned}$$

and the other for child labour,

$$\begin{aligned} Childlabour_t = {} & \beta_{0C} + \beta_{1C}\, Skillendowment_{t-5} + \beta_{2C}\, Tradeopeness_{t-5} \\ & + \beta_{3C}\, GDP_{t-1} + \beta_{4C}\, Tradeopeness_{t-5} * Skillendowment_{t-5} + \varepsilon_C. \end{aligned}$$

In the former, the left-hand term, $Skillpremium_t$, is defined as the ratio of the average wage rate paid by industries classified by the OECD as 'high or medium-high technology' to the average wage rate paid by industries classified as 'low technology' five years after trade liberalization (to allow for the effect to permeate the economy). In the latter, the left-hand term, $Childlabour_t$, is the share of children aged 5–14 reported working, again five years after liberalization. In both equations, the right-hand side term $Skillendowment_{t-5}$ is the share of the adult population with at least completed primary education at the date of trade liberalization, $Tradeopenness_{t-5}$ is the ratio of exports minus imports, to exports plus imports at the same date, FDI_t is foreign direct investment (in PPP US dollars) five years after liberalization, GDP_{t-1} is per-capita GDP (in PPP US dollars) four years after liberalization, and ε_S and ε_C are error terms. The two equations are estimated separately because the two data sets do not totally coincide.

The effect of trade openness on the skill premium, given by

$$\frac{d\, Skillpremium_t}{d\, Tradeopenness_{t-5}} = \beta_{2S} + \beta_{4S}\, Skillendowment_{t-5}, \tag{11.4}$$

is positive, zero or negative according to whether the skill endowment is higher than, equal to, or lower than $\frac{\beta_2}{\beta_4}$. The estimated value of this ratio is

0.79 (almost identical to the sample mean and the sample median). This tells us that trade liberalization raises the skill premium if more than 79 per cent of the adult population completed at least primary education, lowers it if less than 79 per cent did. The effect on the child labour rate,

$$\frac{dChildlabour_t}{dTradeopenness_{t-5}} = \beta_{2C} + \beta_{4C}Skillendowment_{t-5}, \qquad (11.5)$$

is negative, zero, or positive according to whether the skill endowment is higher than, equal to, or lower than $\frac{\beta_{2C}}{\beta_{4C}}$, estimated to be equal to 0.69. The threshold above which liberalization reduces child labour is thus lower than the one above which liberalization raises the skill premium. That may be simply due to the fact that the two equations were separately estimated using not perfectly coinciding data sets, but there is also an economic explanation. Given that productivity is higher with than without trade, liberalization raises the demand for all normal goods, including education. Therefore, trade liberalization has a negative income effect on child labour. Given that trade liberalization raises or lowers the skill-premium depending on whether the country's skill endowment is above or below the 79 per cent threshold, there is also a substitution effect. Above the 79 per cent threshold, income and substitution effects pull in the same direction. Above that threshold, therefore, trade liberalization reduces child labour. Below that threshold, income and substitution effects pull in opposite directions. It thus stands to reason that the net child labour effect of trade liberalization is negative if the country's skill endowment is a little (less than 10 percentage points) below the 79 per cent threshold, positive if it is substantially (more than 10 percentage points) below that threshold.

Gries and Grundmann (2014) use a cross-country panel to estimate the fertility effect of trade liberalization. Coherently with the trade theory sketched out in the present chapter, and with the fertility theory set out in Chapter 2, they find that trade exposure reduces fertility in countries that export skill-intensive goods, and raises fertility in countries that export low-skill-intensive goods. This effect is stronger in middle-income countries characterized by structural modernization, and with a growing manufacturing-intensive export sector. In Gries and Grundmann (2014) as in Cigno et al. (2018), the mechanism through which trade affects the variable of interest (fertility in the former, child labour in the latter) has to do with the skill content of trade. If trade liberalization leads a country to specialize in the production and exportation of relatively high-skill goods, the demand for education will increase (the supply of child labour will fall), and fertility will fall. The opposite will happen if trade liberalization leads a country to specialize in the production and exportation of relatively low-skill goods.

Subject to all possible reservations concerning cross-country estimates and data limitations, these empirical findings are consistent also with the argument in Galor and Mountford (2006) that, in the course of the nineteenth and twentieth century, international trade generated growth in both industrial and non-industrial countries, but not in the same manner. While growth in industrial economies came mainly from productivity improvements fuelled by educational investment, growth in non-industrial economies came mainly from population increases triggered primarily by exogenous medical advances.[8] The implication is that trade liberalization helps GDP growth in any case (although, as noted by Topalova 2010, the benefits do not accrue equally to all strata of society), but encourages education and discourages child labour only if a sufficiently large share of the country's adult population is educated at the level required to attract skill-intensive investments from abroad. Before exposing a country to international competition, a government concerned with development in the broader sense should thus undertake education-enhancing policies like those discussed in the last two chapters.

11.2 Migration, Remittances, and Sanctions

Migration affects wage rates in the country of destination, but also in the country of origin. If the labour force of the country of origin were homogeneous, emigration would raise that country's skill premium. If the labour force is heterogeneous, however, emigration could have the opposite effect, because emigration is selective. Emigrants tend to be better qualified, or to have greater natural ability, than those who remain.[9] That may be compensated by migrants' remittances. Epstein and Kahana (2008) show that, if these are sufficiently large and continue for sufficiently long, the effects are similar to those of the credit-backed policy examined in Chapter 9. Remittances, however, may not be large enough, or stop too soon. Furthermore, the cost of emigration is not negligible, and it is getting higher as the destination countries (essentially North America and West Europe) tend to close their frontiers. As pointed out in Cigno (2024), destination countries unwilling to take in more immigrants could achieve their objective more humanely, and

[8] Recall the role of the μ vector of exogenous survival-enhancing variables examined in Chapter 2.

[9] As shown by Bencivenga and Smith (1997), this may be partly the result of the destination country's recruiting policies.

possibly also at lower cost, by subsidizing education in the countries of origin, instead of letting people drown or freeze to death trying to get in illegally, and imprisoning or repatriating those who succeed. This would make it cheaper for governments in the countries of origin to carry out the policies outlined in Chapter 9, because it would make it unnecessary for those governments to borrow from the international credit market.

International sanctions against countries that use child labour are advocated by some, not only for humanitarian reasons, but also on the grounds that countries applying lower labour standards than the rest of the world give themselves an unfair trade advantage. There is also the opposite argument, however, that preventing poor countries from using child labour distorts comparative advantages in favour of rich countries where children would not work anyway. Like all forms of protectionism, labour standards hurt consumers in the country that imposes them, as well as producers in the country against which they are imposed.

Basu (1999) shows that the effects of an import ban on goods with a child labour content will differ according to whether the ban is imposed on just one country or worldwide, and whether capital is fixed or mobile. Take first the case of a ban on imports from a particular country. If firms in this country cannot easily relocate abroad, shutting off the demand for child labour *may* raise the adult wage rate sufficiently for adults and children to be better off. If firms are perfectly mobile, however, they will flee the country subject to the ban. The adult wage rate will then fall, making adults and children worse off. Take next the case of an internationally agreed ban on imports with a child labour content from any country. As it applies to all countries without distinction, the ban does not cause capital flight. In the countries that formerly used child labour, workers will be better off because adult wage rates rise. In countries that never used child labour, workers also will be better off, because they will no longer suffer unfair competition from abroad. A multilaterally imposed and universally applied ban on child labour is thus preferable to a unilaterally imposed and idiosyncratically applied one.

The argument in favour of multilateral action must be taken with caution, however, because a ban on imports with a child labour content is equivalent to a lump-sum monetary sanction on the exporting countries, and will thus make poor countries even poorer. Without compensatory measures, and given that child labour supply is negatively related to lump-sum income, it is thus doubtful whether trade sanctions or boycotts would have the desired effect.

Labels certifying that a good is not produced with child labour are a milder form of sanction. Consumers rich enough to care for children in distant lands may in fact be prepared to pay more for goods that are certified to be child labour free, but poor consumers struggling to care for their own children may not. It thus seems likely that labelling would be less effective than outright sanctions. The effect could be counterproductive in any case however. Doepke and Zilibotti (2010) in fact argue that sanctions and boycotts lower domestic political support within developing countries for banning child labour. International sanctions and boycotts could thus have the perverse effect of delaying the effective implementation of policies aimed at reducing child labour in the countries where it occurs. Multilateral action is clearly desirable only on condition that it includes not only a ban on goods produced with child labour, but also compensation for countries that give up using child labour.

Conclusion

The main task we set ourselves in the Introduction to this book was to try and explain why children work, whether something should be done about it, and if so what. What have we discovered? The individual optimization assumption underlying mainstream economic thinking implies that public intervention is justified only if there is a coordination failure (efficiency considerations), or on grounds of social justice (equity considerations). This general principle applies also in the case of child labour, but with two provisos. The first is that young children are not free agents. Decisions concerning their consumption, education, and work activities are taken by their parents. This implies that efficiency must reign within the family, as well as in the marketplace. It also implies that there may be a conflict of interest between parents and young children. The second proviso is that consumption at any stage of the life cycle cannot fall below the subsistence level. This constraint is generally assumed away in economics but cannot be ignored in an analysis focussed on developing countries, where a large part of the population is never far above that level. As we saw in Chapter 1, when this constraint is binding, optimization gives way to the algebra of survival. The usual marginal conditions no longer apply.

Chapter 1 revealed that child labour may be inefficiently high or inefficiently low. The former may be the case if the expected return to education is at least as high as the expected return to other forms of investment, but parents are not sufficiently rich and generous to give their children an education as a present and provide for their own old age by saving at the same time. Why? If education is a worthwhile investment, why cannot children, or parents on their behalf, pay for this investment by borrowing, and guard against the risk of an adverse outcome by buying insurance? The problem is not only adverse selection and moral hazard as it is the case with any kind of investment. It is also that young children cannot legally commit to pay a loan back to their parents, or to anyone else. Even if parents could borrow, they would thus be unwilling to do so on their children's behalf, because they could not count on getting the money back from their children. The opposite case, that in which child labour is inefficiently low, can arise if the expected

The Economics of Child Labour. Second Edition. Alessandro Cigno and Furio C. Rosati, Oxford University Press.
 DOI: 10.1093/oso/9780198903000.003.0013

return to education is lower than the expected return to alternative forms of investment. The latter is unlikely to be the case if education yields direct utility, child labour yields direct disutility, or there is a positive education externality. It may arise nonetheless if either school quality, or the demand for educated workers, is low. As we saw in the first section of Chapter 9, the latter may result from a coordination failure between firms investing in skill-intensive technology and families investing in skill-enhancing education. In an open economy, wage rates are affected also by international trade and investment. As shown in Chapter 11, in a developing country, trade liberalization will raise skilled relative to unskilled wage rates, and thus give parents an incentive to invest in their children's education, if there already are enough skilled adult workers in the country to attract skill-intensive investments from abroad. Otherwise, the policy may have the opposite effect.

The theory set out in Chapter 1 implies that education is adversely affected by credit and insurance market imperfections, and by the opportunity-cost of education. Consistently with this prediction, Chapter 3 reviewed evidence that credit rationing and uninsured risk indeed raise child labour. The tests presented in this chapter show that shocks substantially alter household decisions. In particular, a negative shock substantially increases the probability that a child will work. Coupled with evidence from other research that child labour shows a high degree of persistence as in the case of the Rwanda genocide, this finding highlights the importance of protection from shocks for reducing children's labour supply and increasing human capital investment. Risk-reduction schemes, proxied by the availability of medical insurance, also have a beneficial and substantial effect on child work. This is confirmed also by experimental evidence regarding increased access to health insurance. However, we have seen that shocks might also alter the returns to child labour and lead households to increase child labour in the presence of a positive shock. Such changes in the incentives facing the household must be kept in mind when designing actual policies.

Again consistently with the theory, Chapter 4 reported that piped water and mains electricity provision reduces child labour, because it makes it unnecessary for children to spend time fetching water and gathering wood for the home, instead of going to school or doing their homework. If households have to devote substantial time to gather water and fuel, then the opportunity-cost of children's time rises, leading to a reduction in human capital investment. The empirical analysis is made difficult by the complexities of identifying a counterfactual. However, the results presented indicate that access to basic services has a relevant effect on child labour, with the obvious policy implication that, as well as providing schools and health, governments concerned about child labour and school attendance should give a high priority to these basic facilities.

The theoretical analysis carried out in Chapter 1 showed that the equilibrium may be either interior or at a corner. If it is at a corner, small parameter changes (e.g., a small lump-sum subsidy) will not affect education and child labour decisions. This is confirmed by the estimates of the demand for child labour function presented in Chapter 5. This chapter shows the demand side's importance in the determination of child labour. Although the majority of children work in family farms or businesses, both the status of the labour market and the structure of production have a role to play. Cyclical movements in the local adult labour market appear to have an impact on the number of children employed. The effects are differentiated by level of household income, area of residence and age. These findings are consistent with the complex interactions that exist when income effects (reflecting higher adult wage rates) are combined with changes in the opportunity-cost of the children's time (reflecting higher children's wage rates). Also, the presence of relatively child labour intensive industries affects the evolution of child labour. As the productive structure of the economy changes, and child intensive industries become less relevant, child labour decreases. An important role in this context can be played by international trade. As the country moves up along the so-called 'value-added ladder', relatively child labour intensive industries are likely to lose importance, and this will contribute to the reduction of child labour.

The theoretical analysis in Chapter 1 made the simplifying assumption that child labour adversely affects adult earnings only because it takes time away from education. Chapter 6 reported evidence that child labour reduces future earning capacity also because it undermines the future adult's health. The empirical analysis developed in Chapter 6 addresses the complex relationship between child health and child labour. While many working children see their health affected by work, it is difficult to ascertain whether, ceteris paribus, they fare better or worse, in terms of health, than their non-working counterparts. The evidence from rural Vietnam suggests that work has no negative short- term effect on childhood health. In the longer term, however, child work appears to have a negative health impact. Individuals working during childhood are significantly more likely to report illness up to five years later. The nature of the effect differs by gender. For females, work participation appears to provoke illness in the long term. For males, there is no work participation effect, but illness propensity increases with the period of time spent in childhood work. While childhood work raises the risk of future illness, the health impact is not sufficiently large to impede the growth of the child. The analysis of the Guatemalan data reveals that adult health is influenced by the age of entry into the labour market. There are two general pathways through which this effect may operate. First, it may be that a child suffers a workplace accident with long-term consequences for health. Second, it may be that there is a latency period in the development of work-related health problems (for example, of conditions that are the cumulative effects of sustained exposure to chemicals, poor posture, or heavy lifting).

Chapter 2 theoretically explained the nexus between parental decisions affecting fertility and infant mortality, and parental decisions affecting the education of the surviving children. Ex post, the more school-age children a couple have, the more likely it is that those children will work instead of going to school. Ex ante, the more likely it is that children will work when they reach school age, the more children will a couple want. Evidence of the relationship between fertility and child labour was reported in Chapter 7. Such evidence is not very large, but clearly points towards the existence of a strong link between fertility and child labour. Exogenous changes in either of them is likely to significantly affect the other. Moreover, once the endogeneity of fertility is taken into account, its impact on child labour and school attendance increases. Taken together, Chapters 2 and 7 provide the theoretical and empirical foundation for the so-called demographic transition, the switch from the high fertility, high mortality, high child labour, low education equilibrium that characterizes developing countries, to the low fertility, low mortality, low child labour, high education equilibrium that characterizes developed ones. Favouring this transition is ultimately the only way of eliminating child labour, and conquering prosperity.

In Chapter 8, we gave a theoretical explanation of why family rules and social norms emerge and persist. Such rules and norms may be viewed as collectively rational responses to a Prisoner's Dilemma type of situation, where individual rationality on its own leads to inefficiency. We found an example of such a situation in Chapter 1, where we saw that one of the reasons why education may be inefficiently low is that young children cannot legally commit to pay back a loan. The remedy offered by Chapter 8 is a self-enforcing, renegotiation-proof family rule obliging adults to support their young children and elderly parents. We found another example of such a situation in Chapter 2. The problem, there, was that an efficient allocation of tasks between husband and wife will not be implemented if it entails that she must specialize in unpaid domestic (essentially child raising) activities exposing her to the risk of opportunistic bargaining on her husband's part.

A solution to this problem is a self-enforcing, renegotiation-proof social norm imposing specialization, and equal division of the surplus generated by marriage. The same chapter reported evidence that such rules and norms actually exist and influence behaviour.

The theoretical policy analysis carried out in Chapter 9 reached the conclusion that prohibition or coercion unsupported by measures making it in people's interest to obey those obligations is generally not a good idea. Banning child labour or making education compulsory may not even be feasible, because the use children make of their time when they are neither at school, nor working openly on the labour market, is not observable by the competent authorities. The optimal (Second-Best, because parents and children's actions are not perfectly observable) internal policy mix includes not only a ceiling on observable child labour, and compulsory school enrolment, but also educational subsidies, and an international loan paid back by taxing skilled wages. As already recalled, trade liberalization, discussed in Chapter 11, also may help, but only if the country starts out with a ratio of skilled to unskilled workers large enough to attract skill-intensive investments from abroad. Therefore, trade liberalization is a complement rather than an alternative for internal policy. External sanctions, such as a ban on the importation of goods produced using child labour, or 'child labour free' labels on goods produced without it, may be counterproductive.

The empirical studies reviewed in Chapter 10 assess the policies that are carried out in practice in developing countries for the specific purpose of reducing child labour. Redistributing income in favour of families with children (unconditional cash transfers) or giving parents money if they send their children to school (conditional cash or in-kind transfers) turn out to have had the intended effect in the majority of cases, but the size of this effect is often disappointingly modest. Using public works to increase parental income may even raise child work because it induces children to substitute for parents in the performance of domestic chores and in the operation of the family farm or family business. Microcredit schemes aimed at relaxing the credit constraint facing families also have mixed results because they may increase family income on the one hand, but will raise fixed investment and thus the marginal product of children employed in family-run production activities, on the other.

A defect common to many of the policies reviewed in Chapter 10 is that, unlike the prescriptions examined in Chapter 9, and contrary to all that is explained in the present book, they overlook the complexity of the problem they are intended to address. If a policy designed to raise education or reduce child labour does not take into account the fact that it makes parents poorer, or encourages them to have more children, its effect may be the opposite of that which was intended. US President Harry Truman reportedly once said that he wanted a one-armed economic advisor because he was tired of economists saying 'on the one hand, on the other hand'. He was wrong. Complex problems do not have simple remedies.

References

Acemoglu, D. and A. Wolitzky (2020), 'Sustaining cooperation: community enforcement versus specialized enforcement', *Journal of the European Economic Association* 18(2), 1078–1122.

Akerlof, G. and R. E. Kranton (2000), 'Economics and identity', *Quarterly Journal of Economics* 115, 715–753.

Alesina, A., P. Giuliano, and N. Nunn (2013), 'On the origins of gender roles', *Quarterly Journal of Economics* 128, 469–530.

Andersen, E. (1970), 'Asymptotic properties of conditional maximum likelihood estimators', *Journal of the Royal Statistical Society* 32, 238–301.

Angrist, J. D. (2001), 'Estimation of limited-dependent variable models with dummy endogenous regressors: simple strategies for empirical practice', *Journal of Business and Economic Statistics* 19, 2–16.

Angrist, J. D. and W. N. Evans (1998), 'Children and their parents' labor supply: evidence from exogenous variation in family size', *American Economic Review* 88, 450–477.

Ashagrie, K. (1998), *Statistics on Child Labor and Hazardous Child Labor in Brief.* Geneva: ILO.

Ashenfelter, O. and A. Krueger (1994), 'Estimates of the return to schooling from a new sample of twins', *American Economic Review* 84, 1157–1173.

Baland, J.-M. and J. A. Robinson (2000), 'Is child labor inefficient?', *Journal of Political Economy* 108, 663–679.

Balboni, C., O. Bandiera, R. Burgess, M. Ghatak, and A. Heil (2022). 'Why do people stay poor?', *Quarterly Journal of Economics* 137, 785–844.

Bales, K. (1999), *Disposable People: New Slavery in the Global Economy*. Berkeley and Los Angeles: University of California Press.

Bargain, O. and D. Boutin (2021), 'Minimum age regulation and child labor: new evidence from Brazil', *World Bank Economic Review* 35, 234–260.

Barnett, R., J. Bhattacharya, and M. Puhakka (2018), 'Private versus public old-age security', *Journal of Population Economics* 31, 703–746.

Basu, A. M. (1993), 'Family size and child welfare in an urban slum', in C. B. Lloyd (ed.), *Fertility, Family Size and Structure*, New York: Population Council.

Basu, K. (1999), 'Child labor: cause, consequence and cure, with remarks on international labor standards', *Journal of Economic Literature* 37, 1083–1119.

Basu, K. (2002), 'A note on multiple general equilibria with child labor', *Economics Letters* 74, 301–308.

Basu, K. (2011), *Beyond the Invisible Hand*, Princeton and Oxford: Princeton University Press.

Becker, G. S. (1971), *The Economics of Discrimination*, 2nd edition. Chicago: University of Chicago Press.

Becker, G. S. (1976), 'Altruism, egoism, and genetic fitness: economics and sociobiology', *Journal of Economic Literature* 14, 817–826.

Becker, G. S. (1981), *A Treatise on the Family*. Cambridge, Mass.: Harvard University Press.

Becker, G. S. and N. Tomes (1979), 'Child endowment and the quantity and quality of children', *Journal of Political Economy* 87, 1153–1189.

Basu, K. and P. H. Van (1998), 'The economics of child labor', *American Economic Review* 88, 412–427.

Becker, G. S. (1960), 'An economic analysis of fertility', in A. J. Coale (ed.), *Demographic and Economic Change in Developed Countries.* Princeton: Princeton University Press, pp. 209–240.

Becker, G. S. (1981), *A Treatise on the Family*, Cambridge, Mass: Harvard University Press.

Becker, G. S. and Barro, R. J. (1988), 'A reformulation of the economic theory of fertility', *Quarterly Journal of Economics* 103: 1–25.

Becker, G. S. and Tomes, N. (1976), 'Child endowment and the quantity and quality of children', *Journal of Political Economy* 87: 1153–1189.

Becker, S. O., and A. Ichino (2001), 'Estimation of average treatment effects based on propensity score', *Stata Journal* 2, 358–377.

Behrman, J. R. and Wolfe, B. L. (1989), 'Does more schooling make women better nourished and healthier?', *Journal of Human Resources* 24: 644–663.

Behrman, J. R., Foster, A. D., Rosenzweig, M. R., and Vashishtha, P. (1999), 'Women's schooling, home teaching, and economic growth', *Journal of Political Economy* 107: 682–714.

Bencivenga, V. R. and B. D. Smith (1997), 'Unemployment, migration and growth', *Journal of Political Economy* 105, 582–608.

Bequele, A. and Myers, W. E. (1995), *First Things First in Child Labour: Eliminating Work Detrimental to Children*, Geneva: ILO.

Bergstrom, T. C. (1996), 'Economics in a family way', *Journal of Economic Literature* 24: 1903–34.

Bernheim, B. D. and Ray, D. (1989), 'Collective dynamic consistency in repeated games', *Games and Economic Behaviour* 1: 295–326.

Bharadwaj, P., L. K. Lakdawala and N. Li (2020. 'Perverse consequences of well-intentioned regulation: evidence from India's child labor ban', *Journal of the European Economic Association* 18(3), 1158–1195.

Bhalotra, S. (2003), 'Is child work necessary?', *Department of Economics DP 03654*, University of Bristol.

Bhalotra, S. and C. Heady (2003), 'Child farm labour: The wealth paradox', *World Bank Economic Review* 17(2).

Bhat, C. R. (2001), 'Quasi-random maximum simulated likelihood estimation of the mixed multinomial logit model', *Transportation Research* B35: 677–693.

Biggeri, M., L. Guarcello, S. Lyon, and F. C. Rosati (2003), 'The puzzle of "idle" children: Neither in school nor performing economic activity: Evidence from six countries', UCW Working Paper, www.ucw-project.org.

Billari, F. C. and V. Galasso (2014), Fertility decisions and pension reforms. Evidence from natural experiments in Italy, IdEP Economic Papers 1403, USI Università della Svizzera Italiana.

Bingley, P. and I. Walker (2001), 'Household unemployment and the labour supply of married women', *Economica* 68(270), 157–185.

Bjorklund, A. and R. Moffit (1987), 'Estimation of wage gains and welfare gains in self-selection models', *Review of Economics and Statistics* 69, 42–49.

Blundell, R. and R. J. Smith (1994), 'Coherency and estimation in simultaneous models with censored or qualitative dependent variables', *Journal of Econometrics* 64, 355–373.

Boldrin, M. and A. Rustichini (2000), 'Equilibria with social security', *Review of Economic Dynamics* 4, 41–78.

Boldrin, M. and A. Rustichini (2015), 'Fertility and social security', *Journal of Demographic Economics* 81, 261–299.

Boockmann, B. (2009). 'The effect of ILO minimum age conventions on child labor and school attendance: evidence from aggregate and individual-level data', *World Development* 38, 679–692.

Boockmann, B. (2010), 'The combined employment effects of minimum wages and labor market regulation—a meta-analysis', *Applied Economics Quarterly* (formerly: Konjunkturpolitik), Duncker & Humblot, Berlin 61(Supplemen), 167–188.

Bound, J., Jaeger, J. A., and Baker, R. (1995), 'Problems with instrumental variables when the correlation between the instruments and the endogenous explanatory variables is weak', *Journal of American Statistical Association* 90: 443–450.

Boyd, R. and P. J. Richerson (1992), 'Punishment allows the evolution of cooperation (or anything else) in sizable groups', *Ethology and Sociobiology* 13, 171–195.

Boyd, R. and P. J. Richerson (2002), 'Group beneficial norms can spread rapidly in a structured population', *Journal of Theoretical Biology* 215, 287–296.

Brownstone, D. and K. Train (1999), 'Forecasting new product penetration with flexible substitution patterns', *Journal of Econometrics* 89: 109–129.

Buchanan, J. (1987), 'Constitutional economics', in L. E. Blume and S. N. Durlauf (eds.), *The New Palgrave: A Dictionary of Economics*, London: Macmillan, pp. 72–118.

Bureau of Labor Statistics (2000) *Report on the Labour Force*, Washington DC, United States Department of Labor.

Carrasco, R. (2001), 'Binary choice with binary endogenous regressors in panel data: estimating the effect of fertility on female labor participation', *Journal of Business and Economic Statistics* 19(4): 385–394.

Chamberlain, G. (1980), 'Analysis of covariance with qualitative data', *Review of Economic Studies* 47: 225–238.

Chatterjee, S. and F. A. Ionescu (2012), 'Insuring student loans against the financial risk of failing to complete college', *Quantitative Economics* 3, 393–420.

Chaudhuri, S. and J. K. Dwibedi (2007). 'Foreign capital inflow, fiscal policies and incidence of child labour in a developing economy', Manchester School 75, 17–46.

Chiappori, P.-A. (1988), 'Rational household labor supply', *Econometrica* 56 (1), 63–90.

Chiappori, P.-A. (1992), 'Collective labor supply and welfare', *Journal of Political Economy* 100, 437–467.

Chin, Y.-M., S. Cunningham, and P. H. Van (2023), 'The long-term effects of the Rwandan genocide on child work', *Economic Development and Cultural Change* 72, 329–360.

Chong, A. and M. Yáñez-Pagans (2019), 'Not so fast! Cash transfers can increase child labor: evidence for Bolivia', *Economics Letters* 179, 57–61.

Cigno, A. (1986), 'Fertility and the tax-benefit system: a reconsideration of the theory of family taxation', *Economic Journal* 96, 1035–1051.

Cigno, A. (1991), *Economics of the Family*. Oxford: Clarendon Press.

Cigno, A. (1993), 'Intergenerational transfers without altruism: family, market and state', *European Journal of Political Economy* 7, 505–518.

Cigno, A. (1998), 'Fertility decisions when infant survival is endogenous', *Journal of Population Economics* 11, 21–28.

Cigno, A. (2005), 'The political economy of intergenerational cooperation', in S. C. Kolm and J. Mercier Ythier (eds.), *The Handbook of Giving, Reciprocity and Altruism*. Amsterdam: North-Holland, pp. 1505–1558.

Cigno, A. (2006), 'A constitutional theory of the family', *Journal of Population Economics* 19, 259–283.

Cigno, A. (2007), A theoretical analysis of the effects of legislation on marriage, fertility, domestic division of labour, and the education of children, CESifo WP 2143.

Cigno, A. (2012a), 'How to deal with covert child labor and give children an effective education, in a poor developing country', *World Bank Economic Review* 26, 61–77.

Cigno, A. (2012b), 'Marriage as a commitment device', *Review of Economics of the Household* 10, 193–213.

Cigno, A. (2014), 'Is marriage as good as a contract?', *CESifo Economic Studies* 60, 599–612.

Cigno, A. (2022a), 'A strictly economic explanation of gender roles: the lasting legacy of the plough', *Review of Economics of the Household* 20, 1–13.

Cigno, A. (2022b), 'Rules, preferences and evolution from the family angle', in K. F. Zimmermann (ed.), *Handbook of Labor, Human Resources and Population Economics*. Switzerland AG: Springer Nature. https://doi.org/10.1007/978-3-319-57365-6_266-2.

Cigno, A. (2024), 'Can a ban on child labour be self-enforcing, and would it be efficient?' *Journal of Population Economics* 33(3), 1–15.

Cigno, A. and F. C. Rosati (1992), 'The effects of financial markets and social security on saving and fertility behaviour in Italy', *Journal of Population Economics* 5: 319–341.

Cigno, A. and F. C. Rosati (1996), 'Jointly determined saving and fertility behaviour: theory, and estimates for Germany, Italy, UK, and USA', *European Economic Review* 40: 1561–1589.

Cigno, A. and F. C. Rosati (1997), 'Rise and fall of the Japanese saving rate: the role of social security and intra-family transfers', *Japan and the World Economy* 9: 81–92.

Cigno, A. and F. C. Rosati (2000), 'Mutual interest, self-enforcing constitutions and apparent generosity', in L. A. Gérard-Varet, S. C. Kolm, and J. Mercier Ythier (eds), *The Economics of Reciprocity. Giving and Altruism*, London: Macmillan and St Martin's Press.

Cigno, A. and F. C. Rosati (2002), 'Child labor, education and nutrition in rural India', *Pacific Economic Review* 7, 1–19.

Cigno, A., G. Giovannetti, and L. Sabani (2018), 'The role of trade and offshoring in the determination of relative wages and child labour', *Journal of International Trade and Economic Development* 27, 267–292.

Cigno, A. and A. Pettini (2002), 'Taxing family size and subsidizing child-specific commodities?' *Journal of Public Economics* 84, 75–90.

Cigno, A. and M. Werding (2007), *Children and Pensions*. Cambridge, Mass: MIT Press.

Cigno, A. and A. Luporini (2009), 'Scholarships or student loans? Subsidizing higher education in the presence of moral hazard', *Journal of Public Economic Theory* 11, 55–87.

Cigno, A. and C. Pinal (2004), 'Endogenous child mortality, the price of child-specific goods and fertility decisions: evidence from Argentina', in E. Bour, D. Heymann, and F. Navajas (eds), *Latin American Economic Crises: Trade and Labour*, Houndmills: Palgrave Macmillan.

Cigno, A., L. Casolaro, and F. C. Rosati (2003), 'The impact of social security on saving and fertility in Germany', *FinanzArchiv* 59, 189–211.

Cigno, A., G. C. Giannelli, F. C. Rosati, and D. Vuri (2006), 'Is there such a thing as a family constitution? A test based on credit rationing', *Review of Economics of the Household* 4, 183–204.

Cigno, A., G. Giovannetti, and L. Sabani (2018),'The role of trade and offshoring in the determination of relative wages and child labour', *Journal of International Trade and Economic Development* 27, 267–292.

Cigno, A., F. C. Rosati, and L. Guarcello (2002), 'Does globalization increase child labor?', *World Development* 30, 1579–1589.

Cigno, A., A. Luporini, and A. Pettini (2003), 'Transfers to families with children as a principal-agent problem', *Journal of Public Economics* 87, 1165–1177.

Covarrubias, K., B. Davis, and P. Winters (2012), 'From protection to production: productive impacts of the Malawi social cash transfer scheme', *Journal of Development Effectiveness* 4, 50–77.

Dammert, A., J. de Hoop, E. Mvukiyehe, and F. C. Rosati (2018), 'Effects of public policy on child labor: current knowledge, gaps, and implications for program design' *World Development* 110(C), 104–123.

Danzer, A. M. and L. Zyska (2023), 'Pensions and fertility: microeconomic evidence', *American Economic Journal: Economic Policy* 15, 126–165.

Dasgupta, P. (1993), *An Enquiry into Well-Being and Destitution*, Oxford: Clarendon Press.

de Hoop, J. and F. C. Rosati (2014), 'Cash transfers and child labor', *The World Bank Research Observer* 29, 202–234

de Onis, M. and J. P. Habicht (1996), 'Anthropometric reference data for international use: recommendations from a World Health Organization expert committee', *American Journal of Clinical Nutrition* 64, 650–658.

Deb, P. and F. C. Rosati (2002), Determinants of child labour and school attendance: The role of household unobservables, UCW Working Papers.

Deb, P. and F. C. Rosati (2004), Estimating the effect of fertility decisions on child labour and schooling, UCW Working Paper.

Dessy, S. E. and S. Pallage (2001), 'Child labor and coordination failures', *Journal of Development Economics* 65, 469–476.

Diamond, J. (2005), *Guns, Germs, and Steel: The Fates of Human Societies.* New York: W. W. Norton.

Doepke, M. and F. Zilibotti (2010), 'Do international labor standards contribute to the persistence of the child-labor problem?', *Journal of Economic Growth* 15, 1–31.

Dumas, C. (2018), 'Productivity shocks and child labor: the role of credit and agricultural labor markets', *Economic Development and Cultural Change* 68, 763–812.

Dupas, P., C. Falezan, M. C. Mabeu, and P. Rossi (2023), Long-run impacts of forced labor migration on fertility behaviors: Evidence from colonial West Africa. National Bureau of Economic Research Working Paper Series No. 31993.

Dwibedi, J. K. and S. Chaudhuri (2007), Foreign capital, return to education and child labour, Munich Personal RePEc Archive.

Edmonds, E. (2002), 'Will child labor decline with improvements in living standards?', mimeo, Dartmouth College.

Edmonds, E. (2008), 'Child labor', in Paul T. Schultz and John A. Strauss (eds.), *Handbook of Development Economics* vol. 4. Amsterdam: Elsevier.

Edmonds, E. V. (2005), 'Does child labour decline with improving social status?', *Journal of Human Resources* 40, 77–99.

Edmonds, E. V. and N. Pavcnik (2001), Does globalisation increase child labor? Evidence from Vietnam, NBER Working Paper 8760.

Edmonds, E. V. and N. Pavcnik (2006), 'International trade and child labour: cross country evidence', *Journal of International Economics* 68, 115–140.

Edmonds, E. V. and S. Sharma (2004), 'Is investment in human capital influenced by property rights? Evidence from families vulnerable to bondage', Dartmouth College, mimeo.

Edmonds, E. V. and M. Shrestha (2012), 'The impact of minimum age of employment regulation on child labor and schooling', *IZA Journal of Labor Policy* 1, 14.

Edmonds, E. V. and C. Theoharides (2020), 'The short term impact of a productive asset transfer in families with child labor: experimental evidence from the Philippines', *Journal of Development Economics* 146, 102486.

Edmonds, E. V. and C. Turk (2004), 'Child labor in transition in Vietnam', in P. Glewwe, N. Agrawal, and D. Dollar (eds), *Economic Growth, Poverty and Household Welfare in Vietnam*, Washington: World Bank, 505–550.

Edmonds, E. V., P. Topalova, and N. Pavcnik (2009), 'Child labor and schooling in a globalizing world: some evidence from urban India', *Journal of the European Economic Association* 7, 498–507.

Edmonds, E. V., N. Pavcnik, and P. Topalova (2010), 'Trade adjustment and human capital investments: evidence from Indian tariff reform', *American Economic Journal: Applied Economics* 2, 42–75

Ehrlich, I., and J. H. Zhong (1998), 'Social security and the real economy: an inquiry into some neglected issues', *American Economic Review* 88, 151–157.

Ellickson, R. C. (1994), 'The aim of order without law', *Journal of Institutional and Theoretical Economics* 150, 97–100.

Entwisle, B. and C. R. Winegarden (1984), 'Fertility and pension programs in LDCs: a model of mutual reinforcement', *Economic Development and Cultural Change* 32, 331–354.

Epstein, G. S. and N. Kahana (2008), 'Child labor and temporary emigration', *Economics Letters* 99, 545–548.

Eswaran, M. (2002), 'The empowerment of women, fertility, and child mortality', *Journal of Population Economics* 15, 433–454.

Eswaran, M., L. A. Facchini, M. M. Dall'Agnol, and D. C. Christiani (2000), 'Child labor and health: problems and perspectives', *International Journal of Occupational and Environmental Health* 6, 55–62.

Fasih, T. (2008), *Linking Education Policy to Labor Market Outcomes.* Washington, DC: World Bank.

Fassa, A. G., L. A. Facchini, M. M. Dall'Agnol, and D. C. Christiani (2000), 'Child labor and health: Problems and perspectives', *International Journal of Occupational and Environmental Health* 6(1), 55–62.

Feenstra, R. C. and G. H. Hanson (1996), 'Globalization, outsourcing, and wage inequality', *American Economic Review* 86, 240–245.

Fenge, R. and B. Scheubel (2017), 'Pensions and fertility: back to the roots', *Journal of Population Economics* 30, 93–139.

Fentiman, A., A. Hall, and D. Bundy (2001), 'Health and cultural factors associated with enrolment in basic education: a study in rural Ghana', *Social Science and Medicine* 52, 429–439.

Ferreira, F. H., G. D. Filmer, and N. Schady (2009), *Own and sibling effects of conditional cash transfer programs: Theory and evidence from Cambodia (Policy Research Working Paper 5001, Impact Evaluationo Series).* Washington, DC: The World Bank.

Filoso, V. and E. Papagni (2015), 'Fertility choice and financial development', *European Journal of Political Economy* 37, 160–177.

Fogel, R. W. (1993), 'New sources and new techniques for the study of secular trends in nutritional status, health, mortality, and the process of aging', *Historical Methods* 26, 5–43.

Folbre, N. (1994), 'Children as public goods', *American Economic Review* 84, 86–90.

Forastieri, V. (1997). *Children at Work: Health and Safety Risks.* Geneva: ILO.

Francesconi, M. (2002), 'A joint dynamic model of fertility and work of married women', *Journal of Labor Economics* 20, 336–380.

Freeman, R. B. and R. H. Oostendorp (2001), 'The occupational wages around the World Data File', *International Labour Review* 140, 379–401.

Gábos, A., R. I. Gál, and G. Kézdi (2009), 'The effects of child-related benefits and pensions on fertility by birth order: a test on Hungarian data', *Population Studies* 63, 215–231.

Galasso, V., R. Gatti, and P. Profeta (2009), 'Investing for the old age: pensions, children and savings', *International Tax and Public Finance* 16, 538–559.

Galor, O. and A. Mountford (2006), 'Trade and the great divergence: the family connection', *American Economic Review* 96, 299–303.

Gary-Bobo, R. J. and A. Trannoy (2015), 'Optimal student loans and graduate tax under moral hazard and adverse selection', *RAND Journal of Economics* 46, 546–576.

Genicot, G. (2002), 'Bonded labor and serfdom: a paradox of voluntary choice', *Journal of Development Economics* 67, 101–127.

Gilligan, D. O., J. Hoddinott, and A. S. Taffesse (2009), 'The impact of Ethiopia's productive safety net programme and its linkages', *Journal of Development Studies* 45, 1684–1706.

Giuffrida, A., R. F Iunes, and W. D. Savedo (2001), 'Health and poverty in Brazil: Estimation by structural equation model with latent variables', mimeo.

Glewwe, P., S. Kock., and, B. Linh Nguyen (2002a), Child nutrition, economic growth and the provision of health services in Vietnam in the 1990's, Poverty Research Working Paper 2776, Washington: World Bank.

Glewwe, P., S. Kock., and B. L. Nguyen (2002b), Economic mobility in Vietnam in the 1990s, Poverty Research Working Paper 2838, Washington: World Bank.

Goldberg, P. K. and N. Pavcnik (2007), 'Distributional effects of globalization in developing countries', *Journal of Economic Literature* 45, 39–82.

Gong, X., and van Soest, A. (2002), 'Family structure and female labor supply in Mexico City', *Journal of Human Resources* 37, 163–191.

Greif, A. (2006), *Institutions and the Path to the Modern Economy: Lessons from Medieval Trade*. Cambridge: Cambridge University Press.

Gries, T. and R. Grundmann (2014), 'Trade and fertility in the developing world: the impact of trade and trade structure', *Journal of Population Economics* 27, 1165–1186.

Grootaert, C. and R. Kanbur (1995), 'Child labor: an economic perspective', *International Labor Review* 134, 187–203.

Grootaert, C. and H. Patrinos (1999), *The Policy Analysis of Child Labor: A Comparative Study*, New York: St Martin's Press.

Grossmann, H. and J. Michaelis (2007), 'Trade sanctions and the incidence of child labor', *Review of Development Economics* 11, 49–62.

Guarcello, L., S. Lyon, and F. C. Rosati (2003), Child labor and access to basic services: Evidence from five countries, UCW Working Paper, www.ucw-project.org.

Guarcello, L., F. Mealli, and F. C. Rosati (2003), Household vulnerability and child labor: The effects of shocks, credit rationing and insurance, World Bank Social Protection Discussion Paper 322.

Guiso, Luigi, P. Sapienza, and L. Zingales (2016), 'Long-term persistence', *Journal of the European Economic Association* 14, 1401–1436.

Guttman, J. M. (2001), 'Self-enforcing reciprocity norms and intergenerational transfers', *Journal of Public Economics* 81, 117–151.

Hausman, J. (1978), 'Specification tests in econometrics', *Econometrica* 46, 1251–1271.

Hausman, J. and V. J. Hotz (1989), 'Choosing among alternative nonexperimental methods for estimating the impact of social programs: the case of manpower training', *Journal of the American Statistical Association* 84, 862–880.

Hausman, J., R. Lalonde and J. Smith (1999), 'The economics and econometrics of active labor market programs', in O. Ashenfelter and D. Card (eds), *Handbook of Labor Economics*, iii(a), *Handbooks in Economics series*, ed. K. J. Arrow and M. D. Intriligator, Amsterdam: North-Holland.

Hazarika, G. and S. Sarangi (2008), 'Household access to microcredit and child work in rural Malawi', *World Development* 36, 843–859.

Hoff, K. and A. Lyon (1995), 'Non-leaky buckets: optimal redistributive taxation and agency costs', *Journal of Public Economics* 58, 365–390.

Hohm, C. H. (1975), 'Social security and fertility: an international perspective', *Demography* 12, 629–644.

Hotz, V. J. and R. A. Miller (1988), 'An empirical analysis of life cycle fertility and female labor supply', *Econometrica* 56, 91–118.

Ibrahim, A., S. M. Abdalla, M. Jafer, J. Abdelgadir, and N. de Vries. (2019), 'Child labor and health: a systematic literature review of the impacts of child labor on child's health in low- and middle-income countries', *Journal of Public Health* 41(1), 18–26.

Idler, E. L. and Y. Benyamini (1997), 'Self-rated health and mortality: a review of twenty-seven community studies', *Journal of Health and Social Behaviour* 38, 21–37.

Imbens, G. W. and J. D. Angrist (1994), 'Estimation and identification of local average treatment effects', *Econometrica* 62, 467–475.

Immink, M. D. C. and E. Payongayong (1999), 'Risk analysis of poor health and growth failure of children in the central highlands of Guatemala', *Social Science and Medicine* 48, 997–1009.

International Labour Office (2002), *Every Child Counts: New Global Estimates on Child Labour*, Geneva: ILO.

International Labour Office (2004), *Investing in Every Child: An Economic Study on the Costs and Benefits of Eliminating Child Labour*, Geneva: ILO.

International Labour Organization (1998), *Conference Report VI (I) Child Labor: Targeting the Intolerable*, Geneva: ILO.

International Labour Organization (2022), *Global Estimates of Modern Slavery: Forced Labour and Forced Marriage*. Geneva: Walk Free, and International Organization for Migration.

International Programme for the Elimination of Child Labour (IPEC) (1997), *Defining Hazardous Undertakings for Young Workers below 18 Years of Age: A Country Report*, Manila: ILO.

Islam, A. and C. Choe (2013). 'Child labor and schooling responses to access to microcredit in rural Bangladesh', *Economic Inquiry* 51, 46–61.

Hoop, J. d., J. Friedman, E. Kandpal, and F. C. Rosati (2019), *Journal of Human Resources* 54(2), 503–553.

Hoop, J. d., I. Kovrova, and F. C. Rosati (2016), 'Eliminating child labour in El Salvador through economic empowerment and social inclusion: Impact report', retrieved from http://www.ucw-project.org/attachment/07032017224El_Salvador_IE_07042016_web.pdf.

Jacoby, H. and E. Skoufias (1997), 'Risk, financial markets, and human capital in a developing country', *Review of Economic Studies* 64, 311–335.

Hossain, A. (2023), 'Unintended consequences of a well-intentioned policy: Impact of credit on child labor in Bangladesh', *Journal of Human Resources.*

Jensen, P., and H. S. Nielsen (1997), 'Child labour or school attendance? Evidence from Zambia', *Journal of Population Economics* 10, 407–424.

Kandori, M. (1992), 'Social norms and community enforcement', *Review of Economic Studies* 59, 63–80.

Kaplan, G., and A. Camacho (1983), 'Perceived health and mortality: a nine year follow-up of the Human Population Laboratory Cohort', *American Journal of Epidemiology* 117, 292–298.

Kassouf, A. L., M. McKee, and E. Mossialos (2001), 'Early entrance to the job market and its effects on adult health: evidence from Brazil', *Health Policy and Planning* 16, 21–28.

Khandker, S., D. F. Barnes and H. Samad (2013), 'Welfare impacts of rural electrification: a panel data analysis from Vietnam', *Economic Development and Cultural Change* 61, 659–692.

Klimaviciute, J., S. Perelman, P. Pestieau, and J. Schoenmaeckers (2017), 'Caring for dependent parents: altruism, exchange or family norm?' *Journal of Population Economics* 30, 835–873.

Klymak, M. (2023), 'The trade effects of information provision about forced and child labor', *World Development* 167, 106–217.

Kooiker, S. E. (1995), 'Exploring the iceberg of morbidity: a comparison of different survey methods for assessing the occurrence of everyday illness', *Social Science and Medicine* 41, 317–332.

Kosse, F., T. Deckers, P. Pinger, H. Schildberg-Hörisch, and A. Falk (2020), 'The formation of prosociality: causal evidence on the role of social environment', *Journal of Political Economy* 128, 434–467.

Koutstaal, W. and D. Schacter (1997), 'Gist-based false recognition of pictures in older and younger adults', *Journal of Memory and Language* 37, 555–583.

Kruger, D. (2007), 'Coffee production effects on child labour and schooling in rural Brazil', *Journal of Development Economics* 82(2), 448–463.

Laffont, J.-J. and D. Martimort (2002), *The Theory of Incentives: The Principal-Agent Model.* Princeton: Princeton University Press.

Lakdawala, L. K., D. M. Heredia, and D. Vera-Cossio. (2023), *The impact of expanding worker rights to informal workers: Evidence from child labor legislation.* IDB.

Landmann, A. and M. Frölich (2015). 'Can health-insurance help prevent child labor? An impact evaluation from Pakistan', *Journal of Health Economics* 39, 51–59.

Leamer, E. E. (1996), In search of Stolper-Samuelson effects on U.S. wages, NBER Working Papers 5427.

Leamer, E. E. (1998), 'In search for Stolper-Samuelson linkages between international trade and lower wages'in S. Collins (ed.), *Imports, Exports, and the American Worker*, Washington DC: Brookings Institution Press, pp. 141–203.

Lowenstein, A. and S. O. Daatland (2006), 'Filial norms and family support in a comparative cross-national context: evidence from the OASIS study', *Ageing and Society* 26, 203–223.

Lewis, E. (2004), 'How do local labor markets in the U.S. adapt to immigration?' Unpublished manuscript, Dartmouth College.

Lundberg, S. and R. A. Pollak (1996), 'Bargaining and distribution in marriage', *Journal of Economic Perspectives* 10, 139–158.

Lundberg, S. and E. Rose (2002), 'The effects of sons and daughters on men's labor supply and wages', *Review of Economics and Statistics* 84, 251–268.

Maddala, G. S. (1986), *Limited-Dependent and Qualitative Variables in Econometrics*, Cambridge: Econometric Society Monographs.

Maitra, P., and R. Ray (2002), 'The joint estimation of child participation in schooling and employment: comparative evidence from three continents', *Oxford Development Studies* 30, 41–62.

Manacorda, M. and F. C. Rosati (2010), 'Local labor demand and child work', in R. K. Q. Akee, E. V. Edmonds and K. Tatsiramos (eds), *Child Labor and the Transition between School and Work*, England: Emerald Group Publishing Limited. 31, 321–354.

Manacorda, M. and F. C. Rosati (2011). 'Industrial structure and child labor evidence from the Brazilian population census', *Economic Development and Cultural Change* 59(4), 753–776.

Manser, M. and M. Brown (1980), 'Marriage and household decision-making: a bargaining analysis', *International Economic Review* 21, 31–44.

Martorell, R. and T. J. Ho (1984), 'Malnutrition, morbidity and mortality', in W. H. Mosley and L. C. Chen (eds), *Child Survival: Strategies for Research.* Cambridge: Cambridge University Press.

Maskin, E. and J. Farrell (1989), 'Renegotiation in repeated games', *Games and Economic Behavior* 1, 327–360.

McElroy, M. B. and M. J. Horney (1981), 'Nash-bargained household decisions: toward a generalization of the theory of demand', *International Economic Review* 22, 333–349.

Meza-Cordero, J. A. (2023). 'Conditional cash transfers tools to combat child labor: evidence from a randomized controlled trial in Costa Rica', *Review of Development Economics* 27, 220–246.

Moffitt, R. (1984), 'Profiles of fertility, labour supply and wages of married women: a complete life-cycle model', *Review of Economic Studies* 51, 263–278.

Neyman, J. and E. Scott (1948), 'Consistent estimates based on partially consistent observations', *Econometrica* 16, 1–32.

Nordman, C. J., S. Sharma, and N. Sunder (2021). 'Here comes the rain again: productivity shocks, educational investments and child work', *Economic Development and Cultural Change* 70, 1041–1063.

Nugent, J. B. and R. T. Gillaspy (1983), 'Old age pensions and fertility in rural areas of less developed countries: some evidence from Mexico,' *Economic Development and Cultural Change* 31, 809–829.

O'Donnell, O., F. C. Rosati, and E. van Doorslaer (2002), Child labour and health: Evidence and research issues, UCW Discussion Paper.

O'Donnell, O., F. Rosati, and E. van Doorslaer. (2005), 'Health effects of child work: Evidence from rural Vietnam', *Journal of Population Economics* 18, 437–467.

Olsen, R. J. and G. Farkas (1989), Endogenous covariates in duration models and the effect of adolescent childbirth on schooling, *Journal of Human Resources* 24(1), 39–53.

Pellerano, L., E. Porreca, and F. C. Rosati (2020). 'Income elasticity of child labor: do cash transfers have an impact on the poorest children?' *IZA Journal of Development and Migration* 11(1).

Phelps, E. (1961), 'The golden rule of accumulation: a fable for growthmen', *American Economic Review* 51, 638–643.

Pitt, M., M. Rosenzweig, and Md Nazmul Hassan (1990), Productivity, health, and inequality in the intrahousehold distribution of food in low-income countries, American Economic Review 80(5), 1139–1156.

Piza, C. and A. P. Souza (2017), 'The causal impacts of child labor law in Brazil: some preliminary findings', *The World Bank Economic Review* 30, S137–S144.

Pouliot, W. (2006), 'Introducing uncertainty into Baland and Robinson's model of child labour', *Journal of Development Economics* 79, 264–272.

Pratt, J. W. and R. Schlaifer (1988), 'On the interpretation and observation of laws', *Journal of Econometrics* 39: 23–52.

Psacharopoulos, G. (1997), 'Child labor versus educational attainment: some evidence from Latin America', *Journal of Population Economics* 10/4: 377–386.

Quisumbing, A. R., and Y. Yohannes (2004), 'How fair is workfare? gender, public works, and employment in rural Ethiopia', *Policy Research Working Paper 3020*. Washington, DC: World Bank.

Ralston, H. (1997), 'Health as an input to labour: intrahousehold food distribution in rural Indonesia', *Journal of Policy Modelling* 19, 567–586

Rapoport, A. and A. M. Chammah (1965), *Prisoner's Dilemma: A Study in Conflict and Cooperation*. Ann Arbor: University of Michigan Press.

Ravallion, M. and Q. Wodon (2000), 'Does child labour displace schooling? Evidence on behavioural responses to an enrolment subsidy', *Economic Journal* 110, cl58–cl75.

Ray, R. (2000), 'Analysis of child labour in Peru and Pakistan: a comparative study', *Journal of Population Economics* 13: 3–20.

Rivers, D. and O. H. Vuong (1988), 'Limited information estimators and exogeneity tests for simultaneous probit models', *Journal of Econometrics* 39: 347–366.

Robbins, D. J. (1996), Evidence on trade and wages in the developing world, *Working Paper 119*, OECD Development Centre.

Rodriguez, F., and D. Rodrik (2000), 'Trade policy and economic growth: a skeptic's guide to the cross-national evidence', www.ksghome.harvard.edu.

Rosas, N. and S. Sabarwal (2016), Public works as a productive safety net in a post-conflict setting: Evidence from a randomized evaluation in Sierra Leone. World Bank Policy Research Working Paper No. 7580.

Rosati, F. C. (1996), 'Social security in a non-altruistic model with uncertainty and endogenous fertility', *Journal of Public Economics* 60, 283–294.

Rosati, F., R. Straub. (2007), 'Does work during childhood affect the health of Guatemalan adults?', *Review of Economics of the Household* 5, 83–94.

Rose, A. K. (2002), 'Do we really know that the WTO increases trade', *NBER Working Papers*, 9273 (National Bureau of Economic Research, Inc.).

Rosenbaum, P. and D. B. Rubin (1983a), 'The central role of the propensity score in observational studies for causal effects', *Biometrika* 70, 41–55.

Rosenzweig, M. and R. E. Evenson (1977), 'Fertility, schooling, and the economic contribution of children of rural India: an econometric analysis', *Econometrica* 45, 1065–1079.

Rosenzweig, M. and T. P. Schultz (1982), 'Market opportunities, genetic endowments, and intrafamily resource distribution: child survival in rural India', *American Economic Review* 72, 803–815.

Rosenzweig, M. and K. J. Wolpin (1982), 'Governmental interventions and household behavior in a developing country', *Journal of Development Economics* 10, 209–225.

Sachs, J. D. and A. Warner (1995), 'Economic reform and the process of global integration', *Brooking Papers on Economic Activity* 1, 1–118.

Sadana, R., C. D. Mathers, A. D. Lopez, C. J. L. Murray, and K. Iburg (2000), 'Comparative analysis of more than 50 household surveys on health status, *GPE Discussion Paper No 15*, EIP/GPE/EBD., Geneva: WHO.

Schultz, T. W. (1974), 'Fertility and economic values', in T. W. Schultz (ed.), *Economics of the Family*. Chicago: University of Chicago Press, pp. 3–22.

Shah, M. and B. M. Steinberg (2021), 'Workfare and human capital investment: evidence from India', *Journal of Human Resources* 56, 380–405.

Shanan, Y. (2023), 'The effect of compulsory schooling laws and child labor restrictions on fertility: evidence from the early twentieth century', *Journal of Population Economics* 36, 321–358.

Siminski, P. and R. Yetsenga (2020), Rethinking specialization and the sexual division of labour in the 21st century, IZA DP No. 12977.

Sloutsky, V. M. and A. V. Fisher (2004), 'When development and learning decrease memory: evidence against category-based induction in children', *Psychological Science* 15, 553–558.

Smith, J. (1999), 'Healthy bodies and thick wallets: the dual relation between health and economic status', *Journal of Economic Respectives* 13, 145–166.

Spolaore, E. and R. Wacziarg (2021), 'Fertility and modernity', *Economic Journal* 132, 796–833.

Staiger, D. and J. Stock (1997), 'Instrumental variable regressions with weak instruments', *Econometrica* 65, 557–586.

Steckel, R. (1995), 'Stature and the standard of living', *Journal of Economic Literature* 33, 1903–1940.

Stiglitz, J. and Weiss, A. (1981), 'Credit rationing in markets with incomplete information', *American Economic Review* 71, 393–410.

Stolper, W. F. and P. A. Samuelson (1941), 'Protection and real wages', *Review of Economic Studies* 9, 58–73.

Strauss, J. and D. Thomas (1998), 'Health, nutrition and economic development', *Journal of Economic Literature* 36, 766–817.

Strulik, H. (2004), 'Child mortality, child labour and economic development', *Economic Journal* 114, 547–568.

Subbarao, K., C. Del Ninno, C. Andrews, and C. Rodríguez-Alas (2013), *Public Works as a Safety Net: Design, Evidence, and Implementation*. Washington DC: World Bank Publications.

Tabellini, G. (2008), 'The scope of cooperation: norms and incentives', *Quarterly Journal of Economics* 123, 905–950.

Tesliue, E. D., and K. Lindert (2002), '*Vulnerability: A qualitative and quantitative assessment*', World Bank, mimeo.

Topalova, P. (2010), 'Factor immobility and regional impacts of trade liberalization: evidence on poverty from India', *American Economic Journal: Applied Economics* 2, 1–41.

Train, K. (2003), *Discrete Choice Methods with Simulation*. New York: Cambridge University Press.

Waldman, A. (2003), 'India's @@poor bet precious sums on private schools', *New York Times*, 15 Nov.

Waterlow, J. C. et al. (1977), 'The presentation and use of height and weight data for comparing the nutritional status of groups of children under the age of 10 yrs', *Bulletin of the World Health Organisation* 55, 489–498.

Wood, A. (1994), *North–South Trade, Employment and Inequality*. Oxford: Clarendon Press.

Wood, A. (1995), *Nort-South Trade, Employment and Inequality*. Oxford: Claredon Press.

Wooldridge, J. M. (2002), *Econometric Analysis of Cross Section and Panel Data*. Cambridge, Mass.: MIT Press.

World Bank (2001), *Social Protection Sector Strategy: From Safety Nets to Springboard*, Washington DC: World Bank.

World Health Organization, (1995), 'Physical status: Use and interpretation of anthropometry', Report of a WHO Expert Committee, *WHO Technical Report 854*, Geneva: WHO.

Zhang, J. and J. Zhang (2004), 'How does social security affect economic growth? Evidence from cross-country data', *Journal of Population Economics* 17, 473–500.

Index

Please note that page references to Figures will be followed by the letter '*f*', to Tables by the letter '*t*'.